Advance praise for *She's a Badass*

"Badass and kick-ass, these music makers—icons and up 'n comers, avant-garde genre-breakers and hitmakers—open up to author Katherine Yeske Taylor. In sharing their compelling stories and struggles, and addressing sexism and feminism, the through-line of integrity and a 'nevertheless she persisted' disposition shines brightly." —**Katherine Turman**, co-author, *Louder Than Hell: The Definitive Oral History of Metal*

"By capturing the spirit and soul of six decades' worth of female rockers, Katherine Yeske Taylor demonstrates that she's as much of a badass as any of her subjects. This is a book that needed to be written, and she rose to the occasion like few others could." —**Tom Beaujour**, co-author of the *New York Times* bestseller *Nothin' but a Good Time*

"The first time I ever worked with a woman in the music industry was in 1990 when I collaborated with Anne Dudley on *Songs from the Victorious City*. Until that point in my career I had never really considered how profound the struggle was for a woman in a patriarchal industry (having been in an all-male environment since the inception of Killing Joke). From the metaphorical airbrushing and stereotyping to the brutal chauvinism encountered by so many women artists, *She's a Badass* documents the experiences of these influential and brave pioneers." —**Dr. Jaz Coleman**, vocals/songwriter, Killing Joke; composer and producer

"*She's a Badass* is a virtual handbook for women, especially those coming up in the music world. As the son of a strong mother and fierce female role model, and a teacher of countless female students, I believe that Katherine's book is a perfect blend of inspiration and motivation." —**John Sparrow**, drummer (Violent Femmes) and educator

"In *She's a Badass*, Kat Taylor gets twenty of the biggest female trailblazers in rock—from Suzi Quatro and Ann Wilson to Orianthi and Amanda Palmer—to spill their guts on what it's really like to have to fight for every scrap of respect as a woman in music, while dodging gropers and setting sexist managers, agents, band members, and labels straight. Nobody got these stories before—because nobody asked for them. Now Taylor has, and the result is a significant contribution to music journalism that is also a wildly entertaining read." —**Debra Devi**, rock musician and author of *The Language of the Blues: From Alcorub to Zuzu*

"My experience in this world as a woman has never let me down because of people like Katherine Yeske Taylor. The intelligence and bravery to write a book of this magnitude of women whose voices are loud and pure is empowering."
—**Diane Gentile**, musician

SHE'S A BADASS

SHE'S A BADASS

Women in Rock Shaping Feminism

Katherine Yeske Taylor

Backbeat
Books

Essex, Connecticut

Backbeat Books

An imprint of Globe Pequot, the trade division of
The Rowman & Littlefield Publishing Group, Inc.
4501 Forbes Blvd., Ste. 200
Lanham, MD 20706
www.rowman.com

Distributed by NATIONAL BOOK NETWORK

British Library Cataloguing in Publication Information Available

Library of Congress Cataloging-in-Publication Data

Names: Taylor, Katherine Yeske, author.
Title: She's a badass : women in rock shaping feminism / by Katherine Yeske
   Taylor.
Description: Essex, Connecticut : Backbeat Books, 2023. | Includes index. |
   Summary: "Profiles of the female rock performers who took control of their
   careers and transformed the music industry from the inside" —Provided
   by publisher.
Identifiers: LCCN 2023016096 (print) | LCCN 2023016097 (ebook) | ISBN
   9781493072545 (cloth) | ISBN 9781493072552 (epub)
Subjects: LCSH: Women rock musicians—Interviews. | Women singers—
   Interviews. | Women in the music trade. | Feminism and music.
Classification: LCC ML82 .T39 2023 (print) | LCC ML82 (ebook) | DDC
   781.66092/52—dc23/eng/20230519
LC record available at https://lccn.loc.gov/2023016096
LC ebook record available at https://lccn.loc.gov/2023016097

For Maril Yeske, with immense love and gratitude.

Contents

Introduction

When I was sixteen years old, I signed on as a staff writer for my suburban Atlanta high school newspaper—and was horrified to discover that they expected me to cover things like student government meetings. *Boring.* Instead, I asked if I could interview well-known musicians (like ones I'd read about in *Rolling Stone* since I was old enough to scrape up enough allowance money for a subscription). "Sure, if you can get anyone to do it," the faculty adviser said. It was clear that he thought I could not.

My obsession with music fueled my determination. Swallowing my fear, I started cold-calling local artist management offices. At that time, in the late 1980s, Atlanta's music scene was particularly vibrant. Hometown acts like the Black Crowes and Indigo Girls had recently become international stars. Fortunately for me, they and other artists found it hilarious that some kid wanted to interview them for a high school newspaper, so they'd often agree to do it. I didn't care that they were so amused—I still wanted to ask them about how and why they did what they did, because music seemed like some kind of mysterious magic to me (and still does).

Besides writing those articles, I also became a regular at Trackside Tavern and Little 5 Points Pub, two of the main bases for Atlanta's flourishing acoustic singer-songwriter scene. Unlike most music venues, which strictly enforced an eighteen-and-up policy, the bartenders at these two places ignored my underage status as long as I didn't try to sneak any alcoholic drinks. My favorite female singer-songwriters—DeDe Vogt, Wendy Bucklew, Natalie Farr, and Caroline Aiken—eventually took me under their wing, making sure that I was shielded from any older men (or women) in the room that otherwise might have tried to harass me.

My love for rock 'n' roll and writing made it obvious that I should study music journalism in college, and it was equally clear that I must attend the nearby University of Georgia. Not only does UGA have a high-ranked journalism school, but it's also located in Athens, which appealed to me immensely. In the early 1990s, that town was having a heyday as one the most renowned music scenes in the world thanks to being the birthplace of acclaimed bands R.E.M., the B-52's, and Widespread Panic, among others.

I threw myself into the Athens music scene with everything I had (sometimes to the detriment of my coursework). Weeks after arriving, I began my professional journalism career as a contributor to the local alternative magazine, *Flagpole*. The music editor, Hillary Meister, assigned me lots of major interviews, and gave me a weekly column, "Scuttlebutt," where I was free to write about whatever shows and other events that I thought were cool. I finally felt like a "real" journalist.

I got my first big break when I started writing for *Creative Loafing*, Atlanta's weekly alternative newspaper (which I had obsessively read cover to cover for years). It was a hard-won achievement: I had called the music editor every Thursday afternoon for six months straight, begging him to give me a chance. Finally, the week before my twentieth birthday, he relented and gave me the first of what turned out to be many assignments.

My excitement soon turned to bewilderment, and then infuriation, when I heard that several (male) writers on staff were saying that I must be getting assignments because I'd slept with the editor. One particularly snarky writer even asked me, to my face, if I wrote my own articles. I wanted to shout about the years of work I'd already done. I was certain that a young male writer in the same position would be praised as a "go-getter" instead of receiving such degrading treatment.

(For the record, my *Creative Loafing* editor, Tony Paris, never made me feel "less than" because of my gender or my age. He taught me more about being a journalist than I learned in any class, and he helped me make connections that have served me well in my career to this day. Thank you, Tony.)

In the years since, I've conducted thousands of interviews—and I've discovered that many of my female subjects have similar stories about their time in the music business. Most of the women seem to agree that progress has been made on this count, but we still have quite far to go—and keeping up the fight is necessary but sometimes exhausting.

A big lingering frustration is the apparently still-encountered attitude that a woman artist should defer to her male counterparts—even, as Icelandic singer Björk told *Pitchfork* in 2015, if that means essentially making herself disappear. "Everything that a guy says once, you have to say five times," she said. "I've been guilty of one thing: after being the only girl in bands for ten years, I learned—the hard way—that if I was going to get my ideas through, I was going to have to pretend that they—men—had the ideas."[1]

This suggestion that men have the monopoly on good ideas is also met with anger, as L7 co-vocalist and guitarist Donita Sparks recounted to me in 2020: "I've had guys at record companies play me current hits and say, 'Would you guys maybe try to sound like this?' And I'm like, 'Really? Would you say that to Neil Young?' I don't think he would. I think he likes Neil Young just as he is and doesn't want him to do a fucking EDM [electronic dance music] track. So it's just kind of weird."[2]

This is nothing new, of course. Stories abound from the early years of rock and pop music about female artists who were manipulated to fit a certain vision—such as Ronnie Spector's well-documented experience with her superstar husband, producer Phil Spector, to name just one example. When women dared to be brash, overtly sexual, or otherwise defy notions of what a female artist should be—as with Janis Joplin, Marianne Faithfull, and Jefferson Airplane's Grace Slick—they were condemned as deviant.

"Feminism" really got underway in the late 1960s and through the 1970s, when journalist and activist Gloria Steinem brought widespread attention to the movement. At the same time, though, there was another type of feminism happening among women in the arts. Specifically, female rock musicians were pursuing their careers as they saw fit. Instead of being mere "manufactured" pop stars, or relegated to membership in a group where they weren't in charge, suddenly women were controlling their own music, message, and image. This was, in its way, just as revolutionary as any protest demonstration.

As I interviewed the women for this book, many of them proudly proclaimed themselves feminists—but several others had various reasons to reject that label. In either case, the way these artists have led their lives has turned them into role models (whether they actually intended to be or not), thereby promoting gender equality in the music business—and, arguably, in society overall.

In the early 1970s, Suzi Quatro was the epitome of this new breed of female artist. She was the first woman rock star to front her own band, singing and playing bass as well as writing her own songs—but, she recalled, it wasn't easy: "I was always a square peg in a round hole," she told me in 2021. "Never fit anywhere. Which is why I had to find my own niche. Nobody told me to act a certain way, play a certain way, sing a certain way. Because I didn't fit anywhere, I found my own place to fit. So finding that place, you create your own thing, and then nobody can take it away from you. So I found my own voice and I kept it."[3]

A decade later, Joan Jett emulated this approach to great success, finding major stardom thanks to hits such as "I Love Rock 'n' Roll" and her swaggering image. "Other people call me a rebel, but I feel like I'm just living my life and doing what I want to do. Sometimes people call that rebellion, especially when you're a woman," she told *Reuters* in 2010.[4]

Things took another jump forward in the 1990s with the "riot grrrl" movement, which strives to combine music, feminism, and politics in order to enact change. In recent years, there has been a renewal of interest in the riot grrrl culture among young women, who are aiming to make it even more inclusive than its first iteration.[5]

Perhaps the more recent feminist movements, such as #MeToo, will spark further significant change. Still, even as many female artists seem to welcome this latest development, some admit that it's stirring up mixed emotions. "I feel so happy to hear people talking about it, but it also reminds me of stuff I never spoke up about because I was just like, there's too much," Bikini Kill singer Kathleen Hanna told *Pitchfork* in 2019, regarding the public conversations about sexism that #MeToo has sparked. "Like, OK, that promoter groped me. Who am I going to go to? It wasn't like I was going to call the cops. I'm going to go play another show tomorrow and forget about it. It's made me wonder about the times I thought, 'I just want to put this behind me. I have a vision and a mission, and I'm not going to let anybody fucking take me off of my mission.'"[6]

Feminism has always been a complex and controversial topic, as female rock musicians seem to know especially well. When they've stayed true to their own vision, these artists have alternately been adored as role models or denounced as bad influences. Either way, they're asked to cope with certain pressures that their male counterparts don't face. Even now, nearly a quarter century into the new millennium, feminism remains a relevant topic.

In this book, I've interviewed twenty significant women in rock, devoting a full chapter to each one, taking an in-depth look at her most memorable experiences in the music business (and in life in general). They reveal the incredible talent, determination—and, often, humor—that they needed in order to succeed. Their experiences reveal the unique challenges that these women have faced, how they overcame them, and what they think still needs to be done to make sure we don't lose the progress that's been made so far on the equality front. Spanning the 1970s through today, these women's stories prove that promoting feminism—either through activism or by living example—is, undeniably, badass.

Katherine Yeske Taylor, New York City

1

Suzi Quatro

In the beginning, there was Suzi Quatro.

She was the original female rock star. While other women came before her in the music business, she was the first one to lead her own band. A true musician, she sang and played bass, wrote many of the songs she recorded, and had the final say in her career decisions—all things that bucked the status quo in the early 1970s. And it worked: with singles such as "Can the Can" (1973), "48 Crash" (1973), "Devil Gate Drive" (1974), and "Stumblin' In" (1978), Quatro became a multiplatinum-selling superstar, especially in Europe and Australia. Five decades later, she continues to release albums and perform in sold-out shows around the world.

Given her history, Quatro is certain that she broke barriers for women in the music business. "There wasn't anybody before me, so of course I did," she says. "I will take to my grave the fact that I was the first. That's something I'm very humbled by. And when I look at it, that job needed to fall on the shoulders of somebody exactly like me who didn't really do gender, who wasn't out there going, 'I'm a girl.' I didn't have an agenda. I was just being who I was."

This doesn't mean she deliberately intended to be a trail-blazer, though: "I've always had the same view: I'm not a femi-nist. I'm a 'me-ist.' Your job in life is to go inside yourself and find that little light that makes you *you* and switch it on and let nobody ever switch it off. I always did make myself heard."

She shakes her head at tales of other female artists having their opinions ignored or overruled. "No, that shouldn't be happening," she says. "You've got to stand up and be counted. You just do. The strength comes from inside. You can always say, 'Hear me, or I'm walking.'"

* * *

"When I held auditions for my band way back in the early days when I started having hits in '73, I could see by the way they walked in the door if guys had a problem with me being a female," Quatro says. "And they were back out the door before they played the first note, because I don't justify myself to anybody. Absolutely not."

At that time, Quatro was living in London, where she had moved in 1971 after English producer Mickie Most signed her to a solo deal with his Rak Records label. Most had become successful in the 1960s, working with acts such as the Animals, Herman's Hermits, Donovan, and Jeff Beck, among many others. "He wanted to make me the first Suzi Quatro, whatever that might be," she says.

This was a refreshing change of pace for Quatro. Elektra Records had previously offered her a solo deal, but she'd turned it down because "They wanted to make me the next Janis Joplin," she says. Joplin was only twenty-seven years old when she died of a heroin overdose in 1970, but she had become one of the most popular female singers in the world thanks to the massive hits "Piece of My Heart" (1968) and "Me and Bobby McGee" (1971). Still, Quatro bristled at the suggestion that she should follow Joplin's lead (or anyone else's).

"I thought Janis was really good," Quatro says. "I also loved Grace Slick of Jefferson Airplane. But I didn't think of them in the same genre as me because I was a *musician*. There's always been girl singers. I mean, Joplin took it to the *nth* degree. So did Grace Slick. But I was a girl musician. From the time I started to play my bass in a band, I was aware that I didn't have a niche in which to fit. It did not exist. So I created my own."

But it wasn't easy. For a time, it seemed like Quatro might never get her big break. After arriving in England at only twenty-one years old, she had spent a year living by herself in a hotel, writing songs and refining her tough, rather androgynous image.

The experience was, she says, "emotionally, very, very difficult. I knew I was leaving everything I was familiar with. I spent about a year very, very lonely, very tearful, but never considered giving up. Never, never, never. Not in my capacity. That was the path I chose, and I was going to make it—I did have self-belief. I wasn't scared. I was determined. And I knew that if I stuck to 'me,' that would make me happy, whether I made it or not."

In truth, though, Quatro had always felt that *someone* would come along and give her the helping hand she needed to make it big: "When I got the two offers for the solo contract, I wasn't surprised. I was always kind of waiting for the tap on the shoulder."

But after signing the deal with Most, she discovered a problem. Despite his stellar credentials as a producer, "Mickie couldn't capture me on records. He didn't know how to record me. He couldn't get my edge. He knew what I wasn't. He didn't know what I was. But he recognized that I was *something*."

Her debut single, "Rolling Stone," came out in 1972. (Peter Frampton, who would go on to worldwide stardom of his own later in the decade, played guitar on the track.) It was a hit in Portugal—and nowhere else.

It was clear that something had to change. First, Quatro held auditions for a band of her own, quickly weeding out anyone who seemed to have a problem with her leadership position. She ended up choosing an all-male lineup to back her.

Next, on Most's suggestion, Quatro agreed to work with the songwriting team of Mike Chapman and Nicky Chinn. The duo had had success writing for glam rockers the Sweet, and Quatro felt confident they'd create songs for her that would have a similarly edgy style. Although Quatro continued to write as well, this arrangement left her free to explore "artistic" avenues, leaving Chapman and Chinn to create more overtly commercial material.

To build up her fanbase, Quatro signed on as the opening act on a 1972 UK tour with hard rock bands Thin Lizzy and Slade. She says she had no problem holding her own as a petite female, even in that ultra-masculine environment. She credits this to her take-no-shit attitude. "Women do have balls—they keep them in their head where they don't get kicked," she says with a laugh. "Let's say a six foot two guy pisses me off, okay? I will go right up to him with my finger in his face, never thinking for a minute that I possibly could be in danger."

All of these efforts paid off: Quatro's next single, the Chapman/Chinn-composed "Can the Can," was a hit when it was released in 1973. It charted in numerous countries, including making it to the top spot in Great Britain, Germany, Switzerland, and Australia.

Her self-titled debut album, released later in 1973, yielded the single "48 Crash." That did similarly well in the charts, and she repeated this success the following year with the song "Devil Gate Drive." In 1975, she toured North America as Alice Cooper's opening act for his extensive "Welcome to My Nightmare" tour.

As her fame grew, Quatro found herself disputing the rumor that Most had acted as some sort of Svengali for her. "I was doing an interview, maybe in the second year of my success, and Mickie was in the room. The journalist said, 'So, Mickie—you tell Suzi what to do?' And Mickie went, '*Nobody* tells Suzi what to do.'"

Quatro hasn't always felt like she's received due respect from her peers, either. She recalls a 2010 Elvis Presley tribute concert that she played in London's Hyde Park. Tom Jones was also on the bill. So was the TCB Band—the group that had backed Presley from 1969 until his 1977 death.

"Huge gig. It was on the BBC," she recalls. "So I arrive at rehearsal with my bass guitar. Jerry [Scheff], the TCB Band bass player, comes up to me and introduces himself. He said, 'Listen, when you go on, I can back you.'" She was insulted at the implication that she couldn't play the bass herself, but she didn't say anything—instead, she made sure during soundcheck that Scheff saw her doing an elaborate solo.

"I saw Jerry on the side of the stage, and my husband was there, too. I walked over and Jerry looked at my husband and he went, 'I have to follow *that*.' I love these little poignant, poetic justice moments in life," she says.

Even now, after decades in the music business, Quatro admits that she continues to have to prove her musical prowess: "I'm obliged to do a ten-minute bass solo every night, just to show everybody that I play."

Sometimes, she still has to tell people how she should be treated offstage, as well—especially when she's out on the road, where she's often the only woman in the band or crew. "I do have a 'female penalty card,' and I keep it in my back pocket," she says. "If anybody steps over the line with me, out comes the card. So I have my little sensibilities."

An example of when she's had to use this: "One time I went into a room with all the people at the gig, all guys, and they had a blue movie on. Nothing wrong with that. But I said, 'Off. I'm in the room. *Off.'*" Another example: "My ass has been touched a couple of times, and both of those people are singing soprano now. So basically, even though I am a tomboy and I don't do gender, you've got to keep that female sensibility, you've got to keep people's respect: 'Here's the line. Don't cross it.'"

*   *   *

Quatro's unwavering toughness comes, in part, from her upbringing in Detroit. Though she moved away from it more than fifty years ago, she's still fiercely proud to be from there. "It's just a special city," she says. "You've got your Black and white completely coming together. Musically, it's joined somehow. You've got your energy level. You've got your edge. You've got this almost desperation. It's one of the best music cities, if not *the* best music city, in the world."

She credits growing up in a large family with helping her learn to stand up for herself. "You really have to find your voice, and it's not always easy. It's always, 'You're one of the kids.' I'm *not* one of the kids, I am me. So maybe I had even more of a natural need to find my voice, and then once I found it, I wouldn't give it up for anybody. I've remained true to that my entire life, and I'm very stubborn about it. Don't box me in. Don't try to make me change. I'm *me*."

In the Quatro household, she and her three sisters were treated no differently than their brother. "My father didn't want clingy females, so he always gave us the impression that you can do whatever you wanted to," she says. "Maybe that wasn't what he was intending, but I actually didn't grow up even doing gender. It's never occurred to me that there's something I can't do, if I want to do it, because I'm female."

It was a musical family, so there were all kinds of instruments around the house. Her father was the leader of his own jazz band, the Art Quatro Trio. She remembers taking family vacations, which usually entailed road trips in a big station wagon, "and always, we'd have family sing-alongs. Like you do with family, you naturally go into harmony. We're all singing our parts, and I always noticed my dad while he was driving, he'd be going *do do do*," she says, mimicking a melodic bass line. "I used to think, 'That's the best part!'"

Her urge to become a musician herself was actually inspired by someone outside of her household, however: when she was five and a half years old, she saw Elvis Presley on TV singing "Don't Be Cruel," and "I had that little light bulb moment. I said, 'I'm going to do *that*.' It didn't occur to me that I was a girl."

She started off playing percussion instruments and classical piano, as well as learning to read music. She estimates she was seven or eight years old when her father invited her to play the bongos with his band at shows. During this time, she began realizing that she had special talent, even compared to the rest of her creatively inclined family.

"We'd always have family shows because everybody played music, everybody sang," she says. "I would do a sketch or tell a joke or play something. I noticed that whenever I did my bit, the whole room would go quiet and watch me. So this made me aware, even very young, that I had something that held an audience. It's got nothing to do with ego; you're just knowing you're doing something well and it's having an effect. That goes into your psyche and stays with you your entire life.

It's knowing there's something in you that sets you apart. You just have a feeling."

Another pivotal moment in her childhood came when she and her sisters saw the Beatles playing on TV. Afterward, "One of my sisters and me, two other sisters we knew, and another girl down the road were talking—and the idea came up, 'Hey, all-girl band.' I think it was my sister Patti who said it." With that, the Pleasure Seekers were born.

"Everybody quickly chose an instrument. I didn't speak up. I don't know why. I was daydreaming, maybe. [Then] I said, 'Hey, what am I going to play?' My sister Patti said, 'You're playing bass.' I said, 'Okay,' and I went to my dad, and he gave me the 1957 Fender Precision, which is the Rolls-Royce of bass guitars. Now, I did not know this. So I learned to play on the heaviest and hardest bass. I didn't question if there was a lighter one, if there was a smaller neck, because I didn't know I had any options. All I knew was that he gave me a bass to play. I didn't even know it was unusual for a woman to play bass."

She immediately fell in love with the instrument, mastering it quickly. "Being a percussionist, and a pianist—which is also a percussive instrument—I guess I'm very much in tune with the rhythm and the bass elements of music," she says.

The Pleasure Seekers soon became well-known in the Detroit music scene. Eventually, through various lineup changes, all of the Quatro sisters spent time in the band. "It started off with one sister, then another one, and eventually the baby sister joined," Quatro says. "When my eldest sister joined, her husband started to manage the band. So even though I was fourteen years old, I think my parents felt that I was quite safe. And it had to be, because even though I don't do gender, we *are* girls."

Still, she says she can't recall any particularly unnerving experiences that happened to her during this time, perhaps because of her fearless attitude. "I found very young that my best weapon is my mouth," she says. "When you're five foot two, you know this. You've got to develop that quick comeback."

She was equally assertive when it came to declaring her status as a professional musician. "See, I always had the attitude that I come at you with, 'Hi, I'm a bass player.' Not, 'Hi, I'm a girl bass player.'"

Though she was wary of emphasizing her gender, she does concede that there were some positive elements specifically related to being in an all-girl band. For one thing, "We were unique, and so we ended up getting most of the gigs—the club owners wanted us because we brought the customers in." When she's talked to male artists who were playing in Detroit at that time—Alice Cooper, and members of MC5 and the Stooges—she's heard that they had not been welcomed in this way.

But being "cocooned," as she puts it, soon seemed overly restrictive. "We were a show band, changing costumes and doing dance steps, while the other people were out there doing rock and roll gigs." Still, she says, "It was all a great learning process."

As it had been within her own family, Quatro increasingly realized that her natural charisma made her the most prominent member in the band, which she knew the other girls resented. "When I was fifteen, sixteen, we didn't have any money to afford roadies—we set up the equipment ourselves," she says, "and I always remember this: Leo [Fenn, manager] was setting up the lights, and us girls were plugging stuff in and scrambling around onstage, and he said to the whole band, 'You guys realize of course that all the lights have to go on Suzi.' I wanted the stage to swallow me up. But I didn't say it—*he* said it."

The Pleasure Seekers signed a deal with Mercury Records, released a single in 1968 ("Light of Love"), and toured the United States—but it became clear that they weren't likely to break through to major stardom.

Shifting gears, they changed the band name to Cradle and, as Quatro recalls, "we got quite serious, jamming and all that" on harder-edged material. By now, Quatro had been relegated to the back of the stage in an attempt to put more of an equitable focus onto her bandmates. "They tried to change the format of the band so that I was mainly playing bass [and not singing]," Quatro recalls. It didn't work: at a Cradle show, Mickie Most noticed her, then gave her the solo deal that changed everything.

*   *   *

As the 1970s progressed, Quatro kept evolving. Her fame in America grew when, from 1977 to 1979, she switched to acting, portraying musician "Leather Tuscadero" on the beloved sitcom *Happy Days*. True to her character's name, she wore leather outfits that gave her a tough appearance, yet her persona was likeably high spirited. These traits, she says, were modeled on her own image and attitude.

"I said, 'If you want me to do this, I play it for real,'" Quatro says of her time on *Happy Days*. "I had the script, and I wasn't given any different direction than what I did. I played it how I felt it. I was able to use bits of the very young Suzi in it. I played it as me, a real rocker. So that was good. We even got the vintage guitar out. What a great show." She says she remains very good friends with Henry Winkler and Ron Howard (who starred as the characters The Fonz and Richie Cunningham, respectively). Since then, she has continued to act on occasion, including an acclaimed starring role in a production of *Annie Get Your Gun* in Chichester, England, in 1986.

In 1978, she released "Stumblin' In," a duet with Chris Norman of the band Smokie. It was another song that was written by Mike Chapman and Nicky Chinn, but its easygoing vibe marked a significant stylistic departure from her earlier singles. It reached number 4 on both the *Billboard* "Hot 100" and "Adult Contemporary" charts in the United States, making it Quatro's most successful release to date in her homeland.

In the 1980s, though, Quatro was ready for a change. She largely focused on her children: Laura, born in 1982, and Richard, who followed in 1984. (Their father, Len Tuckey, was the guitarist in Quatro's band; they married in 1976 and divorced in 1992.) "I hope I was a good mother. I did my best," she says.

Motherhood, she says, taught her one thing more than anything else: "We are the stronger sex, in many ways. We just are. Physically, no. But boy oh boy, we've got the weight of the world on our shoulders. Women should be treated with the utmost respect. We don't have an easy job."

When shifting between her public persona and her personal life, Quatro says it helps that "I separate between little Suzi from Detroit and Suzi Quatro. Two different things, because you must have a private side, too.

"I've always had to wear many hats—but isn't that just being a woman?" she continues. "Sometimes it is a lot. But I do have big shoulders and I am strong. My strength is that I'm very vulnerable. Very. But I survive it." She pauses, seeming momentarily lost in thought before adding, "Boy, did I just say that? I did. I never thought of it that way until just this second." Then she breaks into a sunny smile.

Since she started her career more than five decades ago, Quatro has watched as other women also try to find that balance between being strong while retaining a certain feminine softness. "There has been progress, very much so. If somebody touches them or does something inappropriate, women are speaking out more now, which is good," she says.

But she also has some words of caution as the struggle for equal rights continues: "Let's not ever lose the difference between male and female. It's attractive. I mean, who doesn't want to curl up in their man's arms at the end of the day? That should never be lost. Just because you're strong, don't castrate men in the process."

* * *

Now in her seventies, Quatro remains a big star in England, where she still lives (dividing her time between there and Germany, her husband's native country). She is enjoying a career renaissance, and she has no intention of retiring. "I am an entertainer in my heart and soul. That's what I love doing very much," she says. And she hasn't become jaded about it, either: "Just before I go onstage, even after fifty-eight years, I find myself thinking, 'I hope they like me.' But that's the right attitude."

She continues to release albums and tour—including a headlining show at London's prestigious Royal Albert Hall just a few days before this Zoom video interview. "I'm still high. It was maybe the best gig of my entire career, I have to say. It was special," she says of that performance.

And, finally, she feels like she's getting due recognition for her accomplishments. An acclaimed documentary about her life, *Suzi Q*, came out in 2019. In it, numerous famed female artists appear: Debbie Harry of Blondie, Tina Weymouth of Talking Heads, Joan Jett and Cherie Currie (who both got their start in the Runaways), and Donita Sparks of L7, among others. All of them sing her praises, crediting her with inspiring them to become musicians.

"Made me cry," Quatro says of those tributes. "That's the first time I realized what I'd done. By me doing what I did, I gave permission to women all over the world to be different. So I'll take that to my grave. I'm proud."

2

Ann Wilson (Heart)

"It's been a long and pretty arduous evolution for females in rock," says Ann Wilson, during a call from her Florida home. She feels this way because rock music is something that was created "by men to get girls and talk about their experiences with booze and all that kind of stuff," she says.

She believes things can change, though. "I think women are deep and emotional and attached to their instincts, and that's what they have to bring into songwriting and rock. I believe that women will really come into their own in rock when they come up with something that's uniquely theirs, where they come from the female sensibility and inject a whole new voice into this thing."

It's likely that many music fans would argue that Wilson herself did just that with Heart. Her powerful vocals (and her sister Nancy's skillful guitar playing) helped propel that band to superstardom in the 1970s with hits such as "Magic Man," "Crazy on You," "Barracuda," "Straight On," and many more. They were the first female-fronted hard rock band to gain international fame. The next decade, they adapted with the times, reinventing themselves into pop rock mainstays with the arena-ready anthems "What about Love?," "Never," "These Dreams," and "Alone."

On the one hand, Wilson doesn't feel that she and her sister should be thought of any differently than their male peers. "I've never looked at our gender as being anything to set us apart from other musicians," she says. "I guess I have a blind spot where that's concerned."

Yet Wilson also recognizes that they accomplished things that no female musicians before them had done—and that made them trailblazers, whether they intended to be or not. "I don't think anybody really knew what to do with me or with Nancy. There was no pigeonhole to put us in. There still isn't, really!" she says with a laugh. "I think that some of the obstacles that were thrown up in front of Nancy and me for being women are just really basic systemic things. By standing up and being bold and not being submissive, do females go against the very basis of their gender, as it applies to culture? If they do, then that's called being rebellious."

*   *   *

Wilson wasn't trying to be rebellious when she started pursuing a music career—she was simply following her instincts: "It was buried so deep down in my psyche. It was the thing that I knew I was aimed at ever since I was a young teenager. For me, there was just no other path."

She pursued her dream relentlessly—even when it was particularly difficult in the earliest days, before Nancy joined the band. "I went through many different bad experiences being the only female [in the group]," Wilson says of that time. "I remember, before it was even called Heart, the band were playing in Montana at this bar. This guy came up to me during a break and said some really insulting things, like, 'You should just hike up your bra straps.' And our drummer stepped in front of me and told the guy, 'She's not here for you, buddy. She's here to sing.' So he acted as a protective big brother.

"That's happened a few times over the years where the males in the band, their protective red flag goes up and they stand in front of you," she says, adding that male bandmates, crew, and other team members have been supportive of the Wilson sisters when it comes to artistic matters, as well. "I don't think anyone in our camp ever really dismissed our contributions as songwriters and performers. But that's a little bubble that you have around you. We gathered around ourselves this small, tight group of people that really believed in it. That's why it worked for us."

Most importantly, even when obstacles have been thrown in front of her because she's female, her own internal drive to succeed has remained steadfast. "It was always the music, the message of the songs, and the feeling of singing," she says. "Just that really basic, primal thing that makes you want to sing, makes you want to be in a band, and makes you want to remember what it was like to be a child before [you understood about] gender."

*   *   *

Wilson's own childhood directly led to Heart, because her and Nancy's passion for music was, she says, "born out of my parents' love of music and their ability to relax and sing in front of each other."

Her parents "didn't have professional aspirations, but my mother was a classically trained pianist, and my father had a beautiful baritone voice. In fact, my parents had met in college, at Oregon State [University], in choir. They brought this love and ease with music with them into their marriage, and then gave it to their children." She recalls that her parents constantly played records, especially hits that were popular at the time like Simon and Garfunkel's "Bridge Over Troubled Water," as well as a wide variety of other music.

Wilson also remembers many get-togethers with her aunts, uncles, and cousins where music played a central part. "They came out of the Second World War, through the '50s where nobody wanted to even know about anything negative," she says of her close-knit extended family. "After World War II, they just wanted to wear their aloha shirts and drink beer in the backyard. So all those people were always gathering at our house with ukuleles. The family had no problem sitting around in a big circle singing together. That gave way to us kids singing for the grown-ups. Then we got guitars so we could accompany the family."

From there, "It wasn't much of a stretch for Nancy and me to want to play at our parents' church on Youth Sunday. And then, 'Hey, that felt so good—let's go get a gig at some coffeehouse!' The coffeehouse led to [shows at] the tavern. And then I was in Heart."

As a child, though, Wilson had no concept that music could ever actually become her full-time job. She was born in 1950 in San Diego, California, but her family moved often because of her father's military career. She, along with her parents and two sisters, "lived everywhere there was a Marine Corps base: Virginia, North Carolina, California, Taiwan, Panama. My mother was in charge of all those moves. [My dad] would be sent ahead, and then she would orchestrate the move to join him. It meant that we had to be like this little platoon. We all had to watch out for each other and had to follow orders and not complain. It was kind of like a little military operation." (This experience, she says, later proved useful in helping her feel at home as a touring musician.)

In 1960, when Wilson was nine years old, her father was transferred to Seattle, where he became the Marine Corps recruiter for the Pacific Northwest. She remembers feeling happy to finally put down roots somewhere. "All the sudden, we weren't like 'the Wilson unit' only. We could actually spread out a little bit and have friends," she says.

By her teenaged years, Wilson was certain that she wanted to become a singer, but it took her some time to become active in her hometown's music scene. "When I was in high school, all the cool clubs were in Seattle, but we lived in the suburbs, so I didn't get a chance as a teenager to get involved in that until after I graduated." She went to art school in the city. "That's when I really entered the Seattle scene, on Capitol Hill."

In the early 1970s, Wilson joined Heart after she met their manager, Mike Fisher, with whom she also became romantically involved. He was living in Vancouver, Canada, after fleeing the United States to avoid the Vietnam War draft. She and the rest of her bandmates decided to move there, as well, and the group soon became popular in that city's club circuit. In 1974, Nancy Wilson also moved to Vancouver, becoming one of Heart's guitarists.

Wilson remembers feeling relief when her sister became her bandmate. "It was great for Nancy and me because we could lean on each other at those moments when only somebody extremely close to you can get you."

With their lineup set, Heart refined a unique blend of hard rock and folk, then tried to get a record deal, but none of the major labels would touch them. "Every single one of them didn't know what to do with me or with Nancy. I remember one guy at one of the labels saying, 'Well, we don't want the band—we'll take her [Ann]." He wanted her to do a cover of a ballad, "Wildflower" (which became a hit in 1973 for the Vancouver-based band Skylark), but she rejected the offer. "At that time, I just went, 'Nah, I'm a rocker.' That's when we were writing songs like "Crazy on You" and "Barracuda." So yeah, we were misunderstood at the very beginning."

They ended up signing with a small independent label, Mushroom Records, and recorded their debut album, *Dreamboat Annie*. Released in Canada in 1975, it quickly became a hit thanks to the single "Magic Man." Later, when it was released in the United States, it was hugely popular there, as well, eventually attaining platinum status (a million copies sold). For Wilson, this was vindicating after having to work so hard to convince music executives to give the band a chance.

"I just think you have to have the goods to back it up—and be pushy," she says. "A lot of women don't want to be pushy because it goes against the grain of the cultural thing of women being submissive and quiet."

Wilson certainly wasn't submissive and quiet—but even so, she was taken aback by the misogynistic culture that permeated the music business at that time. Ironically, one of her encounters with this type of bad treatment also sparked one of Heart's biggest hits, "Barracuda," which was released as a single in 1977. Scathing and soaring, it has become one of the band's signature songs.

"It was probably late '76 or something, '77, maybe," Wilson recalls. "A guy who came up to me in the dressing room after our set said to me, 'Hey, how's your lover doing?' I said, 'He's fine; he's right over there,'" and she motioned to Mike Fisher.

"And then the guy went, 'No, no, no—I meant you and your sister. You and your sister are lovers, right?'

"I had this strange bunch of emotions that hit me right after he said that. At first it was like, 'Wow, *huh*.' And then it was like, 'God damn it, this is a sleazy business after all. What was I thinking?' Because Nancy and I really had this idea that we were songwriters carrying cool messages to the people. We had no idea that we would be perceived, even by a sleazeball, as two porno chicks together in a band. It made me really mad, not only at him but at the industry and at my decision to be so naive and consider myself some kind of spiritual pilgrim with these songs. I got so mad and confused, I wrote the words to "Barracuda." It was mostly just venom that I felt."

Soon after, Wilson encountered another notorious example of how badly women could be treated in the music business. Forty-five years later, she still sounds irritated as she recalls this incident.

"Our record company was really good. They believed in us. But they had this publicist at the time; his idea was to put a full-page ad in *Rolling Stone* that looked like a tabloid cover, and for it they used an outtake from the *Dreamboat Annie* cover session where [Nancy and I] had circles under our eyes and we looked really kind of bad. And the caption was, 'It was only our first time.' So the way it looked was, we just got out of bed from having fucked each other. My parents were offended. We were offended. Everyone was offended—except for the record company, because they sold a lot of records because of it.

"All of it became so distasteful to me that I just thought, 'No, this is going in the wrong direction for our dignity and for our souls. This is not how we want to be perceived. I don't care if it sells records or not. This is just ugly. It's the lowest common denominator, and I'm not going to go there.' So we decided to change labels. Our producer, Mike Flicker, also left over it. We just went, 'We'll take our chances someplace else.'"

Breaking that contract prompted Mushroom Records to sue the band. The lawsuit was filed in Seattle, where the members of Heart had relocated. "That's probably where we lucked out, because if it had gone in front of a judge that was more familiar with the music industry, like in L.A. or something, we might not have prevailed. But we did," Wilson says. "This judge in Seattle went, 'You can't stop these local girls from doing their craft. So back off.'"

Despite winning the case, the Wilson sisters didn't feel entirely victorious, as they were worried that standing up for themselves would get them labeled as "difficult" or otherwise hurt their long-term career prospects. "We felt that no one else was going to want to touch us because we were such divas," she says.

Fortunately, that fear turned out to be unfounded, as Heart went on to ubiquitous radio play through the rest of the 1970s and on into the 1980s, when they became popular on the then brand-new MTV network. Though relieved that they had adapted to the times and remained successful, Wilson recalls that it was difficult for her and her sister to suddenly have so much attention paid to their looks, not just their music.

"It was sort of like you were put on a movie set with trained dancers and people who were actors and actresses, and expected to be one of them," Wilson says of making music videos in the 1980s. "I know in my case, I'd just always been a musician. I'd never been a dancer or an actress or anything like that, so it was really uncomfortable at first to try and measure up to that. And," she says with a laugh, "you can see it in some of the old Heart videos, the styling and the bad acting that both Nancy and myself did!"

MTV provided a new visual-based promotional medium for bands—but in truth, Wilson says, the focus on women's appearance has been the case forever. "I think there's always been an image thing, for all women. That's always been an obstacle. There's a very small window of acceptability that's put on women, image-wise. Or if it's not image, then it's ageism, or it's something else." She says this is particularly true for women in music. "There's always some reason why you shouldn't be doing this if you are a woman."

She worries when she sees how many young female artists these days seem to focus on appearance over talent in order to get noticed. "If you're good-looking and you wear tiny hot pants and all this kind of stuff that is commonplace now for women in the music industry, you can only do it for so long before your body changes. The inevitable decline. So you'd better have a lot more than just your body."

Five decades after Heart began their rise to fame, Wilson sees how women are still treated differently than their male peers—it happens "constantly. All the time," she says. "Sometimes it's disappointing because you're sending the music from your soul, and why does it have to get hung up in the gender issue? It's a human broadcast, not a gender one."

Even though that's discouraging, she also sees reason for optimism: "Now we have so many women doing rock, and involved in every level of the entertainment industry," she says, though she adds that more improvement will "only come with those women pushing it who are the most bold."

She understands that some women don't do this because they're afraid to risk having everything they've worked for taken away. "Such a short, fleeting moment to actually go out and stand in the light in this industry, because there are so many people waiting in line right behind you to be the next you."

She pauses when asked what specific advice she'd give young female musicians who want to know how to make their artistry stand out in this business. "I think if you have to ask what it takes, then maybe you don't have it. It's kind of an instinctive thing. There's not a rule book for it. I just think you have to want it so bad that you're willing to give up everything."

*   *   *

Only one thing has been more important to Wilson than her music: motherhood. And while she didn't give up her music career when she began that phase in her life, it certainly did cause her to change the way she went on tour—which is something she doesn't think tends to be true for male musicians. "Most of the time how it happens is my male counterparts, a lot of them have children, but the wives at home take care of the kids and the guys go out on tour."

Wilson adopted her children, Marie and Dustin, in the 1990s. "I was a single mother, and I brought the kids out on the road.

My son was on a tour bus by the time he was three months old. We made him a special bunk with a guard net so he couldn't roll [out of the bed]. He liked it. He slept really well on the tour bus. He was just [like] a little football to carry around. And by the time my daughter was five, she had been all over Europe, Japan, South America, and a lot of the [US] states. She had traveled more than most kids will travel in their lives."

As a successful artist, Wilson could afford to hire people to make this globetrotting existence possible. "I always had an au pair or a nanny along to help me out because I have to go onstage, and who's going to take care of the kids for that two hours? And I need to sleep; I can't be up all night and do shows and keep my health. It worked," she says.

After struggling with drug and alcohol addiction, Wilson has been sober since 2009. She found further happiness when she got married in 2015, though she admits that while her husband, Dean, supports her career, he's not the biggest fan of her music. "He has his opinions about it because he likes prog music. He is super into art rock and avant-garde stuff. He considers my music to be pretty middle-of-the-road, and kind of pedestrian," she says, amused. "He likes some of the new stuff I've written, but he's in a different headspace. I'm fine with that."

In recent years, Wilson's family has continued to expand as her daughter had three daughters of her own. This has prompted Wilson to think about what their future might look like. When it comes to where women's rights are headed, she's worried about what she foresees for them.

*   *   *

"It's just so painful to me to see us backslide this way in women's rights," Wilson says, referring to the reversal of *Roe v. Wade*, the landmark United States Supreme Court ruling that legalized abortion in 1973. At the time of this conversation, recently leaked documents had made it clear that this case was about to be overturned. (That ruling then happened on June 24, 2022.)

"That just makes my hair stand on end," Wilson says. "All the women my age, we are of a generation where we've all taken advantage of these rights and we know how important they are to a woman's life and liberty and pursuit of happiness." Because of this belief, Wilson has donated to Planned Parenthood, the American nonprofit organization that provides women's reproductive health services, since the 1970s.

Wilson thinks her generation gained this understanding from watching what the women who came before them went through. "My mother's generation and her mother's generation fought and struggled for it, and here it is again. I'm glad my mother is not here to see this. I feel pretty disappointed and frustrated about it. And the women I've talked to that are my age feel the same. It's for the young women now, who've got the energy and the righteous indignation to say, 'You know what? You can't control us.'"

The problem, she says, is that she thinks young women "don't understand all the old stories of back-alley abortions and all that kind of stuff. They weren't alive when that was happening, so they do take [abortion] for granted. I would just hate to see a whole 'nother couple of generations have to go through that struggle all over again because it's one step forward, two steps back."

Though she views this as a crisis for women, Wilson is wary about calling herself a feminist these days. "I'm suspicious of that label, just because it's so exclusive," she says. "I mean that one male feminist is worth about five female ones, in terms of perception and getting the word out, so I wish there was a more inclusive word for it. But since there's not, I'll accept 'feminist.'"

She's also worried that disagreements over women's equality might result in an even deeper schism between men and women. "I think that's so important that we don't separate the genders and politicize the genders—like shove men over onto one side of the line and women on the other side," she says. "That is not helpful in this day and age, when we're trying to knit our society back together. How do we figure out how to work together, men and women, and still have unity? That's a real big question."

From her own experience, she sees how it can be effective to be "pushy but flexible, and not throw the baby out with the bathwater, so to speak. I think as a wife, and also as a woman in a band with men, I've learned a lot about when to be assertive and when to let it ride for a minute, and when to come back."

This is certainly the case, she says, with the band members she has hired to back her in the solo career that she started in 2007, releasing three albums under her own name so far. "It's so amazing how much time I spend in groups of men being the only female there," she says of this part of her career. "I like to think that I know how to relate to them as a person, and they relate to me as a person, and the gender divide doesn't really apply. I think my age helps. I think if I was a young, gorgeous, glamorous twenty-something, it might be harder for the men to see me as a person."

She thinks it also helps that, fifty years since she first joined Heart, she has earned widespread respect for her talent. She, along with her sister, had their musical legacy honored with a star on the Hollywood Walk of Fame in 2012. Later that year, they performed at the Kennedy Center Honors for Led Zeppelin, for which their rendition of "Stairway to Heaven" earned a standing ovation from the audience (which included the current American president, Barack Obama, and First Lady Michelle Obama). Heart have been nominated for four Grammy awards, released sixteen studio albums (several of which have attained gold or platinum sales status), and, in 2013, were inducted into the Rock and Roll Hall of Fame.

Secure in her legacy as one of rock's most iconic singers, Wilson says she feels good about being accepted for who she is now. "They don't seem to have as many conditions as they used to have," she says of the music business. "I think a lot of that is just because you hang around long enough and don't die, people go, 'Well, maybe we do value this person!'"

She laughs, but it's true that she has accomplished amazing things—and led the way for women in rock, now and into the future.

3

Exene Cervenka (X)

Even though she's been credited for breaking barriers for women in rock, X vocalist Exene Cervenka doesn't put much stock in the concept of gender differences. "Because we're not that different, that's why!" she exclaims. "Because there's no difference between men and women in almost every situation. Especially nowadays. Women do all kinds of things."

Because of this, she rejects the "feminist" label. Her issue with it stems from her belief that its definition has changed too much. "I think that the feminist thing doesn't mean what it did in the olden days," she says. "I think that's because, what exactly is your feminist goal? You want to be able to vote? Okay, I'll be all for it. How about if you want to be able to work? Yep, okay. Want to raise your kids by yourself and keep your own name and not have a husband? That's great. So what *is* the feminist struggle right now? I don't know.

"To me, a lot has been accomplished in the last 150 years for women, and I think a lot of people had to struggle *really* hard [for that], and I hope people realize that," she continues. "So women nowadays think they have it rough? I don't know about that. And if they call themselves feminists and if they're fighting for women right now? Yeah, they're fighting to keep abortion legal. Okay. But I just don't like *any* of those labels. I don't like Democrat, I don't like Republican, I don't like feminist—I don't like any of that stuff. I wouldn't want *any* label applied to me, and I never have."

To a certain extent, though, Cervenka is comfortable with being called a role model for other women coming up in the music business—but even there, she's careful to qualify it. "All I did was say yes to having one of my poems put to music," she says of X's early days, "and then I worked really, really hard for the next forty years.

"You know what I *would* like my role-modelship to be based on? That I was uncompromising about who I was, what I looked like, what I did. Compassion for other people, empathy, and being grateful to every single person that comes up and says, 'Thanks—I really like what you do.' I know how hard it is to come up to someone, because a lot of people aren't nice. So I try to be the same person I was growing up, and the same person I will always be. And not be unapproachable, or the kind of person that thinks they're important. I try not to lie to people, except to not hurt their feelings. I don't owe anybody any money. I encourage people and try to help. That's it. Past that, I don't think it matters what people say about you.

"So yeah, if I'm a role model, it's like an aunt. The one that took you places when you needed to go, and talked to you when you felt bad about yourself and told you that the kids were jealous and that's why they made fun of you."

*　　*　　*

Cervenka understands what being misunderstood feels like. When X was starting out, "People told me that I was terrible," she says. "The media told me I was the worst thing that ever happened to music, and if only [my bandmates] would get rid of me, X would be a great band. Or you'd have a producer say, 'Well, I'd really like to work with you guys, but I'd only want to produce the songs John [Doe, X co-vocalist/bassist] sings because I don't really think the songs Exene sings are worth producing.'"

Still, she doesn't blame her gender for this. "It wasn't because I was a woman. It was because I was just too weird for most people. So I understand that. That's a choice. And it's an honest choice."

Cervenka is bothered more by the times she's seen the credit she's due granted instead to Doe, to whom she was married from 1980 to 1985. "There are some people [who say], 'John's wife joined the band, and she really didn't do much except sing occasionally.' I've read that John writes all the X songs, and I'm just a sidekick." She sighs. "John does *not* write all the X songs. We write the songs a lot together. I write lyrics and melodies, which the music then has to follow. So that's why I have song-writing credit for half of everything, because I contribute."

This is one point where she's willing to consider that her gender might have played a role in how people perceive her. "Yeah, I think that is a little bit of something probably, that people just assume that the man wrote the songs—but I can't believe in the 2020s people still would think that way. And so I find that a little odd."

*   *   *

Cervenka's attitude toward gender equality was formed in the late 1960s through the 1970s, during the "second wave" of feminism (the first wave started at a convention in Seneca Falls, New York in 1848, finally culminating in 1920 with the ratification of the Nineteenth Amendment to the United States Constitution, which granted women the right to vote).

Starting with Betty Friedan's best-selling book *The Feminist Mystique* in 1963, second wave feminists sought to expand women's rights even further. Journalists such as Martha Lear (of the *New York Times*) and Gloria Steinem (columnist for *New York* magazine and founder of *Ms.* magazine) wrote high-profile articles advocating on a wide range of issues, including women's reproductive rights, equality within the workplace, and protection from domestic abuse and rape. Steinem also helped to create multiple feminist organizations and spearheaded protest activities around the world, becoming—and remaining to this day—a key leader within the women's liberation movement.

All of this activity made a big impression on Cervenka when she was an adolescent. "That, alongside the Vietnam War, were the two main topics that everyone was thinking about or wrestling with or excited by," she says. "You have to understand that when I was just coming of age, when I was twelve or thirteen, there was no birth control pill. If you got pregnant, you got married and you had a kid—there was no abortion. It was completely illegal." After the United States Supreme Court ruled that abortion was legal with the 1973 case *Roe v. Wade*, Cervenka recalls how "people were excited that they would have some control over that. And that was important."

On a personal level, Cervenka recalls feeling happy that women were gaining equality because it meant that someone unconventional like her would be granted more appealing options in life. "I wanted to work in a gas station. I wanted to be a sports announcer. I was a tomboy. I wanted to do all the fun things that boys could do, and I couldn't. You couldn't: '*You just can't.* Not acceptable.' So that was a nice thing when that was changing."

Yet Cervenka now sees a downside to the women's liberation movement. "There's good and bad to everything, right?" she says. "Like, it's great that women could work outside the home and get better jobs. But then one day it became that both parents *had* to work. There was no choice anymore, because two incomes were required. Then the kids raised themselves. And then you get a generation of narcissists."

Another problem, she says, is that "the changes come from the people—that comes from us. But there's always a lag time between people in power knowing what we want and giving it to us, because they have to adjust everything around it so it benefits them in the end. I was so aware of that."

Still, overall, Cervenka recognizes that the women's liberation movement ushered in necessary changes because in the late 1960s and early 1970s, women were still severely limited. "You couldn't have a credit card. You couldn't sign for a house. You couldn't have a bank account without your husband. So ridiculous. It was time for women to get more out in the world."

*   *   *

In the 1960s, women didn't have as much power and freedom as they later gained, but for Cervenka, it was a magical time to grow up. Born in Chicago in 1956, she then spent her early years in small-town Illinois. She says she's extremely grateful for that time: "You can always experience a city, but you can't always experience the '60s in [rural] Illinois—that's a vanishing part of the world, so I'm happy I did that."

She believes that living in a relatively isolated place at such a young age helped foster her creativity. "Growing up in a town of about a thousand people pretty much in the middle of nowhere, where you live on a gravel road, was such a great childhood because you had your imagination," she says. "You'd see something on TV and you'd want to be a spy, and watch baseball and decide you were going to be a baseball player when you grew up. You'd pretend you were a horse, and you'd climb trees, and go on adventures with the neighborhood kids and ride your bike as fast as you could."

This time in her life also gave her a solid practical foundation. "I got a really sound education—reading, writing, spelling, grammar, math. The fundamentals are the thing that kids don't know anything about anymore. I'm so glad I have that because I use it every day, and I'm so happy that I'm able to have that background."

Her family relocated to St. Petersburg, Florida, when she was fourteen years old. "It was another really amazing place," she says. As a teenager, she began writing poetry and creating her own distinctive style with thrift store clothes. Though she was smart, school no longer appealed to her, and she dropped out of high school when she was sixteen years old.

Though she clearly had an artistic streak, she says there was no inkling that she would one day become a professional musician. "People didn't do that then. We're talking like 1965. You listened to the radio and you heard the Beach Boys, the Doors, the Beatles, Bob Dylan, the Supremes, Ray Charles, Bo Diddley—and it was a magic world that had nothing to do with anything. You weren't thinking you were going to be in a band. There was no chance of even going to see those bands play or have any kind of life like that. You were going to be a nun, a nurse, a mom, a teacher. I had some bigger dreams, but they weren't realistic."

When Cervenka was still a teenager, her mother passed away. "I had to raise my sisters for a couple of years," she says.

After that, she watched one of her sisters and some of her friends leave for New York and California, and it made her want to experience somewhere new, too, "because time to move on: you're twenty years old, so 'Let's go to the big city.'" And also, "All of a sudden, my dad's married again, and I've got to move out." It was clear her time in St. Petersburg was over.

"One of my friends moved up to Tallahassee and she needed a roommate. So I said, 'Well, I'll go there.' So I drove to Tallahassee in my 1950 Cadillac and lived there for three or four months and couldn't find a job. It's the capital of Florida, so it was very bureaucratic and creepy. I couldn't do anything there. It was just really the end of the road."

Fortunately, she was soon given a way to escape this dead-end existence. "My sister's ex-boyfriend called me and said he was moving to the San Francisco Bay area, and he needed someone to help pay for gas, and did I want to go to California?" She jumped at the chance, because "California was the most exotic place on the planet when I was growing up."

Cervenka didn't know anyone in San Francisco, but she did have two friends in the Los Angeles area: Paul Reubens (who later became famous as his Pee Wee Herman persona), whom she had first met when they both were living in Florida, and a girlfriend, Fay, in Santa Monica. Agreeing that she'd be roommates with Fay, Cervenka sold her Cadillac and accepted that ride out to California.

When she arrived in L.A., though, she quickly realized that it was an untenable situation. "I was living with Fay and two friends from Texas who had moved in with her, and her boyfriend, in a studio apartment. I had a bed in the kitchen—a child's bed. It was not a friendly environment. The boyfriend was so upset."

She quickly found a job at a literary arts center and moved into an apartment of her own in Venice, a bohemian oceanside neighborhood in L.A. Soon after, she met John Doe at a poetry workshop. "That really started my musical life, because I hadn't done anything with music up until I met John in '76. I started going to shows with him, and pretty soon X was happening."

Doe had been playing with guitarist Billy Zoom for about six months by the time Cervenka came along. "They were doing cover songs, getting to know each other and just having fun. I came in, and we played with various friends who could play drums, kind of goofing around, and then eventually we got D. J. [Bonebrake]," who had previously been in the band the Eyes with future Go-Go's guitarist Charlotte Caffey. As X, they created a groundbreaking sound that combined punk with rockabilly.

Cervenka says it was an easy decision for her to join X because punk rock's emergence made it okay for someone with no musical experience to play in a band. Also, she adds, "There wasn't anything else to do."

The way she saw it, her current situation meant that she had little to lose by trying a music career. "I was a poet. I was living in Venice in a tiny apartment. I had a black and white TV with one channel on it and a mattress on the floor and a table with two chairs. That's basically all I owned." Her temporary employment was also about to run out, and she was worried about her prospects. "I had to find a job and I had to do something with my life. And I met John, and it was like, team up with him or else just hitchhike around Venice until you get killed. You take a chance on something because you need to have some kind of life."

Right from the start, it was clear that her skills and Doe's would mesh well. "John is a brilliant songwriter, and he would take these poems that I wrote and make music and go, 'Look, here's your song.' I'd be like, '*My* song?' He's like, 'Yeah, now all you have to do is sing it.' I'd be like, 'Well, I guess. How do you sing?' So he really taught me."

She also felt like she had found her place within the punk community at large. "We had this kind of kinship, I thought. Sometimes people didn't get along—we'd get in fights or call each other names because we basically were kids. But feelings didn't get hurt like nowadays. You could say anything you wanted to somebody. If they didn't like it, they'd say something back, and then you'd go have a drink or see a band or go back to rehearsing."

At the time, she was only partly aware that she was involved in a music scene that would become regarded as significant. "I knew that it was influential and important to the people that were in it. I knew that it was probably the most important thing that any of us were going to do in our lives. That this was going to be a magnificent, incredible experience. I sometimes would just stop and look around and know that. I felt really lucky to be there. But I didn't think past that. I didn't care if other people were going to catch on to it. I just knew that for us, being in that moment with those people, creating that music, was an entire universe."

She recalls that her gender was never an issue. "Of course not," she says. "Why would it matter? Everybody was doing everything. There were all kinds of women in that scene. Most of the bands had women in them. There were women doing fanzines. There were amazing journalist women. And women photographers, women managers, women club bookers. There were so many women doing the really important things. It was very normal to turn on the radio and there was a woman singing."

This fit in with Cervenka's attitude that being female was no obstacle to a creative career. It was an opinion she'd formed early in her life "because if you watched *The Ed Sullivan Show*, you would see Lesley Gore and the Supremes. And the next week Connie Francis would be on, then Phyllis Diller." Besides that, "It was the tail end of the '60s, so they'd already been through the beatniks and the hippies." She thought the punk scene followed in that countercultural tradition, making anything seem possible for anyone to achieve. "Everything was up for grabs. People were just doing stuff. You didn't even think about it too much."

That wasn't to say that everything was smooth sailing for her. "There were times when I was just, 'Oh God, this is so *hard* to make a living. There's all these ups and downs!' John and I broke up. And then Billy wanted to quit the band, then Billy got back in the band. And we made some records that we didn't really think were that great. That's a career. A career isn't just, 'I think I'll do this for the rest of my life.' You just go along for the ride."

With hindsight, she lists only one thing she maybe wishes she could undo: "We got tattoos because it was the worst thing we could do. We didn't predict that that would become mainstream popular shit," she says. "So I kind of regret all these tattoos."

But otherwise, "I don't really care what people think." Her bandmates felt the same: "We did everything we wanted to do without regard to what the consequences would be. We're artists and 'out there' people, and just lived our lives."

Four decades after their formation, X are regarded as a highly influential punk band, with eight studio albums so far, and they still tour extensively. Cervenka has been prolific beyond X, as well: as a solo artist, she's released half a dozen albums. She's also put out work through her collaborations with various artists and been a member of the bands Auntie Christ and Original Sinners. Beyond music, she's held successful visual art exhibitions, authored books, and worked as a spoken word artist and poet. "It's not just about being in a band. It's so much more than that. It's about living a full life," she says.

*   *   *

Throughout her career, Cervenka says she has sometimes sensed that she wasn't always held in the same regard as her bandmates—but not because she is female. "I felt like I was getting treated differently because I wasn't a good enough singer, or because I was bratty or mouthy, or because I was maybe not what people wanted." But she believes that being part of a band—and being married to one of her bandmates during the early years—largely shielded her from harassment.

Also, she adds, "I didn't ever get that kind of attention [because] I didn't have anything to exploit. I'm five foot two. I wasn't particularly attractive in the way that they would be looking for someone to exploit. And I was already twenty-one years old—too old. So they were looking for other people to take advantage of."

She wasn't naive about this problem, however. "I was around people that were exploiting women, but I would just look at those people and stick my tongue out at them and stare at them. I would look at them in a way that they knew that I was on to them. I can see right through people. And so they were terrified of me."

She wants to be clear that she isn't dismissing other women's distressing experiences, though. "I'm not saying that people invite it. I feel bad that there are women, especially young women, that have to constantly fend that off and sort through what's real and what isn't. That must be really hard."

She has far less empathy for women who call attention to the sacrifices they must make when they become mothers. "If you don't want to have kids, don't have kids. If you want to have kids, don't complain," she says, "I mean, I know we're talking about the struggle part of things, and I appreciate that. But I think that people focus *way* too much on everything being a struggle and how hard it is to be a woman. It's like, go back in time a little bit."

Remember (or imagine), she says, what parenthood was like "before disposable diapers, when you had four kids in the car and you were taking a trip across the country and two of them were in diapers and you were camping every night. What did the mom do? She washed the shitty diapers out by hand in a bucket by a creek or something and dried them on a clothesline she hung up. And then put them back on the kids the next morning, and they had diaper rash and stuff. Then the dad had to drive, and they were on tiny roads and didn't know if they could get to the [next] gas station. I mean, *that* was a little harder than now."

Yet, hard as parenting can be—then or now—Cervenka doesn't believe that women have a more challenging time balancing those duties with their careers than men do. "I think *everybody* juggles that stuff," she says. As an example, she cites her ex-husband, actor Viggo Mortensen, to whom she was married from 1987 until 1997; they share a son, Henry, born in 1988. "Viggo and I had to juggle our careers to take care of Henry, to take turns. Viggo had just as many decisions. 'Should I do this movie? I'll be gone for three months. What do you think? What are you doing? Are you going to tour? How are we going to take care of Henry?'"

They worked it out, and Cervenka doesn't recall having any particular problems with the situation. "I toured up until a month before Henry was born and played shows when he was still an infant. John and his wife had a baby the same day as me, and he did the same thing: played up until his baby was born and went right back to work afterwards. I mean, everybody has to make accommodations. So yeah, 'Gee, woe is me, I had to nurse a baby *and* play a show.' It's like, that was pretty good stuff. I'm all for both of those things. And I was young. I could do it all."

The logistics required to bring a child on tour are, she says, actually quite straightforward: "You hire someone that you love and trust to be there with you so for that half an hour you're doing soundcheck and that hour you're onstage, someone has your child in their possession and makes sure they're safe and sound. And then the other twenty-two hours, you take care of them."

*   *   *

These days, Cervenka is content. Her son is now a successful actor and director, and she maintains a close relationship with him. When she's not on the road with X, she lives in Orange, a quaint and historic town in Southern California. "It's just the best town ever. Really adorable. I love it here," she says.

She's equally at peace as she looks back on her life. "I stand by everything I ever did, whether it's good or bad," she says. "I had no idea that I would be okay in California. I had no idea our band would ever do anything, or that I wouldn't end up on the street or get addicted to drugs. And then it all worked out. I was kind of stupid and naive with a lot of the choices I made, so I could have ended up dead, easily. Or with the wrong people, easily. But I didn't." She chalks up her good outcome to hard work, and some luck.

Now, four decades after she found her true calling with X, she is grateful. "I just can't believe that we're still together playing music, and we're better than we used to be, in many ways. It's like, 'Oh my God, I love this so much. I love you guys so much. I'm so glad I didn't die! And we're playing shows! This is great!' How could you *not* be overjoyed?"

4

Gina Schock (the Go-Go's)

The Go-Go's first became eligible to become members of the Rock and Roll Hall of Fame in 2006—and it seemed like they should be a shoo-in for it. After all, they were the first chart-topping all-female band who wrote their own songs and played their own instruments. Four decades on, their hits such as "We Got the Beat," "Our Lips Are Sealed," "Vacation," and "Head over Heels" still stand out as some of the most vibrant and memorable pop rock songs of the 1980s.

But for reasons that remain mysterious, it took another fifteen years before they were nominated for this honor. They were finally inducted as members of the Hall's "Class of 2021."

Drummer Gina Schock recalls how, during the years when the band kept getting passed over, "We were like, 'To hell with it—we're never going to get nominated; we're never going to get inducted.' We had sort of given up. So when [the nomination] actually happened, we were slightly in disbelief, because the politics that are involved in this sort of decision-making can be very disheartening. And so we thought, 'Somebody different must be in charge of the Rock and Roll Hall of Fame!' And come to find out, they *did* have a lot of new folks that came in last year [2021]."

Once she and her bandmates found out they would be inducted, they were ecstatic. "We just couldn't believe it was actually happening, because you've got to remember, we came from humble beginnings. As a punk band back in '79, this was about the farthest thing in any of our minds, that's for sure. This was only a dream.

"My whole career has been a dream; what can I say? I thank my lucky stars. This was all meant to happen. I believe in destiny. I believe things are already set up, and we just do our best to put ourselves in the right place to let things happen the way they're supposed to."

*   *   *

It does seem like Schock was set on a path to become a professional musician from the moment she came into the world. "My parents *loved* music," she says. "They were always playing music in the house and dancing. So I had an appreciation for music at an early age."

She remembers a happy childhood where she felt supported, not just by her parents, but by her community at large. Born in Baltimore, she was raised in a suburb, Dundalk, where "everybody knew each other. Nobody locked their doors. We'd sleep on the front porch when it was really hot." Neighborhood parties were common, and often held at her family's screened-in patio.

Her family also had a vacation home on the shore of the Chesapeake Bay, where Schock has equally fond memories. "We'd go down there and catch bushels of crabs. Dad would steam them up and we'd invite the neighbors. Mom and Dad and the older folks were drinking beer while [the kids] were running around screaming and carrying on, having the time of our lives. It was beautiful!"

She adored her brother; he was seven years older than her, and often hung out with their cousins who were close to his age. "Sometimes they'd have to drag me along, but prefer not to," she says with a laugh. But her brother was also responsible for a pivotal moment in Schock's life: when she was eleven years old, he took her to see Led Zeppelin opening for the Who at Merriweather Post Pavilion, in Baltimore's suburbs. It was her first concert. It's also one of the most legendary shows in rock history, as it was the only time that those iconic bands ever shared a bill.

It made an enormous impression on Schock. "I was knocked out. I felt like, 'This is what I've *got* to do—oh my God, if only one day I can be up on that stage. I don't care what instrument I play. I just want to be up there. All these people going crazy—look what music is doing to this audience.'" The fact that it was all men on the stage didn't matter to her. "It never occurred to me, 'Those were guys and I'm a girl.' Music transcends gender, no question."

She immediately started trying to learn an instrument. "I tried bass first because it was four strings, and I thought, 'Oh, that'll be easy.' Not so! Then I tried guitar lessons." This also proved difficult for her. "I was a kid—I just didn't have the patience." Two years went by, but she was still determined to keep searching for an instrument that felt right. "Then I thought, 'Well, I'll try drums and see how that goes.'"

The first time she played the drums, she knew she was finally on the right track. "It seemed easy—I didn't have to think about it. It was a very natural flow. I instinctively knew how to do it, for some crazy reason."

Drumming quickly became her main focus in life. "I saved up money, bought a drum kit, and set it up in my bedroom. I would come home from school and put on my favorite records and play along—this is exactly how I taught myself to play drums. I learned to play by ear."

Despite her skills, she never joined her school band. "Anything to do with school, I wasn't much into," she says, though she adds that there was one aspect of going there that she did like: bringing in albums to show her classmates. "During break periods, [my friends and I] would go to this one room where they had a stereo and I'd put on a record and play it for everybody. We'd all get excited and find out when that band was going to come to the Baltimore Civic Center, and then we'd try to get tickets."

She reels off artists she saw in concert back then: "Grand Funk Railroad, Hall & Oates, Robin Trower, Santana, Foghat, War, Lynyrd Skynyrd, Mountain, Jethro Tull. You name it, I was there." She doesn't mention any female musicians, but she dismisses that point. "Like I said, gender never had anything to do with it—it was just about the music. That gender issue never really came to mind. Color, gender—none of that matters when it comes to music."

She found out that not everyone felt that way when she began joining bands, though. "When I was probably fourteen or fifteen years old, I got in a couple of bands in the neighborhood," she says, "but it was all guys, and when I'd show up to try out, they kind of laughed until I sat down and played." Winning them over with her skills, she was consistently chosen as a band member.

She got even more serious about her craft when, in her late teens, she joined the band Scratch and Sniff. "They were great because we would do four sets [a night]—two sets of covers and two sets of original material. We were a punk New Wave band, although we were also doing stuff like Roxy Music and Genesis and Aerosmith. It was all over the place musically." Playing so much, and across so many styles, made her drumming skills improve even more.

She says her male bandmates in Scratch and Sniff were always good to her. "No discrimination, as far as I could tell—getting put in your place because you're a girl, that never happened, for me."

Audiences were equally supportive, after they got used to the fact that a female could sit behind the drum kit. "I think they were shocked to see a young little teenage girl that could play drums pretty decently. Maybe they were surprised that I didn't get up there and tap the drums—I played with heart and power, more like what you would expect from a guy drummer. Once again, I never thought about being a woman. My ears led me."

Next, she joined an all-female band, Edie and the Eggs, which was created as a star vehicle for Edith Massey, who'd appeared in several films for director (and fellow proud Baltimorean) John Waters.

"That band was not meant to stay together. It was something that was put together to do a little tour of New York and the West Coast, where I had never been. I had never been on a plane.

So, of course I wanted to be a part of this. Honestly, it was more about getting to travel, and also because I loved Edie. The music was not really front and center, in my mind. This was all a first for me, and a wonderful life experience."

During that tour, Schock fell in love with California and became determined to move there. "L.A., that's where all the record labels were. It just felt like that was the place to go. As serious as I was [as a drummer], that seemed like the right place."

But first, she had to return to Maryland to figure out the logistics and save up some money. "It took a couple of years to get it all together, but then I did move to L.A. I was twenty-one years old. My parents must have been so flipped out, but they allowed me to go and had faith that I would do the right thing. And so me and one of my best friends from high school, Babs, put everything in my dad's pickup truck and drove cross-country." She remembers thinking, "'*This is it.* I'm coming out here with everything I own, and my journey is really beginning in earnest. This is what I've been dreaming of.'"

*   *   *

Schock was pleased to discover how welcoming the music scene was in her new city. "L.A. was more like, 'Come on, you guys—let's get together, let's play!' It didn't feel competitive, and so I wasn't intimidated."

When she first arrived in Los Angeles, she moved into a house with a friend named Steve Martin—"Not *the* Steve Martin," she says with a laugh, referring to the comedic actor with the same name. She credits Martin with being one of the main people who'd convinced her to move to California. "He encouraged me. He said, 'Gina, you've got to come out here—you are a great drummer.' So I did exactly that. Steve and I are still great friends."

Martin took her to see various local bands. One day, "He said, 'Gina, there's this band the Go-Go's—you've got to go see them. If you join the band, you'll make them famous.'" Knowing the Go-Go's already had a drummer, Schock was skeptical, but she agreed to see one of their shows. "I thought they were great.

They were having so much fun onstage, and I wanted to be a part of that." However, "they weren't that good at their instruments yet. But they had *something*. There was something about them that made me believe, if they just worked harder at their craft, they're going to happen."

Soon after, Steve Martin's brother, Doug, had a party at his house in Santa Monica. There, Gina met three of the Go-Go's: singer Belinda Carlisle, rhythm guitarist Jane Wiedlin, and bassist Margot Olavarria. They hit it off immediately.

"I invited them over to Steve's house because I had a PA [system], and of course my entire drum kit, amps, and microphones. All they had to do was bring their guitars and bass and plug in. So they came over and we played a bunch of songs. I could feel the minute I started playing with them that this was the band I'd been looking for. We looked at each other and started smiling and got really giggly. It was the perfect fit.

"I know they thought I was really a good drummer because I walked in there and fucking kicked ass. I played hard and fast and from the heart. And I was serious about it. The minute I stopped, I'd burst into laughter—but while I'm playing, I'm dead-ass serious. It's got to be *perfect*. Playing drums is about keeping time. It's about being precise and present. You've got to be real about that. You've got to throw yourself completely into it."

Beyond the instant connection they had through the music, Schock thought she could also bring a certain professionalism to the band. She remembers thinking, "'I could be the person to help them move forward because I have crazy work ethic.' All I wanted to do was practice, practice, practice—that's how I got better at my craft. You just have to put your time in. I'm a firm believer in this."

Soon after that impromptu jam session, the Go-Go's let their drummer go and hired Schock. "This new lineup just happened to be all girls," Schock says. She quickly convinced her bandmates to ramp up their work schedule, telling them, "'Okay, instead of a couple of times a month, we've got to rehearse five days a week.' That's what I brought to the band. And it changed things. It really did."

The band got dramatically better, creating a unique sound that blended punk, pop, and surf rock. They recorded a five-song demo tape in 1979, and on the strength of that, they were asked to open for the popular British ska bands Madness and the Specials for a show in Los Angeles, and then continued on in that capacity for a six-month UK tour in 1980.

Playing the United Kingdom with established bands was a huge opportunity for the Go-Go's—but it wasn't an easy experience for them. At that time, the ska scene was attracting a sizeable skinhead audience. "They were pretty radical and violent, and really didn't want to see five girls from L.A. up onstage playing," Schock recalls. "They thought of us as a joke. 'Show us your tits' and all that crap. Throwing bottles at us and spitting at us. Completely disrespectful. Thankfully, Madness and the Specials were lovely guys, and always treated us respectfully. They were a shoulder that we could cry on when we got offstage."

Difficult as it was to endure at the time, Schock now appreciates this situation as a blessing in disguise. "I'm thankful for that because we became a much better band," she says. "After a couple of weeks, we put the hard hats on, went out there, and were ready for action. Our attitude became, 'Us against them.' Regardless of the audience's behavior, we were still going to do what we loved. And you know what? By the time we got back to the States, we were very, very tight and had a laser focus on becoming successful, in a way that we hadn't been before we left.

"Despite some of the crowd reactions we got, it was a great experience, going all over England for the first time. Flying across the Atlantic. So many firsts. And how exciting when you're that age. Also, being the opening band, you're only onstage for forty-five minutes. And then we had the whole rest of the day and night to have fun, make friends, and go sightseeing, taking in as much as we possibly could in the amount of time that we had."

Shortly after that tour, Margot Olavarria departed the band, and Kathy Valentine became their new bassist. With what's considered their "classic lineup" complete, they had everything in place to take the next big leap in their career.

*   *   *

It was hard work playing the club circuit to continue their upward trajectory, but Schock remembers the Go-Go's always looked forward to shows in L.A., San Francisco, or New York because of the great audiences, and because that's where they had befriended the club owners and promoters. As soon as they started widening their scope to other cities, though, they realized just how chauvinistic the music business could be. "There was a lot of this 'baby' kind of stuff, and innuendo. We saw that a lot when we would go to different towns and meet different promoters," Schock says.

She and her bandmates never felt threatened by this boorish behavior, though, because they had safety in numbers. "Here's the great thing about being in a band: you've got each other," Schock says, "so if anybody's being a jerk, I've got four other girls to back me up. That's yet another reason why I love being in a band."

Overcoming the misogyny aimed their way, the Go-Go's became a popular touring band—but they soon encountered another gender-related obstacle: "We had a problem getting a record deal," Schock says. "Nobody was interested in signing us because there hadn't been an all-female band prior to us that had become hugely successful in the United States. Or anywhere else, for that matter. Some bands might have touched on it a little bit, but not in a profitable way for record labels. So nobody wanted to take a chance on an all-girl band."

In response, she says, "We worked twice as hard to be better at what we do," and finally got a deal with the independent label I.R.S. Records in 1981. That company had been founded two years prior by Miles Copeland, who managed the Police (featuring his brother Stewart Copeland on drums). I.R.S. helped launch the careers of notable bands such as R.E.M. and Concrete Blonde, among many others, but when the Go-Go's signed with them, the label was still getting established.

Later in 1981, things changed dramatically when the Go-Go's released their debut album, *Beauty and the Beat*, which sold more than two million copies in the United States alone. On the strength of the hit singles "Our Lips Are Sealed" and "We Got the Beat," the album reached number 1 on the US *Billboard*'s Top LPs and Tape chart (now called *"Billboard* 200"). They were the first all-female band who wrote their own songs and played their own instruments who had achieved this feat with a debut album.

Schock was not surprised at this success. "I always thought we were going to be big," she says. "I always thought I would be a success if I worked hard enough. That's why I left Baltimore and went to L.A. I told everybody [in Baltimore], 'Next time you see me, I'm going to be a rock star.' How ridiculous is that to say? But I really believed it."

What she wasn't fully understanding yet, though, was just how significant their accomplishments really were. "Unknowingly, we were leaving an impression on lots of people in many ways. The truth is, we were just having fun and doing what we loved, and we happened to be girls."

Their fun-loving attitude certainly comes across in their videos, such as the one for "Vacation," the lead single from their 1982 sophomore album of the same name. In that clip, the band members are shown waterskiing in tandem, wearing tutus and tiaras. That, along with their other videos, made the Go-Go's hugely popular on MTV during that channel's early years.

"Now you get to see that it's five girls in action, making the music that you've been listening to."

*   *   *

Despite their groundbreaking success, intra-band tensions and issues with addiction led the Go-Go's to split up in 1985. After reconciling and getting sober, they've reunited several times. Through the years, Schock says, they've come to realize the importance of what they've accomplished together. "Writing our own songs, playing our own instruments, arranging our own tunes. Nobody played on our records. Nobody was behind the stage playing keyboards or any of that crap. It was us, from top to bottom.

"In retrospect, I know all that really counts. I didn't realize it at the time. I don't think any of us did. We were having success in a way that no other female band had ever had. We were forging a path for any and all female artists that were coming after us."

In this way, Schock says she and her bandmates are following the lead of someone like journalist/activist Gloria Steinem, a feminist icon who has been one of the trailblazing figures in the women's liberation movement for the past five decades. "And certainly for us, after being in the music industry for decades and seeing the pushback, I know what it's all about. Thank you, Gloria Steinem—I understand what you've been fighting for now. And the fight is nowhere near over. It takes time to change people's minds.

"The journey for women has gotten better, but it will be a continual thing. Women have to be proactive. In your neighborhood, in your state, in this country. You've got to participate. You can't just talk about it. You've got to get out there and make the change happen."

Schock believes that she, and her band, have done exactly that. "People ask, 'Are you a feminist?' And I say, 'Yeah, but I believe I'm a feminist by my actions and not as much by my words.' It's your actions that count at the end of the day."

*   *   *

Looking back on everything she's accomplished prompts Schock to give particular credit to her mother and father. "I had the best parents in the world," she says. "This is kind of hokey, but I feel like I owe everything, my success and all, to my parents because of the way they brought me up. You're a winner when you put time in and you do things for the right reasons. And that's the way I've approached everything in my life. I never do things for money. I do it because I love it and I feel there's something inside of me that makes me know it's the right thing to do."

Schock, who felt that her career would always be her main focus (leading her to choose never to marry or have children), was finally compelled to change her priorities when her parents needed her in recent years.

"When they started to not be able to function that well on their own, I stopped working and I brought them out here," she says. (She's lived in San Francisco since 2005.) "For the last six years of their lives, I took care of them. They took care of me my whole life; now it was time for me to take care of them. I have a two-story Victorian [house], and I had the whole downstairs redone to accommodate them. And I had twenty-four-hour caregivers in here. Plus, I was right upstairs. And that's the way I wanted it to be. I told them, 'I'm never going to put you in a [nursing] home. You're going to stay with me.' And everything I told them I would do, I did. And I feel very good about that."

With both of her parents now gone, Schock is recalibrating. "This year, I am just starting to get my life back and figuring out how to move forward," she says. "I've got a lot I want to do, and I feel like now I need to address it all." She plans to start by renovating her house and traveling. She also wants to continue touring to promote *Made in Hollywood: All Access with the Go-Go's*, a book of her photographs and essays focusing on the band's early years (with writing contributions from her celebrity friends, including actress Jodie Foster, singer Kate Pierson of the B-52's, and former MTV VJ Martha Quinn). She also hopes to hold more exhibits for her photography.

Most of all, Schock looks forward to getting back to her music career. Besides her work with the Go-Go's, she has also found success as a songwriter: the pop stars Miley Cyrus and Selena Gomez have recorded songs that she cowrote.

Whether it's with the Go-Go's or on her own, "I'll keep writing songs. It's what I do," she says. "I'll keep drumming. That's what I do. These are things that are deeply rooted in my being. I've worked so many years to be in the position that I'm in. Now it's about giving back, being grateful, and having a voice that can hopefully help make a difference."

5

Lydia Lunch

In her immaculate and cheerful Brooklyn kitchen, Lydia Lunch has prepared a feast from scratch: Moroccan-style lemon chicken, spinach pie, ginger tea, and brownies. "Cooking—knives, fire, my DNA going into people's mouths. What's not to love?" she quips with a sly grin.

She may be most famous as a performer, but she also authored a cookbook in 2012, *The Need to Feed: Recipes for Developing a Healthy Obsession for Deeply Satisfying Foods*. Even the stage name "Lunch" (she was born Lydia Koch) is a reference to her ability, in 1970s New York City, to ensure that she and her friends were well fed during what would've otherwise been their "starving artist" days.

But make no mistake: beyond her stellar culinary skills, Lunch definitely isn't the typical domestic type. Her all-black attire—lacy dress, fishnet stockings, and stiletto heels, along with perfectly applied dramatic makeup—makes her seem more ready to head onstage than to sit down for an interview in her living room.

Settling into an armchair, she veers between kind offers to refill a glass or plate and acerbic answers on a variety of subjects. The first topic in her crosshairs is the women's liberation movement, which she dismisses. "We need a *human* liberation," she says. "Right now, it feels like we're in a backward cycle of everything. It just feels so ridiculous and outdated in this country. I find it outlandish that we're still dealing with the abortion issue. I mean, we have the right to vote. Amen. But women had the right to control our bodies, and now we don't in half the states? What the fuck?"

Despite her anger over US abortion laws, Lunch resists being called a feminist, however. "I have always tried to avoid *any* category," she says firmly. But, she will concede, "I think I'm a humanist, in the sense that I think both genders—and now there's many genders—are fucked by the powers-that-be. I feel that the problem is the patriarchy, and I think everybody that's not a rich white male suffers under it. So I don't think *feminist* is a radical enough term for what I am. I'm a confrontationalist."

After noticing that her artistic friends seemed particularly likely to suffer from what she terms "mental collapse" brought on by sociopolitical ills, Lunch (with filmmaker Jasmine Hirst) has recently been working on finishing a documentary, *Artists: Depression, Anxiety and Rage*. In it, Lunch interviews numerous musicians, artists, and writers about their psychological and emotional struggles, as well as their advice on coping strategies.

For her part, Lunch dealt with childhood trauma by creating avant-garde songs and scathing spoken word performances, which in turn became her livelihood. "My rage, I take it to the stage," she says. "My rage is on a *humongous* level. It's not on a personal level. I'm dealing with societal issues, but I'm hoping to inspire the individual."

Her outspoken subversion is front and center on the more than seventy albums on which she's appeared (as a solo musician, spoken word artist, band member, or collaborator), along with her prolific work as a writer and actress.

In 2019, director Beth B made a documentary, *Lydia Lunch: The War Is Never Over*, so named because, Lunch says, "I have been screaming about the war, which I think is many things. The war against the individual. The war against women. The war against minorities. The war against immigrants. The war against poor white men. So to me, the war is never over."

She juts out her chin, defiant, when asked how, nearly fifty years into her career, she is able to stay motivated to keep fighting. "The problem doesn't go away," she shoots back. "Why should I?"

*   *   *

When Lunch was seventeen years old, she rented her first apartment on her own. It was in New York City's East Village neighborhood, on 12th Street between Avenue A and Avenue B. These days, this is a trendy area, but during the 1970s, it was catastrophically crime ridden. Burned out buildings were ubiquitous, including on either side of her new abode. "There were a lot of dangerous things going on. There were drugs everywhere. It was a war zone," Lunch says.

"They didn't want to rent the apartment to me because the guy that had lived there right before me was electrocuted and his dog ate his face off and there was a hole burned in the paint and it smelled like death," she says. "I said, 'If I can get rid of the smell of death, will you rent it to me?' They said okay. So I went around the corner on Avenue B to a *botanica* and they gave me this little bottle that said nothing but had a skull and crossbones [on it]. A few drops, and it got rid of the smell. And so I had this shitty, dark apartment—but it was only $75 a month."

It was 1977, when things weren't going very well in New York City as a whole. Serial killer David Berkowitz (a.k.a. "Son of Sam") effectively held the city hostage by shooting people indiscriminately; he later was convicted of eight murders, for which he received six consecutive life sentences. Also that year, a citywide blackout on July 13 and 14 resulted in extensive looting and arson. Lunch says living through these times was "very interesting."

It was also an era when, she recalls, "The streets of New York were very misogynistic. There was so much aggression. It's really even hard to think of how it was at that point. You couldn't walk five steps without hearing some kind of, 'Hey, baby, are you married?' You can't box everyone on the street, so I dealt with it with humor because they would be laughing, and I'd be halfway up the block."

Still, she never felt scared. "I grew up in a ghetto. I was not afraid. And that's probably why I was never attacked," she says. "What are you going to fuckin' do? I've got nothing. No, I didn't have any fear, probably from flatlining out of trauma."

She is referring to her childhood in Rochester, New York, when she endured years of living with a father who, as she describes it, had no impulse control. "His sin was, he couldn't keep his hands to himself. But at nine years old, I saw the behavior mirrored in my uncle. The same insanity. I think most people that have a traumatizing experience as a child might think, 'It only happens in my family,' and then they have this sense of shame. Recognizing at a very early age that it wasn't just in my house, but was a universal problem, spared me a lot of horror." In fact, she adds, "I didn't feel my situation was the worst. Far from it."

Arriving at such clarity when she was so young also prevented her from becoming what she terms a "forever victim," where a person turns the trauma inward. "Even though you've been victimized, it doesn't mean you have to continue to be," she says.

Armed with these insights, she was able to view her father with a certain level of understanding and empathy. "My father was a door-to-door salesman. He was a badass, a gambler, a hustler. Everyone loved him. He was charismatic. He didn't drink. He beat me once with a shoe—I'm sure I deserved it, trust me," she says with a laugh.

"I recognized that [the abuse] didn't start with him, so that means it must have been passed down, as it often is, from generation to generation," she continues. "It's very complicated, and most men don't wake up in the morning and think, 'I'm going to beat the shit out of my girlfriend.' Or, 'I'm going to abuse this child.' They weren't born to do that. So why do they do it? I had to start to analyze the cycle of abuse, understand it, and find a way to talk about it."

By her adolescence, she'd discovered that music was a good way to escape her problems. "I was lucky because there was a college radio station in Rochester that would play really interesting music. One day, when I was twelve or thirteen years old, I went and knocked on the door, and this DJ that looked like Gregg Allman answered it. I'm like, 'Look, I need tickets to concerts.' And he said, 'Okay. I'm going to introduce you to a promoter.' It was that simple. Sometimes you just have to ask. I'm not afraid of asking for anything. There's only two answers, yes or no."

Through the promoter, Lunch got free tickets to any show she wanted to see. "My father would have to drive me to all the rock concerts, probably because he felt guilty. He'd pick me up at two in the morning, to which my mother would say, 'What are you doing?' 'It's for my career.' 'What career?' 'Don't ask.'"

At thirteen years old, she ran away to New York City, hoping to meet the influential glam rock band New York Dolls. She didn't find them, and soon spent all her money and had to return home. It took her three years to save up enough to try again, but finally, in 1976, she snuck out of her bedroom window and boarded a Greyhound bus bound for Manhattan.

This time, everything seemed to work out right. She went directly from the bus station to Mother's, a rock club on 23rd Street that she'd read about in *Creem* magazine. As soon as she walked in the door, she saw Wayne County (who later changed her name to Jayne County as one of the first openly transgender singers in rock). Lunch had written a fan letter to County the year before, and had received a reply, so this in-person meeting on her first night in the city seemed like a fine case of kismet. She remembers thinking, "I'm home."

That same evening, "There was a terrible band playing and I picked up the lead singer and went to the band's loft, which was right around the corner in Chelsea, and just inserted myself," Lunch says. "I had sex with the lead singer once or twice, became friends with the rest of the band, they said I could stay there, and I moved in. That was pretty lucky."

Through that circle, Lunch became involved in New York's "no wave" movement, an amorphous musical genre that favored rebellious lyrics and dissonance over melody. It seemed tailor-made for Lunch, who is sometimes even credited with coming up with the "no wave" name in the first place. She soon formed the band Teenage Jesus and the Jerks, writing the music, playing guitar, and taking on the lead vocalist position. They released a few singles and EPs, as well as some compilation albums, earning them cult artist status.

In the mid-1970s, New York's music and arts scene was very male dominated, though Lunch maintains that she and the other women working in it didn't feel oppressed. "There were so many women doing so many different kinds of things: making films, taking photographs, in bands. I think poverty brought us all together. And the creative urge. I think most of the women at that time were creating because we weren't dealing with mainstream media. We were dealing with a very underground, liberated section of nihilistic, creative people."

This egalitarian attitude was also true within Teenage Jesus and the Jerks: Lunch's bandmates—all men—treated her with respect, and the feeling was mutual. "I don't hate men," she says. "I hate men in positions of power that abuse it."

Concurrent with her music career, Lunch also began working as a spoken word artist. She believes that this art form gained momentum in the 1970s "because people, like myself, thought the '60s fucking failed. [US President Richard] Nixon was an idiot. Something had to be said. And then we had [President Ronald] Reagan. And shit had to be said."

Lunch's first spoken word performance had been at an acid party in Buffalo, New York, when she was fourteen years old, but her drug intake means she can't remember anything about it other than the fact that it happened. Her professional debut a few years later at New York City's Pyramid Club was far more memorable; this is when she first performed "Daddy Dearest," which became one of her signature pieces. "I started right in with this indictment against my father. Because my target was always 'The Father': the Father of our country, God the Father—all fuckers," she says.

Using her spoken word performances to reveal the abuse she'd suffered, and working through her emotions surrounding it, was cathartic for Lunch—like a form of "public psychotherapy," as she puts it. It was also a way for her to bring taboo topics out into the open, so that they could be dealt with properly. "Somebody had to open the dialogue," she says. "People didn't speak about those things when I started speaking about it. There was no conversation about it."

However, she found that audiences often reacted with intense discomfort, or even outright hostility, when she brought up controversial subjects. She responded by doubling down on her confrontational style. Her first spoken word sets were only ten minutes long, but they would still sometimes devolve into chaos. She also had to develop an effective way to deal with hecklers—who have been, she says, almost always men.

"One time I was at a festival called 'The Feminist and the Misogynist Together at Last,' maybe in the early '80s," she says. "This is when I used to dress pretty much militarily for my spoken word [performances], including [weapons such as] a blackjack or a nightstick or a police Maglite. Because I had to. And some guy from the back of the audience says, 'Suck my dick.' So I said, 'Come up here.' And he's stupid enough to come up. And I whacked him in the neck with a blackjack and he went down. And I said, 'Now suck your own dick.' There was no more heckling." She sighs. "If it has to be violence, I'll do it. But I'd rather address it with humor."

Incidents like that prompted Lunch to build preemptive fake violence into her set to quiet aggressive male audience members. "And it worked, because then they were terrified. Sometimes I would have two women onstage with baseball bats standing beside me. Just in case. That kind of leveled the playing field."

Spoken word events have remained a central part of Lunch's career to this day, though she concedes it only appeals to a niche market. She doesn't expect that this will ever change and become more commercially viable, especially for artists such as herself who use the medium to address difficult topics. "I just think the truth is not a popular commodity," she says. "It never has been."

*   *   *

Lunch's airy, well-appointed Brooklyn apartment gives little indication of her previous precarious living situations. She is happy here, but she doesn't let herself get *too* comfortable—she knows she could fall on hard times again: "I've been homeless many times in my adult life. I could be homeless again." She shrugs.

With a sweeping gesture, she indicates the elegant furnishings. "I've had to sell my stuff over and over again. Most of the stuff I have now, I found in the trash. I just paint it white and then it looks good. Somebody gave me that table, those chairs, almost everything in this room."

She's lived in this particular apartment for a year and a half now. Before returning to New York, she lived in Barcelona, Spain, for eight years, which was one of her longest stretches in one place at a time. She's also resided in a wide variety of other cities, including London, Los Angeles, New Orleans, San Francisco, Pittsburgh, and Louisville, Kentucky. She usually stays for two to five years before moving on.

Her nomadic lifestyle hasn't lent itself to settling down in her personal life—not that she ever wanted that, anyway. "I don't believe in marriage. I think it's ridiculous," she says. "I've had many relationships that lasted for seven years, which is more than enough for any one person, I feel. I mean, how much time does any one person deserve? Two years, it's still hot. Five years, it gets platonic. Seven years is enough. After that, it's usually, 'Get the fuck out of here.' But I'm friends with 99 percent of my exes."

She also has no interest in becoming a mother: "All of the people I know are infants. I don't have time for another one. No, not for me to do. Absolutely not. I don't have the money, the time, the energy. There's enough human beings in this world and enough people that need attention."

Instead, Lunch pours her energy into her work. She returned to New York four years ago because, she explains, "I think I have to be here as the deliverer of America: to report on stupidity, arrogance, and violence." She mainly does this via her weekly podcast, *The Lydian Spin*, which she started in 2020. In it, she interviews musicians, artists, and actors, as well as using it as a forum to express her own sociopolitical viewpoints.

She also fronts the band Retrovirus, which draws from material across her entire career (during which she estimates she's written four hundred songs). "It's like the 'Lydian Jukebox,'" she says. "It's a bit more interesting to me than just having a band that is one concept."

With Retrovirus, Lunch can show how incendiary her music has consistently been throughout the past five decades. She knows this relegates her to the artistic fringes, and she's fine with that. "I've never dealt with mainstream record companies. The reason I've never even been approached by the mainstream is, they can take one look at my face and realize I'm not going to buckle to anything they want."

She is unimpressed with the contrived provocativeness that so many commercially successful artists seem to portray these days. "I think a real conundrum of our times is that we have what I call 'the new Puritanism.' And then we have this really extreme hypersexuality," she says. "I don't think it's that liberating to wear a leotard onstage in a surgically enhanced body that other women will never live up to, claiming you're doing this for women's empowerment, when you're a corporate prostitute to a mainstream mega-conglomerate."

This leads her to another thing that often bothers her as she watches the next generation of women. "I don't understand the new, 'He looked at me—that's an assault.' 'He touched my back—that's an assault.' I don't understand why, at this point, women aren't tougher about it. That if they think it's bad in this country with the misogyny, open your eyes to the rest of the world. And it may never go away. But that doesn't mean you have to play victim to it by every glance or touch. Women should realize what real rape and abuse is. You have to put it in a real perspective.

"My generation, we had to know how to handle ourselves because we had things to deal with that many women right now might not want to, have to, or need to deal with. So I think that women my age are tougher. They weren't coddled. They had to know how to handle themselves."

To illustrate her point, she goes to a shelf filled with colorful pieces of art, many of which she made herself. She selects a voodoo doll and hands it over—it's shockingly heavy. She explains this is because it has an iron pipe embedded at its core, because "Then you can just hit someone with it if the curse doesn't work."

She's not joking. "I wish [today's] mothers would teach their daughters how to be less of a victim. To verbally and physically not take [abuse] and realize that you can defend yourself. I think every woman should know how to punch. A death blow. You might need it. And also, one of the weakest parts on a man's body is the shins. Just to let you know."

She understands that this type of talk can be triggering for younger women, but she's going to unapologetically continue saying these things because she's intent on making more people wake up to the (sometimes unsettling) truth. "You have to realize what reality is. You can't pretend it's not what it is, or hope it's something different," she says.

"This is why I sleep with a bucket of knives beside my bed," she adds, her words in sharp contrast to the peaceful vibe in her home. Here, as on any stage she graces, there will be no more abuse: "Trust me: I'm not going to take it."

6

Suzanne Vega

In 1987, when folk rock singer-songwriter Suzanne Vega was twenty-seven years old, she had her first widespread hit with "Luka." That song charted in the Top 10 in a half dozen countries (including the United States, where it reached number 3 on both the "Hot 100" and "Adult Contemporary" *Billboard* charts). It also earned her three Grammy nominations.

Later that same year, away from the spotlight, an even bigger event unfolded in her personal life when she reestablished her relationship with her biological father, Richard Peck. There had been no contact between them since she was eighteen months old.

When she was two and a half, her mother and stepfather took her from Santa Monica, California, where she'd been born, to live in New York City. "My stepfather and my mother forged my birth certificate and put his name over Richard's, and they changed my [last] name," she says. This is why Peck hadn't realized that the newly famous "Suzanne Vega" and his daughter were one and the same.

But in a way, Vega's professional achievements had led her to Peck. "I guess I started to have more confidence once I saw how successful I was," she says, which in turn sparked her to seriously pursue her other long-held goal of finding her father.

Her manager, Ron Fierstein, offered to help, hiring a detective who soon found Peck still living in Southern California.

Vega sent Peck a letter that included her phone number; he called her a week later, on New Year's Eve. Though they'd been separated when she was too young to have any conscious memories of him, she instantly recognized his voice.

As if being reunited with Peck wasn't remarkable enough, what he told her was even more astonishing: he had only recently been back in touch with the rest of his biological family, too. "His older sister had found him through the Motor Vehicles Bureau. And so he had been reunited with his brother and two sisters. I had grown up with my mother, but I didn't know my father, and he had grown up not knowing either of his parents.

"But the real surprise was that my grandparents were touring musicians. That was a big shock. My grandfather was a trumpet player, and my grandmother had been a drummer in an all-girl band in the vaudeville circuit in the '20s and '30s."

Later, Peck showed Vega photos of her grandmother, all dressed up with her bandmates. Vega was impressed. "She looked very happy in her career. She looked like a very glamorous woman. There she is at her drum kit, and I thought, 'This is so damn cool.'"

As surprised as Vega was to find out about her lineage, it also made absolute sense, because suddenly she understood why she'd always had innate musical talent. It's something she shares with many of her kin on her paternal side: besides her grandparents, she also discovered that several cousins play instruments, and her father has a natural talent for playing piano by ear.

But there was a dark side to her family's story, too. "My grandmother had all these children—and then, while she was pregnant with my father, my grandfather left her during the Depression," Vega says. "So her way of dealing with the issues between her touring and her children was to give my father away to the foster care system. Then the other children, she put in an institution, like an orphanage, for short periods of time while she went on with her career. But the children didn't fare so well."

Fortunately, all those children grew up to become happier as adults. Vega takes great pleasure in her bond with them (especially her father, with whom she has remained close), and she still sounds amazed as she recounts how she felt when she first found out about these relatives: "I remember thinking it was a miracle that I had been born into this family."

*   *   *

Growing up in New York City, Vega was part of a very different family. Her mother's second husband was Ed Vega (a.k.a. Edgardo Vega Yunqué), a celebrated novelist who was originally from Puerto Rico. Her mother and stepfather had three children together. Vega recalls being there when each of them was brought home from the hospital; she didn't realize they were half siblings to her.

"I've always really liked the name 'Suzanne Vega,' and I think it united me with my brothers and sisters—we grew up as Vegas," she says. "I was very well loved by Ed's side of the family and felt happy being a Vega, even though other people in the neighborhood could see that I was not half Puerto Rican. That wasn't something I could see. That was confusing for me because I didn't have any knowledge of myself from the outside. I knew myself on the inside. And the inside of me was happy being Suzanne Vega."

The family lived in New York's underprivileged but proud East Harlem neighborhood, then moved to the then slightly more affluent Upper West Side. Although their living situation became better, "New York City in the '70s was horrifying in some ways. It was a very dangerous place. I remember seeing *Taxi Driver* and thinking, 'Yeah, that's what it's like right now,'" she says, referencing the 1976 film depicting a loner who works as a night cabbie in the violent city.

It was not always a happy childhood, but Vega recognizes it as an unusual one, largely because Ed Vega was "a singular character. He was larger than life. He did have an influence on me, in some very good ways and in some not-so-good ways. At his best, he taught us to really express ourselves, especially artistically. Reading, art, literature, plays—anything that was cultural, he pushed us towards that. So that was, in some ways, a really great atmosphere to grow up in."

In this setting, her natural interest in music flourished. "Ed's mother, my Puerto Rican grandmother, sang to me a lot. I really loved her, and we had a nice bond," she says. "There was also always music in the house. My stepfather played a beautiful nylon string guitar. He would play folk music. Pete Seeger songs, Lead Belly songs. And he wrote a song that was very similar to a Bob Dylan song. This impressed me, so I was drawn to it from an early age."

Guitar playing also appealed to her because she could do it in solitude. "If I ever sat down at the piano, somebody would join me after about five minutes—Ed, or one of the kids. It was very public. It was in the hallway, so I could never sit down and work things out privately. Whereas with the guitar, it was quiet, and it just seemed perfect for my temperament. I could take the guitar into my room and work on my ideas privately." She started writing full-fledged songs when she was fourteen years old.

Initially, though, Vega was most drawn to dancing, for which she was accepted to study at New York's highly prestigious High School of Performing Arts (now named Fiorello H. LaGuardia High School of Music & Art and Performing Arts). This school became widely known after it served as the setting for the 1980 film *Fame* (and the 1982–1987 television series of the same name).

She was keenly aware of how competitive it was to earn a spot at that school. "I was very proud that I had gotten in, and I didn't want to waste the opportunity," she says. At the same time, though, she quickly recognized that a dancing career probably wasn't going to work out for her. "I realized that I was never going to be a lead dancer, and I wasn't particularly good at being in the chorus, either. I just never had the technique to really stand out as a great modern dancer on my own, and I didn't like having to work for some of the choreographers."

Instead, she felt drawn to the musicians who played the accompaniments for her dance classes. Once they realized she was writing songs on the side, they began to give her advice. One of them suggested that she should play in local coffeehouses.

At sixteen years old, she had an unexpected advantage as she entered that scene: "As a dancer, by the time you're eighteen years old, you're heading into your prime, so I was very aware of my limitations—[but] I was thrilled to find out that once I got into this other world of songwriting, I was considered really young."

Her teachers at the High School of Performing Arts also initially encouraged her, inviting her to take music classes in addition to her dance coursework, but this plan soon fell apart. "Unfortunately, I have a type of dyslexia, I guess, where I could not learn to read music and I could not learn the theories," she says, "but I think it has helped me in some ways because I find, if I have an obstacle, I can work my own way through it, and it makes it sound original. It's not really like anybody else's style, how I play guitar."

After graduating from high school, she attended Barnard College in New York City, which is a women's liberal arts college affiliated with Columbia University. Her inability to read music meant she could not study music at this level, either, but this didn't upset her. "I always wanted to be an artist, so in a sense, it didn't matter to me what I majored in. So I majored in English literature and minored in theater. I ended up doing my thesis on the life and work of the writer Carson McCullers."

During this time, she also continued to pursue her singer-songwriter ambitions. She successfully auditioned to play at Gerdes Folk City (usually known simply as "Folk City") in New York's West Village neighborhood. From 1960 until its closure in 1987 due to losing its lease, it was one of the most well-known and influential music clubs in the world. Bob Dylan, one of her primary influences, played his first professional show there. Despite this illustrious history—and the fact that she remembers that setting being "very male-dominated"—she felt immediately accepted there.

"I went down to Folk City when I was twenty; I was probably twelve to fifteen years younger than a lot of the men there. But it didn't bother me—I felt that I was equal to them," she says. "I had this body of work already, and it was clear that I was very smart, so I caused a lot of interest. I had a ton of songs by then, and everyone seemed impressed that I was so young. That suited me fine, so I settled right in. I did feel that I was respected and taken seriously, and I enjoyed that."

This was the early 1980s, when artists such as Madonna and Cyndi Lauper were promoting an exaggeratedly sexy style, but this wasn't the way Vega wanted to present herself onstage. Instead, she looked to musicians such as Patti Smith and Chrissie Hynde of the Pretenders, who had more of an androgynous appearance. In particular, she liked that they wore jackets, so she adopted that look for herself.

"I loved wearing my jacket because I felt protected in it," she says. "I could cover myself from my neck all the way down to my knees. It allowed people just to see my hands and my face, which is what I wanted them to be looking at, anyway. So that's become a trademark [of mine]."

Even so, she recalls, "I would still get the occasional catcall from somebody in the audience asking me to smile more and stuff like that, which is nonsense. I just ignored them and continued the show with my normal face, which was not a particularly smiling or happy one, especially at that time."

Vega's performances caught the attention of A&M Records executive Nancy Jeffries, who helped Vega secure a record deal. "I felt that she really got what I was doing. It definitely helped that she was female," Vega says of Jeffries. "She was helpful in making sure the music had not-conservative production, but something freer and a little wilder."

To that end, Jeffries suggested that Vega should hire Lenny Kaye to join Steve Addabbo in producing her debut album, and Vega jumped at the opportunity. She had already been working on demos with Addabbo, a highly respected recording engineer and producer, while Kaye is best known as Patti Smith's long-time guitarist.

Jeffries also proved instrumental when it came time to choose a photo for the album cover. "She kept an eye out for my image, which I found hard to do for myself because I wasn't aware of having one," Vega says. "The first time we had a photo shoot, I looked so conservative I couldn't stand it. I was like, 'Oh my God, what happened?' I was wearing makeup, what I might wear on a stage, but I think the girl who had done my hair had teased it and fluffed it up into one of these crunchy '80s 'dos.

"The men in the room were all going, 'This is great—this will sell a lot of records.' And Nancy looked at it and said, 'That doesn't look anything like her. We're going to have to do this again.' She was fearless. She just said, 'She's going to do her own makeup; she's going to dress herself.'"

The second photo shoot took place in New York's Meatpacking District, where Vega was living at the time. "The wind had whipped my face and my mascara was running, and because we'd been walking around all day, my lipstick finally faded. Nancy said, 'Now *that's* what you really look like.' And that image became my first cover." This experience also led Vega to make sure that a clause was added to her contract ensuring that she will always have final say over her own image.

Her self-titled debut album was released in 1985. Though it only got into the high reaches of the US charts, it did well in Great Britain, where it achieved platinum sales status. It also received many favorable reviews in well-respected music publications, and eventually sold a million copies worldwide.

The next year, Vega and Steve Addabbo wrote the song "Left of Center" specifically for the film *Pretty in Pink*, with the lyrics sung from the point of view of the main character, Andie Walsh (portrayed by Molly Ringwald). Popular artists such as the Psychedelic Furs, the Smiths, New Order, INXS, Echo & the Bunnymen, and OMD were also on the soundtrack album, and it became a bestseller. This helped to significantly raise Vega's profile just in time for her sophomore release.

* * *

For her next album, *Solitude Standing*, Vega again worked with Lenny Kaye and Steve Addabbo as the producers, but this time, she found herself sometimes becoming exasperated with them.

"There were times when I would be frustrated because I would say to Lenny, 'This just doesn't have enough edge.' And he'd go, 'It has edge—don't you hear the edge?' And I'm going, 'No, I don't hear the edge. That's why I keep saying that I want more.' And Lenny's worked with Patti Smith, who was *pure* edge," Vega says. "So I learned over time that one person's idea of edge is one other person's idea of really boring."

In the end, they worked the songs out to everyone's satisfaction, and Vega says that "most of the time, [Kaye and Addabbo] were very respectful." However, she also adds that they could be "sometimes a little condescending. I remember for a while, from time to time, I would feel that I was being pacified.

"I have a bit of a sweet tooth, so if I was in a cranky mood, they would get me these certain cookies that I liked, and these really sweet juices that were red. And I would know I was being pacified—and it made me even crankier because I felt that my artistic objections weren't being taken seriously. Maybe that was because I was young and I was a female. I'm saying this very affectionately because I love Steve and Lenny and I love what we did together, but there were times when I would be frustrated."

Solitude Standing came out in April 1987, but the first single, "Gypsy," didn't chart. Things significantly changed the following month when "Luka" was released as the second single. Deftly tackling the difficult subject of child abuse with empathy (and shimmering musicality), "Luka" immediately set Vega apart from other artists. Based on that success, *Solitude Standing* reached the Top 20, and attained gold or platinum sales status in more than a dozen countries. She was also chosen to headline the prestigious Glastonbury Festival in England in 1989—the first female artist to do so.

Despite this huge success, Vega made a big change when it came time to make her third album, *Days of Open Hand* (1990).

"I went from being sort of affectionately coddled by Lenny and Steve to deciding, 'No, I'm going to do this myself, with Anton Sanko.' He was my keyboard player, and we were also boyfriend and girlfriend at the time."

She came to regret this decision. "[It] was *unbelievably* difficult. So it went from being like, 'Now I'm going to be all empowered' to really hitting a wall. There was so much pressure on that third album—I found it very daunting. And I think Anton did, too. So that didn't quite work out the way I had expected that it might." While it sold respectably worldwide, this release failed to achieve the same heights as her previous album.

Determined not to repeat this experience, she decided to audition producers for her next album. She ended up hiring Mitchell Froom, who'd had significant success in the 1980s producing Paul McCartney and Crowded House.

She chose Froom, she says, because he was "the most articulate. He said, 'I'd like to give these songs more edge'—that was what I was always looking for. And he gave me very specific suggestions. He said, 'Because your voice is so small, I would like to record it very close up and very dry, so you keep all the grain and texture.' I thought, 'Wow, that sounds really interesting.' Because usually, people put reverb around my voice, which makes it sound very angelic and clean and kind of pure. But it turns out if you take that away, the actual voice underneath it has a lot more character. So I thought that was a really cool idea. I just liked everything I heard, so I chose him to work with."

Froom also helped her develop a sound that veered away from straightforward folk rock, incorporating more electronic elements. The resulting album, *99.9F°*, was released in 1992, and earned positive reviews. Proving that she finally had found the edge she so desired, her single "Blood Makes Noise" reached number 1 on the *Billboard* "Modern Rock Tracks" chart in the United States.

Beyond their professional success, Vega and Froom also found happiness personally. They had a daughter in 1994 and married in 1995. The next year, they worked together again on her album *Nine Objects of Desire*. But by 1998, their relationship had derailed, and they divorced, a situation she addressed on her next album, *Songs in Red and Gray* (2001).

More than twenty years later, Vega can be objective as she looks back on that time. "We had this great chemistry, and we really did love each other. In the end, I thought that love would conquer all, and it just didn't. But I'm very proud of the work we did together, and I learned a lot from Mitchell about music and my particular form of edginess and how to express myself. And we have a wonderful daughter, too. So I don't regret any of it. But I was pretty sad when it all fell apart."

*   *   *

These days, Vega is happy in her personal life. In 2006, she married Paul Mills, a civil rights lawyer who also works as a spoken word poet under the moniker Poez. They had actually dated in the early 1980s but met up again nearly a quarter century later and wed almost immediately.

She also maintains a close relationship with her daughter, Ruby, who initially seemed interested in a music career of her own (even joining her mother onstage at some shows) but is now working on earning a PhD in biology.

Her daughter's decision to become a scientist instead of a musician, Vega says, likely came about because "She wanted something that was more stable and, I think, something that had more of a salary and was more predictable."

Ruby's career choice also probably stemmed from her childhood experiences. "I started touring with Ruby when she was quite young, two years old," Vega says, adding that she brought along a nanny to help. "But Ruby got really sick of that lifestyle. She let me know in various ways that touring was not fun for her. So when she was about eleven years old, she started to go to sleepaway camp with her buddies in the summer. That was great; she could go off and be with her friends, and I could go on tour."

It wasn't always easy, though: "It all required a lot of juggling, and I think sometimes she resented that I wasn't there. But

I tried to explain to her that I tour for two months, and then I'm home with her for ten months."

In the end, Vega figured out how to successfully balance her private and professional lives. Beyond her happy marriage and motherhood, she still enjoys a well-established career, touring the world and releasing nine studio albums so far. She is currently writing material for her next release, which she hopes to put out in 2023.

No doubt Vega's vaudevillian drummer grandmother, who'd been such a pioneer in her own way, would've been very pleased to see her granddaughter's accomplishments—and how far women in music have come.

7

Cherie Currie (the Runaways)

"Everybody's so afraid to be canceled. But you know what? I'm not afraid. I could give a rusty rat's ass."

Cherie Currie, looking cozy in an overstuffed chair with a vape pen in hand, had seemed relaxed at the beginning of this Zoom video call from her home in West Hills, California. But as the conversation progressed, she became increasingly animated as she offered her opinions on a variety of topics.

She's been publicly outspoken since 1975, when she became the lead singer for the Runaways when she was only fifteen years old. The Runaways—which also launched the careers of Joan Jett and Lita Ford—were notable for being an all-female, all-teen group who played their own instruments and were involved in writing their own hit songs (such as "Cherry Bomb," which went all the way to the top of the charts in Japan). By the time she left the band in 1977, Currie had become notorious for her onstage swagger and snarling vocal style, challenging the demure persona that young female musicians were usually encouraged to adopt during that era.

Despite believing that the Runaways broke barriers for other women in the music business, though, Currie refuses to be included in the feminist narrative. "I kind of feel like this whole feminism thing, it just has not been my story," she says.

"Does feminism exist anymore? I don't think it does. When you talk about feminism, I don't even know what that means now. What is it? Is it, 'Because I don't have a penis, give me special powers or privileges?'" She shakes her head. "As feminism has morphed and changed, now I don't know what it is. All I know is what feminism used to be before the radicals took it over."

What she means by that is, in her view, "Men have been emasculated," she says. "Now, men don't feel comfortable to even tell you, 'You look very pretty today.' I wouldn't blame men if they ran for the hills."

She believes that there is a significant contingent of women who, in their quest for equality, are unfairly maligning men. She points to the music business to illustrate this. "I've always seen the glass half full with how far women have come," she says. "I see so much good in the music industry now. I'm looking and going, 'Wow, I see so many women in music now at the very top.' And yet I still hear them talking down about men. I just don't see it, personally. We are living in a completely different world from what was just a few years back. I just don't see men taking advantage of women like what was happening in the '70s."

She references her experience in the Runaways as proof of this progress: "I think if people could have sat where the five of us girls sat in 1975, 1976, and 1977, they would have really seen that women were just not around [in the music business] at all. And I'm not saying it was the fault of men. I'm saying it was that women just weren't doing it. Especially teenage girls—they were in school or planning families."

But as far as women have come, she adds, it's problematic to expect that the genders can ever truly become equal in everything, anyway, because "Men and women are *different*. Period. We are. We're *always* going to be different. That's why we attract each other."

Ignoring these innate contrasts is, she believes, resulting in a worse outcome for everyone. "When you start blurring those lines, it all becomes boring and unhealthy, in my opinion.

There's a magic about the differences between men and women that is being destroyed." She uses songwriting as an example: "Women can deliver songs and lyrics in a way that men cannot, and men can deliver songs and music and everything else in a different way."

She worries that there may be a rift between the sexes that can't be undone if things don't change. "I don't see any way of us achieving more without tearing it absolutely into shreds where we never recover," she says. "You can't demonize men to lift yourself up."

Instead, she tries to show how powerful it can be for one woman to offer support to another. "I think that women should be kinder to each other," she says. "Even on the street or in the supermarket, if I see a gal and something about her shines, I tell her so. And it makes her day."

But even as she makes a point of encouraging other women, she also reserves her most severe derision for the ones she thinks are invoking their right to equality in order to mask mediocrity. "If you're doing what you're supposed to be doing in life, it will work for you," she says. "You can't use gender all the time as an excuse for poor workmanship. If you fail in life, it's your fucking fault. Nobody else's. And that I know for a fact. You can't blame other people."

She wishes everyone—male or female—could tap into their own inner self-confidence, as she has worked hard to do. "People will have stickers on their mirrors, 'You're wonderful! You're fantastic! You're the best there is!' What the fuck is the matter with you, where you have to actually see it to believe it? It comes from within. And that's coming from a girl who grew up very insecure."

*　　*　　*

Currie's childhood in Encino, California, initially seemed typical. One of four siblings (she has an older sister, an identical twin sister, and a younger brother), she recalls that she was much more reserved than the rest of her family, preferring to spend her time surfing. "I was the least popular of my sisters," she says. "My twin sister ran with the 'It Crowd.' I was not so much that. I was very meek."

In 1974, when she was fourteen, she went to the Universal Amphitheatre in Los Angeles to see David Bowie, who was touring to support his just-released *Diamond Dogs* album. As she watched him, she had an epiphany: "It was like the skies opened. I thought, 'This is what I want to do!'" At that point, though, she didn't know how to pursue this dream.

Later that year, her life took a harrowing turn because of her twin sister's boyfriend. "He knew I was alone in the house and came and knocked on the sliding door. I said, 'My sister is not here.' He forced his way in and raped me. I was angry. I was bitter because something was taken from me: I could never get my virginity back."

Currie says that he was never punished, except for having her sister refuse to ever see him again. "My mother said, 'We don't talk about this kind of a thing.' Back then, it was just so different. It was such a different world. There was nothing I could do about it.

"The way I coped with it was, I embodied David Bowie. I guess it was a way for me not to deal with my feelings. I cut my hair into this shag look and would dress up like a guy in the suit and the tie."

By the next year, at fifteen years old, she had already established herself as a familiar figure in the L.A. rock club scene. Through connections she made there, she ended up auditioning for the Runaways, an all-girl rock band that had formed a few months earlier.

For someone who had only occasionally sung just for fun, the audition was an intimidating experience. "As far as being a *singer* singer, I hadn't done it until the Runaways. When you sing in the car or in the shower—that's the best I had done. I'd never auditioned for anything. It was scary to have a mic put in front of me and have to sing."

She had arrived ready to sing a Suzi Quatro song but found that nobody else knew how to play it. Instead, they created the song "Cherry Bomb" on the spot. While songwriting credit is officially given to rhythm guitarist/vocalist Joan Jett (who'd go on to achieve success as a solo artist in the 1980s) and producer Kim Fowley, Currie says that she also played a significant role in crafting that track. "I wish I would have asked for some writing [credit] on it, because I really did come up with the melody," she says.

Fowley, who was steering the group's career, was already notorious for the way he treated the band members, frequently insulting them or calling them names. On the day that Currie auditioned, though, he showed a softer side.

"Kim Fowley knew that I was so scared," she says. "He turned all the lights off in the studio and gave me a handheld mic so I could dance around and pretend I was onstage doing the song, because I was just horrified to be standing in a studio with lights on me and having to sing with people looking at me. He did whatever he could. That was one thing he did understand. He could be very compassionate at times. But otherwise, he was tough as nails."

While it was hard to endure Fowley's often unkind treatment of them, Currie now thinks she understands why he did it. "He knew what we were going to be dealing with out there," she says. "How do you prepare teenage girls to go out on the road, doing something that had never really been done before? It's unfortunate, but this dog-eat-dog world that Kim Fowley would talk about all the time, he was absolutely right."

Though it was already clear that being in the Runaways would be a challenging situation for her, Currie readily accepted when they offered her the lead singer position because it seemed like it was fated. "I decided I wanted to be in a band and *boom*, it happened, just like that. Just by being in a club at the right place at the right time, with the right look. A huge part of this business, being successful, is luck. Meeting the right people at the right time."

With their lineup set—Currie (lead vocals), Jett (rhythm guitar/vocals), Lita Ford (lead guitar), Jackie Fox (bass), and Sandy West (drums)—the Runaways began refining their sound, mixing hard rock, glam rock, and punk. Currie recalls that it took some time for them to adapt to their new roles, though.

"Joan [Jett] emulated Suzi Quatro; I was David Bowie. Because we didn't know who we were. We were too young, too insecure, so what we did is pretend to be our heroes. Then we gradually grew into finding out who we were, and what felt right, what was comfortable." She adds that part of their uncertainty was due to the fact that they were entering uncharted territory. "There weren't any teenage girls doing rock and roll. We knew that we were the first."

Their efforts paid off when, the next year, they had built up enough of a reputation that they signed a record deal with Mercury Records. To outsiders, it looked like everything was ideal. Within the band's inner circle, though, the girls were contending with Fowley's increasingly controlling management style.

"We were warned," Currie says of Fowley's questionable methods. She remembers her family, and the other band members' parents, all asking questions about things that didn't seem quite right. "But Kim Fowley would just turn around and say, 'I'm going to wash my hands of this and walk away. And if I walk away, there's no [record] deal. I'm just going to stop this.' The intimidation occurred to keep people from looking further into it."

In the end, Currie and her bandmates all signed the record contract without pushing for details. "When you're offered a record deal, what do you do? What's my family going to do, say no? Absolutely not," she says.

The band also seemed like a good distraction from Currie's home life, which was in a state of upheaval at that time. When she was thirteen, her parents divorced. Two years later, as she was joining the Runaways, "My mom was just remarried, and she moved to Indonesia with my baby brother," she says, "so my dad, my twin sister and I, my grandmother, and my Aunt Evie lived in a house in Reseda."

Still, she says it was "a tiny little house full of love and support. I had a very loving family." But it was not a well-off family, as they tried to exist on what her father earned as a bartender.

She wishes her Runaways work could've helped support her family, "But I just didn't have that kind of income people would have thought we would have had," she says. The deals Fowley struck for the band meant that none of the members ever seemed to profit. "We never made any money in the Runaways. It was all stolen from us. They stole, and I mean all the people—the agents, managers, [and] the record company was involved, I'm sure." She estimates the most she ever got paid, at the conclusion of a tour, was $1,700.

Beyond not being paid well, the members were also worked to the point of exhaustion. "We never got a break. That's why we ended up breaking up. If we weren't on tour, we were in the studio, we were doing photo sessions or rehearsals. They never gave us a break, and they never gave us any assistance, as far as if we'd have just been able to talk to each other when there were jealousies or whatever was going on. If we had had someone, a mediator, I would have lasted another record. But we didn't have that. Anything that cost money, we didn't have."

*   *   *

Being in the Runaways wasn't all bad, though. Their 1976 self-titled debut album earned favorable reviews. They embarked on several extensive American tours opening for a diverse range of headlining acts, including Van Halen and Talking Heads. In 1977, with the release of their sophomore album, *Queens of Noise*, they graduated to international touring, becoming hugely popular in Japan.

On the road, the band was only accompanied by a roadie and a tour manager (both male), but Currie says it felt like a safe situation. "We didn't ever feel vulnerable because we looked out for each other. We didn't do crazy things. We weren't going out and partying all night with guys. We just didn't do that. We were on the move all the time. I'm not saying that we didn't partake here and there on the tour with different guys or girls or whatever it was. I'm just saying that we were the only ones that had each other's backs, and we kept an eye on each other. We kind of had to grow up and be our own parents."

Having to mature quickly had some benefits, at least. As Currie recalls with a grin, "Did people want to have sex with us? Of course they did. We wanted to have sex with them! Back then, an older man was attractive to us. We didn't want *boys*. Come on, you want to be grown up when you're a kid!"

Currie is also careful to point out that there were men who genuinely seemed to want to help them. "There were guys on the road with us, like Tom Petty and the Heartbreakers and Cheap Trick, who were as supportive as they possibly could be. Just great guys."

Not everyone was compassionate toward them, though. "People like [the band] Rush? They weren't so kind. They didn't take us seriously." She describes a show at Cobo Hall (now Huntington Place) in Detroit on February 10, 1977, when Rush members threw sheets of paper onto the stage, making it hazardous. "I jumped off Sandy's drum riser, happened to hit one of those pieces of paper, and I slid right to the end of the stage, [where] there was an orchestra pit. And all I remember is thinking, 'I'm going to go off this stage.' I caught myself at the very last minute."

She knows that Rush's members are beloved, so what she's saying about them will be considered controversial, but she shrugs it off. "People get really upset when I tell that story, but the thing is, that's what they were doing. They thought we were a joke."

*   *   *

By 1977, Currie had had enough of the chaotic life that came with the Runaways, so she left the band. She released a solo album, *Beauty's Only Skin Deep*, the following year. In 1980, she and her twin sister, Marie Currie, released the album *Messin' with the Boys*, which spawned a successful single, "Since You Been Gone." She also tried her hand at acting, with a notable appearance alongside Jodie Foster in the 1980 film *Foxes*.

But drug addiction, and exhaustion from intensive years of working without pause, were taking their toll, so she took several years away from the spotlight to recuperate. While she was out of the public eye, though, she was determined to remain productive.

"It was very important to me to work—to go and have a normal life," she says. "I started working at a linen store right across from a record store where my [Runaways] records were. I'll never forget Rosanna Arquette, who is a friend of mine, coming in and saying, 'What are *you* doing here?' I said, 'What's it look like I'm doing? I'm working.' And she was shocked. But the thing is, I wanted to experience that. There's nothing shameful about any of it. But yet, there's stigma. It doesn't matter what you do: be great at it. I've watched plumbers who are far better people than some of these people with platinum records on their walls, I'll tell you that much."

She was married to actor Robert Hays from 1990 to 1997; their son, Jake, was born in 1991. She credits becoming a mother for truly grounding her. "When you have a baby, everything changes. The love is a completely different realm of understanding. I mean, it's overwhelming, the love that you feel for that child. And it really puts things into perspective: what's important in life and what is not," she says.

Another life lesson Currie learned in her post-Runaways years is that "There is strength in letting things go." Specifically, she means her animosity toward her former manager, Kim Fowley. "I hated that man. *Hated* him," she says. "But when you look at things through the eyes of an adult rather than a child, you see things so completely differently."

She remembers encountering Fowley at a party, and "I wanted to shove him into a pool—I was so angry. Then I just had this reckoning about who was suffering through all of this. And it wasn't him. *I* was the one that was suffering. *I* was the one that was bitter and angry and resentful. And that was hurting me, not him. It washed over me that I didn't need to be angry anymore. I didn't need to hurt myself anymore."

After running into Fowley at another party, which she thinks was in 2007 or 2008, the pair started talking again. Those conversations led her to another realization: "That this man, as cruel as he could be, had a crappy childhood. Terrible relationship with his mother. Didn't know what love was. All those things mold people."

Currie and Fowley's reconciliation led to an incredibly deep bond. "I took care of him toward the end of his life here in my home, when he had bladder cancer," she says. She feels good that she resolved things with him before he passed away on January 15, 2015. "It meant a lot to be able to have good memories with him."

*   *   *

Currie is also at peace with her time in the Runaways and the legacy it has granted her: "I feel incredibly blessed that I was able to do something that is now profound to some people," she says.

She still occasionally releases new music—her latest solo album, *Blvds of Splendor*, came out in 2019 (via Blackheart Records, the label that Joan Jett and songwriter/producer Kenny Laguna founded in 1980).

Music is no longer her main focus, however. Instead, "I sling a chainsaw for a living," she says. By this, she means her chainsaw art—intricate wood carvings (many on a large scale) that are created using a chainsaw, which she sells through galleries as well as via direct commission. "It's a hard ass thing to do. I just happen to do it well. It's a blessing for me that I can make a living doing something that mainly men do. But it was a calling." In fact, she adds, she has to leave this Zoom call soon because she's on a deadline to finish carving a cane for a client.

"You have to trust yourself. You have to believe in that inner voice. The reason why I picked up a chainsaw was this inner voice that would not stop. I was going down the street on a motorcycle, passing a couple of guys chainsaw carving at the side of the road. Didn't stop, but that voice would not leave me alone. If it wasn't for that voice, I would not have this house I'm in, because I didn't get any money from the Runaways. We push that voice down, because a lot of times, it's telling you things you don't want to hear.

"There comes a point of reckoning where you stop believing all the bullshit around you and look inside for the answers. Because the answers are there. They've *always* been there, I promise you. I pray that people start listening to that inner voice and stop just going with the narrative.

"Do what you were put on this planet to do. Follow your path. If there's stones, you move them aside. Or climb over them. Whatever you've got to do. But it's your path, and yours alone, and nobody can walk that path with you. So don't expect people to understand your feelings or ambitions or desires. They're yours, and that's a gift that you get from the universe when you're born. So believe in who you are as a human being, and trust that voice. That voice is never wrong." If you do that, Currie says, "You will go as far as you could ever possibly dream."

8

Joan Osborne

After a performance on August 3, 1997, at The Cynthia Woods Mitchell Pavilion (a.k.a. The Woodlands Pavilion), an amphitheater near Houston, Texas, Joan Osborne was banned from ever playing at that venue again. Her offense? Standing up for Planned Parenthood, the American nonprofit organization that provides women with reproductive health care, such as options for birth control, sex education, and—in the states where it is legal—abortions.

That fateful show was part of that year's Lilith Fair concert tour, a massive traveling festival featuring female artists performing across multiple musical genres. Founded by Canadian singer-songwriter Sarah McLachlan, Lilith Fair happened annually from 1997 through 1999, with a revival in 2010. Besides Osborne, other top-billed artists who participated included Jewel, Emmylou Harris, Indigo Girls, Suzanne Vega, Mary Chapin Carpenter, and many more. Selling out arena after arena, it became one of the most successful touring events of the 1990s. "It was a bigger cultural moment than I expected it to be when I first said yes to it," Osborne says. "It ended up being this touchstone for people in a way that I didn't expect."

Besides the music, Lilith Fair also hosted a number of information booths for female-oriented nonprofit organizations, including Planned Parenthood. When the tour came to metro Houston, "We were playing this big outdoor arena, and it was a sold-out show. And the people who ran the venue said, 'This is wonderful, all of these people can come in here—but Planned Parenthood is not allowed to set up their information booth.' We were like, 'What? This whole festival is about empowering women—you can't just single out this one organization and say that they can't come in, because this is part of what you get with this festival.'

"We had a big meeting backstage about it. And there was a big press conference. Finally, it was agreed that Planned Parenthood could have their information booth in the arena, but that no one could talk about it from the stage. That was the compromise that they reached. And I was like, 'Fuck this.'"

During their set that night, Osborne and her band all wore Planned Parenthood T-shirts. "And after the very first song, I said, 'I would like to reach out and especially welcome our friends at Planned Parenthood, and the booth is right over there.' So that got me in trouble. [The venue executives] said, 'Well, you can never play here again, Joan Osborne.'"

Twenty-five years later, Osborne still feels fine about this banishment—which, as far as she knows, is still in effect. "But it's not like I'm filling an arena by myself anymore, anyway, so it hasn't really impacted me that much," she says.

She still gets upset when she thinks about that incident, though. "I was *livid*. I could not believe they would do that. They wanted to make all the money and host this festival and pretend like they were feminists, or women-friendly, but not allow in Planned Parenthood? It was bullshit. That's the bedrock of being an actual full citizen of the United States, is being able to make decisions about your own body. So I was having none of it."

This wasn't the first time Osborne had shown support for Planned Parenthood through overt activism. She first became involved with that organization in the 1980s, which she recalls was "a time when doctors at abortion clinics were being shot and killed."

Back then, her apartment in New York City was near a Planned Parenthood branch, "and I saw how these anti-abortion protesters would camp out on the sidewalk and harass women and teenage girls as they were going in to try to get health services, whether it was an abortion or whether it was just a test or birth control or whatever it was. They had these grisly signs which were just horrible, and they were shouting abuse at these women. I was like, 'I need to do something about this.' So I volunteered."

In that capacity, Osborne walked women in and out of the Planned Parenthood facility, helping to shield them from anyone acting in an aggressive manner toward them. She also organized concerts to benefit the organization.

Osborne is extremely distressed to watch how, in 2022, access to abortion became more restricted in the United States, with each state's government being granted the power to decide whether or not the procedure will be legal within its borders. "Back then [in the 1990s], the people who were protesting [at abortion clinics] were, I think, generally thought of as being very much on the fringe," she says. "It's horrifying to think that this is something that we've had to continually fight for, and that it's worse now than it was even back then because [opposition] is happening at the legislative level now."

Having a daughter (whose name and other details Osborne prefers to keep out of the media) makes the situation even more worrisome for her. "It makes me really, really sad that she is growing up in a time where this thing that was taken for granted as a human right is no longer [in place]. I mean, I know that she's going to be fine. If she ever needs an abortion, I will do whatever I have to do to make that happen for her. But it's the people who are more at risk who are not going to be fine. And those are the people who need the help and support."

Although Osborne feels discouraged by the current state of some aspects of women's rights, she hopes she's been able to make a difference—both with her activism and by simply showing that it's possible for a woman to have a successful performing career that has been done entirely on her own terms.

*   *   *

But her singing career, Osborne admits, "was kind of an accident."

While attending New York University, she lived in New York City's Gramercy neighborhood. One night, a guy in her building invited her to go to a bar that was on the same corner where they lived. It was called the Abilene Café. "It was a little blues and jazz club. It was kind of late at night, so the band had finished, but the piano player was just playing for himself and the people who were still there. And this guy dared me to go up and sing and said that he would buy the drinks if I did."

It was a tempting offer, as she was perpetually almost broke because of paying her NYU tuition. "I would have to stop taking classes and work some jobs to save up some money, and then I could go back [to school]. I was always worried about money." So she accepted the dare.

"I went up to the piano player, and we figured out that we both knew this Billie Holiday song, "God Bless the Child," and I sang that. The piano player said, 'That's good—why don't you come back? We do an open mic night here once a week.'

"So because this place was right on my corner, and there was something about singing—I knew I could do it, and I liked it—I started going to this open mic night every week." There, she befriended fellow singers who told her about more places in town with open mic nights. "Mostly blues clubs. But the further I went, the more that I realized there was this whole amazing scene going on of roots music and other kinds of music."

Initially, she found singing on New York stages to be intimidating, but she didn't let her discomfort show. She remembered the tough, talented female rock singers she'd admired when she was growing up, such as Patti Smith, Chrissie Hynde of the Pretenders, and Debbie Harry of Blondie.

Blues music was also an important inspiration for her. "I loved B.B. King and Otis Redding and all those guys. And not just the male singers, of course, but [also] Etta James, Tina Turner, and Mavis Staples—people who came out of that gospel tradition but really turned it into this very powerful feminist statement."

Osborne especially admired this "very empowered and very sassy" attitude. "For me, I think that was part of the appeal. It wasn't just the music; it was [also] this celebrating themselves as they are and not taking any bullshit from anybody. At least, that's the persona that they were projecting. Now, the reality of being an African American in the music business and being female at the time when they were coming up, it probably wasn't all like that. But that's the image they were presenting."

So as she started her own career, Osborne deliberately emulated those women. "I knew that I wasn't that confident, and I didn't have that kind of swagger, but I could pretend to have it while I was onstage singing those songs. And I think little by little, that confidence started to seep into the rest of my life, and I started to have a bit more of a feeling of, 'You don't have to be the nice little girl in the corner accommodating everyone else's needs.'"

Her confidence and performing skills growing, Osborne threw herself into New York's club scene. Along the way, she got to know many talented musicians who would also go on to find fame, such as the singer-songwriter Jeff Buckley. "And I slowly but surely became a part of it and ended up putting together my own band."

Even so, it took her a little while to line up paying gigs—there were "a lot of refusals from the different clubs." She persisted until she got her foot in the door. After that, it wasn't long before she began making enough money to support herself entirely through her singing.

At that point, it became clear that she would not have the capacity to keep pursuing a music career while continuing her university studies. When she really thought it through, "I was like, 'I feel like I will regret this if I don't see where it will go. If I just stop here, then I'm probably always going to wonder what could have happened. So I need to see this through and see where I can take it.'" She dropped out of NYU.

That gamble paid off: Osborne has released eleven critically acclaimed studio albums, earning seven Grammy award nominations. She continues to tour the world, drawing audiences that appreciate her emotive singing in a wide range of genres, including rock, blues, jazz, soul, and country.

*   *   *

Even after those achievements, Osborne knows it's not guaranteed that she (or any other female artist) will always be treated with respect. "There is certainly casual sexism in being a performer and being onstage," she says. "If you go up onstage, especially as a young woman in a bar or club, some guys are going to talk about your boobs or whatever. Guys in the audience can be jerks sometimes. But the way that you get around that is just by understanding what your purpose is. You start to sing, and they realize that you've got something going on. You start to reach them in a different way, at an emotional level. And that shuts them right up."

This advice should work for anyone, not just performers. "If you can own that space, you can ignore people like that who are going to be assholes, because they're everywhere, in anything that you want to do. You just have to develop a little bit of a thick enough skin where you don't let that stop you. And mostly, if you're doing what you love to do, people are going to see that, and they will stop saying stupid shit to you because they realize that you are legitimate."

She knows this is easier said than done sometimes, though. "We live in a world that doesn't necessarily raise girls and women to believe in themselves. So that can be a rare thing, and it can be harder for women to get to that place of, 'I understand what my power is' if they haven't been raised like that. So it's not like I'm saying it's your fault if you don't feel this way about yourself. But in my experience, that has been the key to getting around sexism and misogyny—do the work that you have to do in order to fulfill your own potential and understand your own power."

At the same time, she cautions women against getting *too* sensitive about male attention, as it isn't always cause for concern. As an example, she points to her own early experiences as an entertainer: "It's a music scene, and part of that music scene is people wanting to meet each other for romantic partnering up. That's part of the reason that I thought it was exciting, too: 'Maybe I can meet some cute guys.' It wasn't just that the women were out there being exploited or hit on all the time. Certainly that happened, but I don't recall any situations where somebody was like, 'Okay, I'll give you this gig only if you date me.' It wasn't like that for me."

In fact, Osborne says, she encountered many supportive men as she was establishing her career. "I think the first guys who really took me under their wing was a group called the Holmes Brothers. They would have you crying in your beer one second doing a beautiful Hank Williams song, and then they'd have you sweating on the dance floor the next second with this super funky groove. They were amazing.

"Sherman Holmes, the bass player, was running one of these open mics at a place called Dan Lynch Blues Bar [in New York]. So I started showing up to this place and doing my two or three songs, and he was really supportive. Just a great guy." (She later repaid this kindness by producing two albums for the Holmes Brothers, *Speaking in Tongues* in 2001, and *Feed My Soul* in 2010.)

Before long, Osborne was playing up to five nights a week, eventually expanding beyond New York City until she had established herself in the club circuit throughout New England and the Mid-Atlantic states.

In 1991, she put out her first release, *Soul Show: Live at Delta 88*. Unlike most debut albums, this was a recording of her performance at a New York club, not in a studio. And she did it via Womanly Hips, a record label that she'd set up for herself.

It was an innovative approach. At the time, though, she felt she was simply doing the most straightforward thing. "After the show, people would be like, 'I want to buy your album.' And I was like, 'I don't have an album for you to buy. I guess I'd better get on this.' There was an example that you could look to in the punk scene of people putting out their own records. So I was like, 'I can put a record out on my own—I don't have to wait for [a record deal].'"

She did need some help when it came to funding, though. "Here's another example of a guy who was very supportive, a guy named Peter Honercamp. He did, and he still does, run a club on Long Island called The Stephen Talkhouse. We had started playing there, and I was talking to him after the show one night and saying I was planning on putting out a record. And he said, 'I'll front the money because I know that you'll pay me back, because I know that it'll be a success.' So he put up some of the money." The rest came out of her own pocket.

Although the album was released independently, receiving little radio support or national distribution, it sold so well at her shows that record company executives took notice. "That's when major labels started to be like, 'Here's somebody who's taking it to this point on their own, so maybe if we stepped in right now, we could put our energy behind it and expand on this.'"

She signed with Mercury Records, where she felt respected. "The person who I ended up working with at Mercury, [producer] Rick Chertoff, had had a lot of success with Cyndi Lauper and Sophie B. Hawkins. He was looking for what was unique about somebody. I think he felt, and rightly so, that that's how you find an artist who is really going to connect with people. You don't just fit somebody into a preconceived mold. You find out what is unique and beautiful about them, and then you help to bring that out."

To do that, Chertoff brought in Eric Bazilian and Rob Hyman from the rock band the Hooters to collaborate with her on writing and recording her album *Relish*. "One of Us," written by Bazilian, was a particularly good showcase for Osborne's emotive and intimate vocals as she sang about what would happen if God were leading a mundane existence among the humans. Released as the album's first single in November 1995, it was an instant smash hit, charting in more than a dozen countries, including reaching the top spot in Australia, Belgium, Sweden, and Canada. In the United States, it attained gold sales status (500,000 copies sold).

"Suddenly, it was a worldwide thing," Osborne says. "I was certainly excited. The fact that people were appreciating this song and this record and it was getting a lot of positive feedback—obviously, that's what you want if you are an artist. So of course it was incredibly gratifying."

But there was a downside to this sudden fame, too. "The job of being the person who is the face of that, and who needs to go to the photo shoots and do the interviews and be on television—it's flattering up to a point, but it was hard for me. Some people, I'm sure, love that part of it. But I really didn't. I would never say that I regret that it happened; it was just a part that I didn't like so much."

Some of that discomfort stemmed from having a big part of the attention focused on her appearance, rather than her music.

"The emphasis on looks and on slotting yourself into a particular way of looking that is considered attractive, I think that was on my mind more than it probably would have been if I wasn't female," she says. "I would turn things down back then because I thought that I didn't look the way that I should look. I got offered a guest spot acting on an episode of [the hit television show] *Friends*—and I turned it down because I didn't want to be standing next to these skinny TV actresses. I thought that I would feel embarrassed because I don't look like that."

She doesn't believe this kind of self-doubt is limited to female performers. "That's just the life that you live as a woman: your looks are so much the way that people make decisions about you and the way that you are able to move around in the world. I don't like that, but that's how it is. And I think very few women are able to really love themselves for the way that they look. Or just not care what anybody thinks. You can say that, but I think it's a lot harder to really feel that in your heart and in your mind."

But she finds it's getting easier for her to do so as time goes on. "That's one of the things about getting older that I like, is that I really have stopped giving a shit about what people think about the way I look and been more accepting of the beauty that I have—that we *all* have."

*   *   *

Growing up in Anchorage, Kentucky, just outside of Louisville, Osborne never imagined that she'd one day become a world-famous singer.

"I had a kind of idyllic childhood, in a lot of ways," she says. "We lived in a small town. Everybody knew everybody in the town, and it was safe. I'm one of six children, and myself and my brothers and sisters would go out and play in the woods around our house, and then come back in time for supper."

Born in 1962, she is the second oldest of her siblings, which she thinks had a profound impact on her. "I was mom number two, in a way. I did a lot of caretaking for my younger siblings, and they looked to me for breaking up fights or being something of an authority figure. Certainly not at the parental level, but I did have responsibilities to take care of my younger siblings. I think that probably gave me a sense of being a person who can be in charge, who can take care of others, and who can be listened to and appreciated. So this feeling that people are going to listen to what I have to say and respect it probably had something to do with me being able to stand up on a stage and sing."

As an adolescent, she started singing in her school choir. "We had a very good music teacher at my little public school, Caroline Browning. We would do these intricate six-part harmonies, and Olde English madrigal songs. Maybe that's not unusual for a choir, but I felt like, 'Wow, this is challenging stuff.' My teacher was always very encouraging to me and would give me some of the more difficult parts to sing and would work with me on solo pieces. So I did have a pretty thorough education [in music]. I think that was certainly a real help to me in later years."

Singing was also a favorite pastime for her outside of school. "I remember going into the woods from the time I was six or seven years old and taking my little red Radio Shack transistor radio. I would build forts and listen to the radio, and I remember singing along to that [1975] Minnie Riperton song, "Lovin' You," where she does the super-high part. The birds would sing, and I would imitate them and try to sing like they did. So I always knew that I had a voice—but I don't think that I thought of it as being anything special. I think I just figured, 'Everybody can do this.'"

Even though it seemed like the most natural thing in the world, Osborne never entertained the thought of singing professionally. "Growing up in the place that I grew up, that would have been considered a real pipe dream, like, 'Who do you think you are, thinking you're going to become a singing star? Yeah, right. And I'm going to be the president of the United States.' So it was not something that I thought of in any kind of serious way, or even really fantasized about."

Still, her artistic streak led her to study theater at the University of Louisville. She became the director for a school play there, "and I thought, 'Wow, this is really cool. I can see trying to do something with this.' But I'm a practical person." She realized that, much as she loved theater, the audience for movies was far larger. "So I was like, 'Hmm, maybe I could get into movies somehow.' Not being an actor or performer but being behind the camera. So that's when I decided to apply to NYU [film school], and was very excited when I got in."

She moved to New York City, never dreaming that her life would take such an unexpected turn there.

*   *   *

After successfully navigating all the twists and turns she encountered along the way to making it as an internationally famed singer-songwriter, Osborne still hesitates when asked if she believes she helped pave the way for other women following her in the music business.

"I mean, that's really hard for me to say," she says. "I've certainly had people come up to me after shows, saying, 'I fell in love with your record and that's what made me want to sing,' or 'I grew up in a very conservative place and I knew that I was gay but I couldn't say anything about it, but your music really gave me some hope and some strength that there was another way to look at things aside from the way that my family and community look at things.'

"But that's part of the thing about doing music, is that you don't always know: you send these things out into the world, and you don't have any control over the way that people experience them. And in fact, the audience, by way of listening and taking it into themselves, are sort of completing the creative act. I can sit on a mountaintop and sing all I want, and that's wonderful—but until someone hears that and interprets the meaning that they get from it, then it's very one-sided."

So far, fans around the world have made it clear that they like the messages Osborne is sending with her music, so it's highly likely that her work (and that of other talented women) will endure. As she puts it, there is an "eternal fascination with women in rock."

9

Donita Sparks (L7)

L7 vocalist/guitarist Donita Sparks remembers the moment toward the end of the 1990s when she realized just how much the notion of "female empowerment" had been embraced on a mainstream level. "I was on a treadmill in Las Vegas before a show. There were video screens [showing] MTV and I'm watching the Spice Girls and it said 'Girl Power,'" she says. "It was only a matter of time that what we were toiling away at in the underground was co-opted by a pop singing group."

Since forming the band in 1985, the (female) members of L7 have used their uncompromising hard rock songs and tough image to transmit the message that women are strong and self-determining. They achieved success with hits such as "Pretend We're Dead" (1992) and "Andres" (1994)—but at the same time, they weren't always given full respect. Even in an otherwise supportive interview with the group (which told readers, "Simply, they kick ass, regardless of gender"), the influential British music magazine *Melody Maker* still started it with: "Are L7 really Californian white trash bitches from hell or is [the article's writer] just having another wet dream?"[1]

By then, Sparks was well familiar with this type of negativity because she'd encountered it during her early days in the Los Angeles music scene. "That is not foreign to my ears, because I experienced that even when we were in the underground," she says. "I think that there was such vitriol toward the word *feminist* from the male community, and even from other females. Goddamn, if I identified myself as a feminist pre-L7, even in the underground, the mean punk guys would really start trying to antagonize me. They really hated that word. It was so threatening to them."

It has especially disturbed her to see women rejecting the "feminist" label: "It really surprises me when it's a punk woman or a woman from the underground. That really blows my mind. I actually think it's contradictory to the way they live their lives. I'm just like, 'Wow, where were you during women's lib?' It's so bizarre."

So it was with mixed emotions that Sparks watched the Spice Girls on MTV that day. While she was glad to see how her own band had helped pave the way for making a feminist message palatable in such a widespread way, she also viewed this outcome with some suspicion. "I don't hate them or anything," she says of the Spice Girls. "I've got no problem with them, but to see that co-opted was just very like, 'What the fuck?' It was funny and infuriating at the same time. You can't just dance in front of a neon sign that says 'feminist.' You've got to do more than that."

A quarter century later, Sparks continues to monitor the progress on this front. "I think a lot more people are proclaiming themselves feminists. It's much more in the zeitgeist, especially with young women, so that's great, and I hope they know what it fuckin' means."

She certainly still does. "I am a dyed-in-the-wool feminist," she says. "My mother raised me that way."

*   *   *

"I was always fighting the power, even in grade school," Sparks says. "We were in a public school and our principal made this random rule: 'You can't wear pants if you are a girl.' He was just making up these rules that he had no legal basis for. So I led a rebellion. The principal would actually come into the classroom to pass out report cards, and I got as many girls as I could to wear pants that day because it would always enrage him. I was always doing little rebellions like that."

Sparks was born in Chicago in 1963, the baby in a family with four girls. Her father was a high school principal in the inner city, while her mother worked a union job as a clerk for the railroad. "My parents were very tolerant people," she says. "As a kid, I was always aware of social issues that were going on."

When she was young, her family moved to the city's suburbs, where it quickly became apparent that they weren't like most of their neighbors. "I had a liberal family, so I always felt kind of like an outsider. Even though I was a popular kid, I felt like our family was different than the others. Because we were," Sparks says. "The community there was highly Catholic and pretty conservative." In contrast, her family attended a Unitarian church on the South Side of Chicago, "but I hated going to church like any other red-blooded American kid."

She was much more interested in artistic endeavors. "I always fantasized myself being a dancer or something in show business. I took dance classes and was in the choir. But I never thought, 'I'm going to be in a rock band.'"

Although she wouldn't characterize her family as being particularly musical, she now sees how her childhood prepared her for her future career: "My dad had been a drummer in a drum and bugle corps as a kid. He was constantly tapping all these really cool military beats on our cutting board with his drumsticks," she says, "and my sisters and I would sing in rounds a lot. We'd have fun and harmonize to pop or rock records." She recalls her sisters playing rock albums, but as a young girl she also loved the soundtracks to *The Sound of Music* and *West Side Story*.

Formal musical training was required in the Sparks household. "Every kid in our family had to take a musical instrument whether we liked it or not," she says. "I played the clarinet. My sister played flute. We had a piano in the house."

When Sparks was nineteen years old, she decided it was time to leave the Chicago area. "I wanted to get out to California," she says, though she admits her vision for what she'd actually do once she got there was rather vague: "I was into punk rock art. I thought I'd surf and be a beach bum."

She ended up in Hollywood, where she "found kind of a loose punk community." She got a job at *L.A. Weekly*, a hip alternative newspaper. At first, she worked as a messenger, driving all around her adopted hometown, but she soon got a pivotal promotion.

"I was quite the dresser back then. Much different than my L7 look. I was always doing thrift store fashion mashups, [such as] a Kiss backpack with a '50s skirt and socks with sandals," she says. "The Art Department liked my style and said, 'Hey, want to work [here]? Do you want to be an apprentice?' All the sudden, I was in the building with all these artists and writers and musicians. It was a really cool little hub of creative people who were pursuing the arts as a career. That was like, 'Wow, this is cool.' And they were liberal, too, most of them, and there were some people who were civically minded. So I felt good there."

Sparks thinks it was 1984 or 1985 when she first got to know singer/guitarist Suzi Gardner. "We had mutual friends. Suzi had worked at the *L.A. Weekly* before I did and had also waitressed at a place called Millie's before I did. So it was like I was following her, a couple years apart. But we were both on the scene. There were so few women playing guitar and into rock at the time that a couple mutual friends said, 'You and Suzi should meet.'

"I was playing in a band that was pretty horrible, and she came to see me," Sparks continues. "We started hanging out and listening to records together and had some long weekends with using substances that kept us up for days at a time. We got to know each other a bit. She had a demo tape of some songs that she had just recorded herself, and I really liked them a lot because they were heavier than what I was playing in this [other] band—it was the direction I wanted to be. I just loved a lot of her riffs."

Sparks and Gardner formed a band together soon after. "Suzi and I wanted to be the guitarists/singers, and we were cowriting, as well, so it was very much going to be fronted by us, but we didn't care if [the other members] were male or female." This approach informed what they decided to call themselves. "I was like, 'I don't want any gender reference in our name. I don't want anybody to even be able to tell if we are male or female.'" They eventually picked L7, which she explains "is a slang term for a person who is a square."

Even with their open-minded approach, it took Sparks and Gardner time to find permanent bandmates. "We went through many bass players who were all women, just coincidentally." They finally hired bassist Jennifer Finch in 1986.

This early iteration of L7 also included a male drummer. "Then we kicked him out of the band. He'd get drunk and call us bitches or cunts or whatever. When he was sober, he was really sweet, but he just had this dark streak, like a lot of people do." His departure marked the beginning of L7 as a female-only band.

"When we got rid of him, it was like, 'Okay, no more of this. We are not dealing with any sass from any dudes. Fuck that. Let's look for a female drummer.' Which was incredibly difficult. We went through a lot of auditions until we finally got Dee [Plakas]. The way she played was exactly what Suzi and I were looking for. It really made the difference between us even remaining as a band, the fact that we got Dee in there."

Their lineup set, L7 began playing around the Los Angeles scene, but they found that their hard rock songs confounded many people. "We were different, other than just being female," Sparks says. "We sounded different. We weren't playing jangly stuff or hardcore punk. We were playing distorted guitars. We were playing a musical mashup of punk and metal and a little bit of surf and a little bit of blues. We were going for something that was pretty fresh in the underground at the time."

Their scruffy image also made them striking: "Our style of dress was different than what was in vogue in the underground at the time. We didn't look New Wave. Our hair was long and was not teased and coiffed. It was just kind of grungy looking, before 'grunge' was used as a musical style term. When we were doing our band at first, [people said], 'They're trying to be guys. They look like guys.' Even other women would be like, 'They're doing all these male posturings.' We were just being ourselves."

When they encountered sexism in the city's music scene, Sparks says they just shrugged it off. "Listen, there are people who are going to be pig-o's everywhere," she says. "I remember being at a couple of parties where the guys were jamming and I said, 'Hey, can we play?' And they said no. That kind of shit. They were too busy wanking to give up the guitars. Just stuff like that."

Although L.A. was then the epicenter of the so-called hair metal scene, which could be notoriously misogynistic, Sparks says she and her bandmates didn't actually get any grief from that quarter. "We didn't have to contend with that—they played different clubs than we did. Some of those guys supported L7. I've got to say, Taime Downe from Faster Pussycat, Slash from Guns N' Roses—some of those guys really liked us. They thought we were cool."

L7's first big break came from a connection Jennifer Finch had with Brett Gurewitz, who was the founder and lead guitarist for the influential punk band Bad Religion. "Jennifer was like the baby on the scene; she was in that hardcore punk scene as a kid. She knew Brett when Bad Religion was starting out," Sparks says. Gurewitz signed them to his then-fledgling Epitaph Records, which put out L7, their 1988 debut record. It was one of the earliest releases on that label, which has since gone on to become one of the most prominent independent record companies in the United States.

Epitaph was still limited in its scope when L7 were on the roster, though, so it was an easy decision to switch to Sub Pop, an influential Seattle-based record label. "It was a great break that we got on Sub Pop, for sure. Sub Pop was hot shit," Sparks says.

At that time, Sub Pop was considered an arbiter of the so-called Seattle sound, and would prove instrumental in helping to launch the careers of several notable Washington grunge bands, including Nirvana, Soundgarden, and Mudhoney. Even though L7 were from California and didn't consider themselves grunge, "To be lumped in with them was a good thing. It gave us a whole new world of exposure. We got out to a lot more people. If we hadn't gotten on Sub Pop or another cool label, we probably would have broken up at that point, because it was just so difficult. But Sub Pop gave us that shot of adrenaline that we needed."

Through Sub Pop, L7 released a single, "Shove" / "Packin' a Rod" (1990), then a full-length album, *Smell the Magic* (1990). The album received favorable reviews, but otherwise didn't result in substantial commercial success, so another change was in order.

"Sub Pop was great, but we wanted bigger distribution, so it was time for a jump to a major label," Sparks says. "We went to Slash Records, which had been an independent L.A. label of very cool bands, and they had just gotten a distribution deal with Warner Bros. Records. So we felt really comfortable with the people from Slash because they were still kind of underground art people."

This time, the change paid off: L7's next album, *Bricks Are Heavy* (1992), brought the band their first hit single, "Pretend We're Dead," which charted in the United States, Australia, the United Kingdom, and Belgium. But Sparks, who wrote the song and performed lead vocals on it, thought that it was prevented from becoming as successful as it might have been if L7 were not an all-female band.

"We were told by some of the radio people working at Warner Bros. that some of the morning shock jocks had a 'no chick' policy: they just wouldn't play you," Sparks says. "Other radio stations had an allotment of how many female-fronted bands could be played within an hour. Some crazy bullshit. So we didn't get played as much as some of the other bands like Soundgarden or Nirvana, but there wasn't anything we could do about that at the time. It definitely affected the sales."

As they'd always done, though, Sparks and her bandmates simply shrugged off this bad treatment, which she says is "probably the way to cope for all females on this planet. You're going to encounter a monster every now and then. You're going to encounter someone that really dislikes you just because you are female. What else can you do? You've got to ignore them, get around it, quit altogether, or laugh it off."

Most often, she says, the members of L7 have chosen that final option: "Our most effective weapon of war would be humor. So these people, if they were pig-o's, we would laugh at them, or laugh behind their backs. There's that quote that says, 'Women's biggest fear is to be murdered by men. Men's biggest fear is to be laughed at by women.' Some men were kind of terrified of us. The ones who were terrified were probably terrified for a reason, because they had things to maybe hide."

She notes that this fear didn't go the other way. "Nobody ever scared us," she says. She credits "safety in numbers" for shielding them from ill treatment, at least to a certain degree. "The thing that was cool about L7 is that because we were four together, you're in a gang. [Despite] whatever things that you might not like about each other, you are united as a band. Even when we were onstage having a bad show, we were *all* having a bad show. There was a unity with that. And if anybody fucks with your band or one of your bandmates, it's like, 'Oh, now you're at war with *us*.'"

Even so, Sparks admits that there have been some incidents. "Maybe an occasional guy in another band would say something really gross to one of us or something. That happened a couple of times," she says. "But that'll happen. That's that person's chemical imbalance. They've got problems, anybody who would say something gross."

She gives an example of how she and her bandmates have dealt with this kind of disrespect: "We were playing our first tour of Australia [in 1995] and we heard that the promoter, after a Red Hot Chili Peppers show, said over the PA, 'All right, come see L7 next week—great tits, great ass, great band!' We heard about that, and I was like, 'Okay, tell him that if he's going to speak of us like dames, we want to be treated like dames. I want an opal for every one of us in our dressing room by the end of this tour.' We ridiculed him until, the last date, there was indeed a little velvet box for each one of us with an apology note and an opal."

There have been times when Sparks has been more confrontational, though. In one infamous incident, during L7's appearance at the prestigious Reading Festival in England in 1992, Sparks flung her used tampon into the crowd. That ignited a firestorm of indignation across global media. Thirty years later, Sparks has this to say about it: "We were having a bad show. In addition to technical difficulties, the crowd was hitting us with big clumps of mud our whole set. It sucked. So I went performance art on their asses. I like absurdity, activism, and humor. They threw mud, I threw blood. Period, ha ha."

Another controversial incident happened that same year when Sparks pulled down her jeans and underwear during L7's performance on the British TV show *The Word*. "I dropped my pants because there was a men's naked bum contest going on [during the show], which I found offensive: 'Why are they rating those guys on their asses?' It was so objectifying and stupid," she says. "It was like, 'Okay, they want to see some ass cheeks? They're going to see mine.' That's what I did. It was live TV, and I also knew I'd blow some minds. That's always fun, to be on live TV—and that probably stopped us from ever being on live TV again. They got a full-frontal view on that one, too.

"Some British writer gave this big backlash about it, that if I had been Madonna, I would have taken it to this sexually liberating place," she continues. "*My* absurd moment, *he* wanted to have some meaning. It was weird."

*   *   *

Sparks has also channeled her anger into activism, such as organizing shows to benefit Planned Parenthood, the American nonprofit organization that provides women's reproductive health care, when she was in her first band in L.A. That evolved into L7 spearheading Rock for Choice, a series of high-profile concerts to benefit the abortion rights movement.

"Heat was coming down on the abortion issue," Sparks says of the sociopolitical climate in the early 1990s. "I was like, 'Hey, you guys, let's do something for abortion rights. They're trying to chip away at this stuff.' And everybody was into it. Then we got together with a writer from *L.A. Weekly* named Sue Cummings, and also the Feminist Majority Foundation, and that's how Rock for Choice started."

The first Rock for Choice show, in 1991, featured L7, Nirvana, and Hole, among others. More concerts were held multiple times throughout the next ten years. After the first couple of years, with Rock for Choice well-established, L7 stepped back so other bands could take a turn at the helm, though Sparks notes that nobody else took possession of it in quite the same way that L7, as the founders, had done.

The 1990s also marked the emergence of the "riot grrrl" feminist movement, which uses a confrontational punk aesthetic to advocate for women's equality. "Thank gods for Bikini Kill and these other bands that went very political," Sparks says of the women who helped to popularize that movement's message.

L7 have been erroneously labeled as riot grrrls, even though they predated that scene by several years, but Sparks appreciates that they all have the same goal in mind. "They were leading by political manifestos: 'Girls to the front' and all that stuff. We had Rock for Choice. We were leading by example; that's how we chose to do it. Between us, I think we actually made a dent with that." Ultimately, she says, "Everybody breaks barriers for everybody else. There were others before us who got it even worse. You've got to honor that."

*   *   *

L7 went on hiatus in 2001, but the members reunited in 2015. Now, Sparks says, they're granted respect for being an influential hard rock band. This was evident in the 2016 documentary *L7: Pretend We're Dead*, which included effusive homages from other musicians such as Joan Jett, Shirley Manson (Garbage), Lydia Lunch, and Krist Novoselic (Nirvana), among others. In 2019, L7 released the critically acclaimed album *Scatter the Rats*, and they often tour.

"We're really enjoying the experience," Sparks says of being active with L7 again. "We are filled with gratitude. It's cool that we get to do these little victory laps, and we don't feel the pressure of the industry at all. All we have to concentrate on is putting out music every once in a while and enjoying the live experience with our fans."

Since L7 began four decades ago, "We've been through life. We've had health issues. We've had loss," Sparks says. There have also been many good developments, such as artistic endeavors outside of the band, long-term happy marriages, and gratitude for being recognized as trailblazers. All of these experiences, she adds, helped the members gain new perspectives that have given them a deeper appreciation for each other, and for what they've done together.

"Even through our personal turmoil with each other at times, we can also dig the fact that we accomplished this thing together," Sparks says. "It couldn't have been done without any one of us. I think that we're able to cope with each other's flaws a little bit better, with a more mature eye and ear. We're proud of what we've done. Not only musically, but the dent we made for women. That's fucking cool."

10

Amy Ray (Indigo Girls)

"There are a lot of different kinds of women, and I think it's important to always know that," says Amy Ray. "A masculine woman is a thing."

Ray has gender dysphoria, which the Mayo Clinic defines as "the feeling of discomfort or distress that might occur in people whose gender identity differs from their sex assigned at birth or sex-related physical characteristics."[1]

It is something that Ray says she wrestles with "all the time—but I would never be able to commit to being a man because I feel completely split down the middle [between male and female]. That's something that you should embrace because it's a blessing. But it's been hard for me to see it that way in my life because women are just not allowed to be that in society."

Indigo Girls, the Georgia-based folk rock duo Ray formed with Emily Saliers when they were still in high school, have achieved international acclaim with numerous charting singles from fifteen studio albums (one of which, 1989's *Indigo Girls*, won a Grammy Award for "Best Contemporary Folk Recording"). In 2022, they were inducted into the Women Songwriters Hall of Fame. Still, Ray understands from personal experience that success doesn't automatically eradicate self-doubt.

"I was so angry when we were first signed [to a record deal] and touring around," she says. "I'd get mad at the smallest things because I was just *mad*. I didn't know why. Everything was brewing inside. And there was so much that you're dealing with, all this homophobia and sexism and self-hate, that your anger comes out in ways that aren't really right—and [directed] at the wrong people, usually."

In Ray's case, this meant engaging in "really ridiculous punk rock stuff. I would throw a guitar across the stage at the monitor person. I kicked in a wall and broke my foot. I broke my hand knocking a wall in. Just repeatedly doing things that hurt myself. It didn't hurt the person I was mad at."

Looking back, she can see how being in one of the era's few openly gay bands exacerbated her feelings of alienation, though she didn't realize it then. "Our people at Epic [Records] were great; they were super friendly and supportive of us," she says, "but even they, behind the scenes, were talking about how they were going to deal with us, and trying to fend off the gay press because they didn't want us to play that up. We didn't totally know what was going on at the time. There would be people that were really on our side who later would say to us, 'Oh yeah, we tried to do this and this, but the label told us we couldn't because they didn't want us to promote you as gay women.'"

As a result, the band's rise to fame actually left Ray feeling worse about herself. "I was so self-hating," she says. "But it wasn't me. It wasn't my problem. But you don't know that when you're in your twenties—especially when it's the early '90s and you're trying to navigate things. You just think it's all your fault. All something that you should have done differently, [or] better. No matter how much your exterior is defiant, in a way that's like a front because you feel so bad about yourself."

Through the years, she's learned to have empathy for herself, and she hopes that humanity overall will also become kinder to anyone who's experiencing identity confusion similar to what she once endured. "It's hard when you have so much experience of self-hate and untangling the world and society that you can't really get clear about who you are," she says.

* * *

Despite Ray's insidious insecurity, there was one thing she never doubted: the music she created with Emily Saliers.

By the time they were both attending Emory University in Atlanta, they had already been performing together for several years. College life granted them the freedom to play frequent shows, and they also took advantage of the city's vibrant nightlife to go out dancing with their friends or hang out in the lesbian bar scene.

They played gigs just for fun, never seriously considering that they could become full-time professional musicians. "Back then, life was very different because you didn't have access to all this knowledge about how you could do a [music] career," Ray says. Instead, they looked for guidance from other women who were successful in the local club circuit, especially the singer-songwriters Caroline Aiken and DeDe Vogt. "Those were our role models. Those two were very, very, very influential on us, and helped us a lot."

There were also male musicians in the Atlanta scene who were extremely encouraging, especially Drivin n Cryin leader Kevn Kinney. "Kevn is one of my favorite people," Ray says, "and he always has been, because he never had an ounce of disrespect or condescension with women musicians."

Sometimes, however, Ray and Saliers could be confused by others' input. Some of their mentors were separatist, politicized lesbian feminists who told them they ought to focus on playing exclusively for women like themselves. Others warned that doing so would severely limit their opportunities. "So we were informed by two different sides, and kind of struggling with it," Ray says.

In the end, they chose to line up gigs wherever they could within Atlanta's flourishing music scene. They regularly performed at popular venues such as the 688 Club and the White Dot, and they became something of a house band at Little 5 Points Pub, which Ray recalls being like a "little oasis. The guy that ran the place, John Blizzard, was a gay man who was very supportive of our whole career, and the person that did sound was the same. We felt very at home [there]."

Things became harder when Indigo Girls began venturing outside of Atlanta, playing shows as far afield as Texas and New England with only a female tour manager to help them. "Emily and I were pretty obviously dyke-y, so you even felt scared to go into some truck stops where you had to go to make phone calls because there weren't cell phones back then," Ray says. "It was a lot of catcalling, and you didn't feel safe all the time. There would always be people that would call us dykes or make fun of us. I mean, that was constant." The insults came from women as well as men.

The disrespect often continued at their shows, where male venue employees would question their capabilities, such as "a sound person who does not believe that you know anything about sound. It was maddening, because we were used to playing gigs where you had to set up your own sound system, so we would do everything for ourselves.

"But also, here's the problem: when you're that young, you actually *don't* know everything about sound yet, but you're so disparaged and patronized by these soundmen that it doesn't even give you a chance to learn. Your reaction is so knee-jerk: 'You don't need to tell me what the EQ should be; I know what I need.' In the end, though, what you really needed was a teacher—a soundman that says, 'Come over and listen—this is a trick I've learned.' You can't win, because no one's taking the time to teach you because they don't think you're worthy of it. And you're not given any credit for what you already know."

The negativity often seemed to come from the top. "The promoter would always be a guy and would be kind of sexist. They're either making passes at you, and they think that that's okay, or they're taking advantage of you—they don't think you know what you're doing, so they're cooking the books and saying, 'This many people came,' when you know that it was twice as many. Or they'd try to pay you less. In the '80s, they even would try to pay you in drugs. It was just very sleazy."

Though Ray suspects that male musicians also encountered this type of bad behavior, she believes that female artists were treated even worse because the men in charge could more easily intimidate them.

"At some gigs, when I was trying to get paid, I didn't feel safe enough to say, 'Hey, you're shorting me,'" she says. "I was pretty street-smart and knew when I was in danger. Sometimes I really did feel scared, and I would take less money and go, because you just don't know what you're up against." Sometimes the bullying could be almost cartoonish: she remembers one promoter in Maine who attempted to underpay after a show, and when she called him on it, he grabbed a stick and menacingly beat it against his hand.

In contrast, other men in positions of power were immensely helpful toward Indigo Girls. Perhaps the biggest example of this is Russell Carter, a lawyer whom Ray and Saliers first met in 1986, and he became their manager two years later—a role he has held ever since.

"Russell is a total feminist," Ray says. "That's lucky. I think about all the friends that started out with male managers that were so heavy-handed and took advantage of them or hit on them. But with us, Russell never blurred any lines, ever. And never talked down to us and never tried to take advantage of our inexperience in the [music] industry. He would help us make the best deals possible—and always look out for ways that we would be screwed over, because he was aware of what's out there."

By the time Ray and Saliers graduated from Emory University (both earning degrees in English, with Ray additionally receiving one in Religion), it was obvious that they should pursue a music career full-time. They continued touring relentlessly and, in 1987, released a debut album, *Strange Fire*, on a record label they created for themselves, Indigo Records. The album found traction on college radio, resulting in bigger audiences at their shows.

Major record companies took notice, and Indigo Girls signed a deal with Epic Records in 1988. Their first album on that label,

Indigo Girls, came out the following year and quickly became a massive success. Lead single "Closer to Fine" became the band's first charting song, performing well in the United States, Canada, and Australia. *Indigo Girls* went on to win a Grammy award in 1990 for "Best Contemporary Folk Album." Fellow Georgians R.E.M., who by then were a major force in the alternative rock scene, gave Indigo Girls an opening slot on an extensive tour. By any measure, these were impressive accomplishments.

Unfortunately, success didn't stop Ray and Saliers from encountering discriminatory attitudes or, sometimes, outright abuse. "Emily got socked by some guy in Virginia Highlands," Ray says, referencing an affluent and normally safe neighborhood in Atlanta. "Some drunk guy hit her and called her a dyke. We were known, so he knew who she was. It was totally a terrible experience for her."

Ray also found herself being targeted. "I was walking through The Castro [neighborhood] in San Francisco and got egged. In the early '90s, hooligans would drive through gay areas and throw eggs at people." She feels fortunate that she never suffered anything worse, because "there would be gay bashing, literally. So you weren't always safe."

Ray and Saliers also felt hostility from mainstream radio staff, who were often far less welcoming than college radio personnel had been. "There were places you didn't get played, but the reason you didn't get played was hard to discern," Ray says. "That was hard for us because it was like, 'Is it because the song's not right? Or is it because we're two gay girls and they know it?' We could never quite tell."

Even when Indigo Girls succeeded in setting up on-air interviews at radio stations, they still felt ostracized. "That's when we really ran up against DJs that were so misogynist about women, and so homophobic. A morning show interview is always very full of jokes—but it was always jokes at our expense. Always little ribs. They didn't say the word 'gay' outwardly; it was just sexist jokes. But it was a constant trope."

Male DJs weren't the only ones to blame. "We would walk in with our guitars, and it would be some dude [DJ] and a cohost that was female, and I don't think they knew what to do with us," Ray says. "We were not the normal fare, so the guy couldn't flirt with you, and the woman couldn't compare notes, making jokes about husbands. So that was hard. It makes you hate yourself. It's like you're a kid and you can't see that it's not your problem, it's theirs."

*   *   *

In truth, though, Ray had learned early in life that some people weren't going to approve of who she was.

She grew up in Decatur, an inner suburb of Atlanta, Georgia, with two older sisters and a younger brother. Her family was close-knit, but then they hit a snag: "We were all three gay," she says of herself and her sisters, "so there were a lot of hard knocks dealing with that.

"For a while, my parents just didn't agree with it. They were pretty devout. We were raised in the Methodist Church, and we all loved church and were really involved. But when we started to have our own ideas and be apparently gay, it was *very* hard for my parents at first. Their friends were not very nice about it and disowned them for a long time. Not very Christian—it was very the opposite of what you're supposed to be."

Her parents eventually accepted their daughters as they are, but by then, Ray had internalized the stress that this situation had engendered. "I was prone to depression and being very intense about everything. Not really having a lot of filters, as far as what I saw in the world and how it affected me."

She found that music was a saving grace amid this emotional turmoil. She'd begun her training years before, initially taking piano lessons. She switched to the guitar when she was nine years old because she realized that instrument would work better for playing along with her sisters' rock records. She took guitar classes at the YMCA, and by the time she was in the eighth grade, she was good enough to join a band with friends of hers from church.

Unfortunately, her membership was short-lived. "I showed up one day for practice and my friend told me I was out of the band because I was a girl. That was my first experience of that happening. That was pretty formative—that really set my whole path.

"It's so funny because I see him when I go back to church [in Decatur] for holidays. He says, 'Oh man, I'm *so* sorry.' It's so awesome," she says, amused. "Believe me, I laugh about it now. But back then, I was *furious*."

Her "firing" turned out to be a blessing, though, because it left her free to begin playing music with Emily Saliers the next year. Ray had first met Saliers in grade school, but they hadn't been friends because Saliers was a year older, which had seemed like a vast gulf then. By the time they were both enrolled at Shamrock High School, however, their age difference no longer seemed insurmountable, especially after they both joined the school chorus. When they discovered they also shared a love for the acoustic guitar, they began practicing together.

They started out learning cover songs, but soon incorporated their own original material, as well—though, Ray concedes, Saliers was far ahead on that count: "Emily was already writing a lot. I was writing, but probably not anything worthwhile."

Shamrock High School (which has since changed to become Druid Hills Middle School) was a fertile place for their budding musical ambitions. "We had a few teachers there that really encouraged us," Ray says. "One in particular, an English teacher, Ellis Loyd, was a really good supporter. He would have us sit in the classroom and play after school, and people would come by, listen, and give us advice."

Loyd's English classes were also an important influence on their lyric-writing skills: "We were really fascinated by words. Metaphor and imagery and irony and all the things you're trying to learn when you're a senior [in high school]. We read a lot of really great books, and that really informed what we were thinking about musically."

Ray's history teacher, Coach Sutherland, also helped her gain a pivotal new perspective. "I could be combative at times with him," she says. "He was really patient with me because I didn't know what I was talking about for the first few years of my life. He really helped mold the idea of listening to other opinions and thinking about history in a different way. Which, as a songwriter, has really informed how I write: I try not to be didactic; I try to talk about the humanity of things. There's a lot of different places people are coming from, and he really taught me that."

When Ray and Saliers decided it was time to start playing for audiences besides their classmates, they chose the band name "Indigo Girls" after spotting the word "indigo" while flipping through a dictionary. Even though they were under-age, they convinced their parents to help them persuade the manager of Good Ol' Days Bar & Grill to allow them to perform at the weekly open mic nights. That went well enough that they procured fake IDs so that they could also play at other popular Atlanta bars.

Saliers went off to college at Tulane University in New Or-leans, but whenever she returned to Georgia on breaks, she and Ray would perform together. Sometimes Ray would visit Saliers in Louisiana so they could do a show there. It was fun, but it wasn't quite as good as when they'd lived in the same place and could line up frequent gigs.

That same year, things took another difficult turn in Ray's personal life. "I fell in love with a girl in my senior year in high school and was very bold about it," she says. "Her parents really did not like me and did not agree [with the relationship], and I think my parents probably were hoping it was just a phase."

She didn't find support among her classmates, either. "Me and my girlfriend hung out all the time together, but no one really knew what 'gay' meant, honestly. Some people were still in denial. I mean, it was '82 and it was the suburbs. There re-ally wasn't anybody to talk to about it. So everybody made fun of me, but I was pretty defiant. I didn't know who I could tell or not, so I was out because I didn't know what else to do, and because it was just who I was."

Even Saliers could not relate, as she hadn't yet realized that she, too, was gay. When Ray told Saliers about her girlfriend, "she didn't know what to do with it, honestly. She really didn't know how to react." (Saliers ended up coming out during her time at Emory University.)

These responses to her homosexuality left Ray with a nagging feeling of "tension and awkwardness." This worsened when she enrolled at Vanderbilt University in Tennessee, and then her romantic relationship ended due to the combined pressures of being physically separated and her girlfriend's parents' continuing disapproval. The breakup plunged Ray into severe depression. "That's when I started to absorb all that hate and sexism and misogyny. It really dragged me down," she says.

Homesick and despondent, she returned to Atlanta and enrolled at Emory University, where Saliers had also transferred after two years at Tulane. Finally together in the same city on a full-time basis again, they could find solace in their music—and begin Indigo Girls' rise to fame.

*   *   *

After struggling to feel comfortable with herself for many years, Ray credits "becoming politicized and realizing that there's activism that you could be doing" for helping her finally find inner peace. "You have to learn that you're okay and have what I call 'authentic anger' about the right things, not anger just because you hate yourself so much," she says.

Ray, along with Saliers, has used Indigo Girls' prominence to help bring awareness and financing to a diverse list of causes: women's rights, environmental issues, LGBTQ+ support, death penalty opposition, gun control, and voter education, to name just a few.

Through this wide-ranging work, Ray says, "We really started learning about intersectionality and how everything is related, and your own part in racism or homophobia. When you start to untangle all those things, then your energy is so much clearer—you don't waste anger on things that you can't change."

She knows not everyone agrees with her liberal sociopolitical views, and she's fine with this—though she admits there is one disagreement that arose that still bothers her: Indigo Girls' falling out with Michigan Womyn's Music Festival, an annual feminist gathering that started in 1976. "I have this really conflicted sort of relationship with them," Ray says.

The festival had a strict "female only" policy for attendees, workers, and performers—males were only admitted if they were very young children. Indigo Girls performed there many times, an experience that Ray calls "formative to me, and the place where I really learned how to be my full self. I learned about gender. I learned that being a masculine female is okay. I learned about the history of feminism from talking to women who were in their eighties and nineties."

But Ray's feelings shifted as the festival organizers increasingly came under fire for excluding transgender women. In response, Indigo Girls donated their earnings from their 2013 festival appearance to transgender causes, then declined to perform there again. They had been one of the more major acts to participate throughout the years, so their sudden absence was significant.

In a lengthy Facebook post on April 21, 2015, Michigan Womyn's Music Festival's producer announced that that year's festival—the fortieth one—would be the last. She did not give specific reasons for the decision, though she stated, "The Festival has been the crucible for nearly every critical cultural and political issue the lesbian feminist community has grappled with for four decades. Those struggles have been a beautiful part of our collective strength; they have never been a weakness."[2]

"We tried for so long to help solve that whole controversy, in any way that we could, and tried to frame it as, 'These are communities that need to talk to each other, and we need to figure out a solution because trans women have done so much for the gay movement generally, and for women generally,'" Ray says. She sighs, obviously still troubled by the outcome even though the dispute occurred a decade ago.

Fortunately, she and Saliers have no such reservations about other activism work they've done through the years. She is particularly proud of Honor the Earth, an initiative they cofounded with Winona LaDuke to support cultural and environmental sustainability on Native American lands via efforts to raise awareness and funds. Ray was drawn to "the environmental work and seeing things through the Native lens, and supporting the Native-led groups that were so smart and strategic and grass roots—they really were good at changing things and setting precedents in corporate and government responsibility. Winona LaDuke was the force that really drew us in at first; she opened our eyes to the work being done in the Indigenous-led environmental movements."

Ray explains that gender has also played a part in why she and Saliers decided to take on this particular work: "The cofounders of the group are mostly women. Most of the [Honor the Earth] board members came out of a group called the Indigenous Women's Network. They were our mentors, and they were the most feminist, evolved badasses that we'd ever met. A lot of their activism comes out of the matriarchy. They really taught us about activism, which really helped us form our activism in the queer world, as well."

When not busy with music or activism, Ray is happily settled into a peaceful private life. She lives in the North Georgia Smoky Mountain foothills with Carrie Schrader, her partner of almost twenty years. It is a relationship that they have fought hard to maintain.

"We have been through a lot, like breakups and getting back together, and most of it is because either one of us is figuring out how to juggle a career and relationship. I hadn't done the greatest job because in the beginning I would be like, 'I'll probably retire in five years'—I would say anything to get her to stay with me because I didn't want the reality of my life, which is touring all the time, to scare her away. So the first thing I had to learn was to be honest."

Ray isn't exaggerating about the amount of time she must spend on the road—and in fact, for this interview, she calls from the back of a tour bus as it rumbles across Texas. She stays busy with Indigo Girls, as well as her frequent work with her side project, the Amy Ray Band. Meanwhile, Schrader's career as a filmmaker can be demanding, too.

But Ray and Schrader have worked out the logistics, not only for themselves, but also for the sake of their nine-year-old daughter, Ozilline. "I know so many male crew members and band members with kids, and they'll be gone for three months, and it's [considered] okay because they're 'bringing home the bacon.' But my partner would not put up with that—no way," Ray says. "And I wouldn't want to be gone [that long], anyway—and I think that's because I am a woman. I do think there is an upside to some of the things women have been socialized for, which is caretaking and multitasking."

Having a daughter also provides Ray with another reason to nurture her own hard-won self-confidence: "You want your kid to know about herself as a strong person, so you're thinking about it for yourself, as well." She hopes anyone who hears her music will also absorb her message of redemption, healing, and joy.

11

Tanya Donelly (Throwing Muses, the Breeders, Belly)

The first time Tanya Donelly encountered what seemed like blatant sexism, she reacted with disbelief. It happened as her alternative rock band, Belly, were riding high with their 1993 single, "Feed the Tree," which had reached the top of *Billboard*'s "US Alternative Airplay" list and charted in the United Kingdom and Australia.

"I was doing a photoshoot for the cover of a magazine, and the publisher showed up and asked if I was free for dinner. I said yes. I brought my A&R woman and my manager with me. The publisher was visibly disappointed that they showed up with me, and then through the course of the dinner, it became pretty clear that he had thought that this was a date." She politely deflected his advances. Then, "Within forty-eight hours, we were told that Belly wasn't getting the cover."

Even though, with hindsight, it's obvious to her that he was punishing her for rejecting his romantic interest, "I immediately thought, 'It's not possible that that's the reason we lost the cover.' Now, with the distance of time, who fucking cares? But at the time, it was something that bummed the people around me out. The people who had worked for that moment, like our PR woman."

Donelly stresses that she didn't respond this way because she was naive ("Because I really was not naive ever in my life, really")—rather, it was "because I had never experienced any-thing like that so overtly. I never blamed myself for a second. I went to a much weirder place, which was, 'This has not been my life experience, so this cannot possibly be the cause of that.'"

But another incident in the 1990s made it even more evident that women were not always being treated fairly in the music business. She recalls "sitting in a program director's office and having him say to me, as if this were completely understandable, 'Well, we can't pitch your single to radio because there are too many women on the radio right now.' And I remember being like, '*What?*'

"Just to give you an idea of how bone-level this kind of systemic thinking was at the time, he wasn't even being a dick about it. It was just like we were comrades in the same battle, and I should understand that this was part of the war, basically: 'Well, you understand. There are too many women right now, so we just have to wait a few months.'"

This time, Donelly wasn't in denial. Instead, she objected immediately. "I said, 'That seems ridiculous to me.' Later on, when my manager and I were talking about it, I said, 'Is it just that people can't hear one woman's voice after they've just heard another woman's voice? Like, what does that *mean?*'" Considering that radio playlists have always consisted of consecutive male artists' songs, the double standard was glaring. "I couldn't believe it. Obviously, we pushed back, and had multiple written and spoken exchanges around that conversation."

All that protest came to nothing, though. "At the end of the day, the argument was, 'Hey, this is out of my hands; this is what I'm getting from radio.'" And, she adds, "Let me be clear: this included college radio, too."

That last part was particularly galling, because in the 1990s, college radio stations were believed to be far more broadminded than commercial outlets. College radio was also the arbiter of taste for modern rock—and within that genre, few artists have been as accomplished and influential as Tanya Donelly.

She cofounded three of the most admired alternative rock bands: Throwing Muses, the Breeders, and Belly. Her work has twice been nominated for Grammy awards. As a solo artist, she's put out more than a dozen releases. She's also collaborated with a long list of well-regarded musicians, including Juliana Hatfield, Catherine Wheel, and Mission of Burma.

So, as a woman who has experienced intractable disrespect because of her gender despite achieving such success, Donelly knows that more progress still must be made—and that is exactly why she identifies as a feminist. "The only thing I dislike about that label is that it's unfairly charged with negativity," she says. "But in the name of every woman that came before me and worked under horrible conditions to move that feminism forward, I will never throw that label away easily."

*   *   *

Three decades after first encountering her own eye-opening experiences with sexism, Donelly has two more significant reasons to keep fighting for gender equality: her daughters, Gracie and Hattie, born in 1999 and 2006, respectively.

Donelly is particularly upset about the US Supreme Court's June 2022 ruling overturning the landmark 1973 case *Roe v. Wade* (wherein the right to an abortion was granted at the federal level). Now, each state's legislature will determine abortion's legality for their citizens. Talking about it makes Donelly emotional.

"What's happening with *Roe* right now, I am unsurprised by, sadly," she says. "I have been saying for a very long time that that is a place of vulnerability, and always will be. But to experience this with my children right now is just heartbreaking. Just something that I don't know how to galvanize around, to be honest. I have two daughters who are directly impacted because this is the present they live in, the future they live in. This backward move is devastating to them."

And yet, despite her dismay over where women's reproductive rights now stand in the United States, Donelly also sees reason for optimism because she knows how far women's rights have expanded overall. "I mean, I was born to a mother who couldn't get a checkbook unless my dad signed off on it. Who couldn't get a bank account unless my dad signed off on it. Who couldn't get a job unless my dad signed off on it. In the

'70s! So coming from that perspective, yes, I absolutely feel like the movement is [going] forward. And even what we're going through right now, I feel like this challenge will be met."

*   *   *

Donelly learned about the power of activism from her very liberal and politically minded parents, who made sure she and her younger brother got involved, too. "My mom took us on every march—for [abortion] choice, and for any LGBTQ [issue]," she says. "My parents marched and protested throughout my childhood. And to this day, they are still active."

She was born in Newport, Rhode Island, in 1966, as the countercultural movement was underway. Her parents identified strongly with that ideology, so when she was about three years old and her brother was a baby, "they sold all their furniture and we headed west, with no plans other than that they wanted to land in Haight-Ashbury," she says, referring to the neighborhood in San Francisco that was then the epicenter of the hippie ethos.

Unfortunately, after the family arrived in California, "My parents did not experience the love they had expected to find out there. And so it wasn't really for them; they just weren't feeling it so much. They wired home for money, I believe," so that the family could then make their meandering way back across the country. Some of her earliest memories come from that long drive.

"I remember—and I say this drained of all drama—I remember sleeping on a floor. I remember sleeping in the Jeep. I remember camping. And I think we went through a lot of desert. I think I felt excited by it at the time. The general vibe was one of excitement and adventure. My parents were extremely positive about it the whole time. We had a lot of fun. There was a lot of laughing."

By the time her family arrived back in Rhode Island, she estimates they had been gone for almost a year. "I remember being thrilled to get back to my grandparents," she says. "We spent quite a lot of time with them when I was a kid. They were very instrumental in my childhood."

She remembers her early home life as being happy, but also chaotic and unconventional. "We had kind of a revolving door of characters coming in and out. So never a dull moment, never a quiet moment," she says. "I grew up with parents who were very focused on dismantling any system that existed."

Traditional gender identity was one of the things that her parents questioned. "I mean, there were obviously going to be these low, thrumming systemic things woven into any upbringing up to this point, but my parents did not lay gender on us for the most part, in terms of what was expected of us. Who we were going to be or what our behavior should have been—that was never put on us." For example, Donelly was a tomboy, but "My mom would bristle at that word and say, 'Don't let anybody call you that.'"

Not everyone in her family had the same attitude that her parents did, though. "I remember feeling from external family a *tsk*-ing around some of my behavior that was rough and tumble." Some relatives gave her a hard time for not wanting to play with dolls like they thought a girl should. "As a kid, I was terrified of dolls, never mind wanting to play with them," she says. "I would always be surprised when someone commented, 'Oh, there are no dolls in your room.'" With a laugh, she recalls what she wishes she could've retorted to that: "Dolls want to kill you at night. Perhaps you're not aware!"

Her parents separated when she was six years old, then finalized their divorce a couple of years later. After that, she and her brother split their time between each of their parents and their grandparents.

Donelly is sympathetic to her parents' situation. "They were extremely young when they had me," she says. "Having a child doesn't automatically bump you forward in life. They had to go through all the stuff they had to go through as teens and people in their early twenties. But through it all, they were very kind with each other, and with my brother and [me]. We never felt like we were going to fall through any cracks or anything. There was just so much that went on, but it's stuff that we've all worked out as a fragmented family. So I kind of leave that there."

Around the time that her parents divorced, Donelly met a girl at school, Kristin Hersh. Like Donelly, Hersh was musically inclined—they were both taking violin lessons. They were also only three weeks apart in age. It wasn't long before they became extremely close.

But they were taken aback when Donelly's father married Hersh's mother. Instead of being thrilled about becoming stepsisters, Donelly recalls that this change was "Much to our chagrin, actually, at the time. We were best friends, and some of that relationship had to do with creating an oasis for ourselves. And so when our families blended, that little bubble was less separate, less protected."

Also, she says, "I don't want to say that we had any prescience around what would come, but we just had our gut instincts that it was not going to be good for us. I think all parties involved at this point would say it was not the best marriage choice for either of them." But she quickly adds, "So many good times came out of that marriage, though. We had some really undeniably happy moments in there."

Living in the same home also gave Donelly and Hersh more time to play music together. By now, Hersh was playing guitar, Donelly was taking lessons on the bass, and both of them played the keyboard. At fourteen years old, "We started playing some Beatles songs, and then we played a Yoko Ono song. And Marshall Crenshaw. We had a brief time of experimenting with other people's songs. And then Kristin started prolifically writing her own stuff. She was very, in her own way, ambitious for us to move forward and be a band and record and play shows. She was an engine. That's really the only word for it."

As their skills grew, they invited their friend Elaine Adamedes to join them, with the three of them switching off on vocals, guitar, bass, and keyboard parts for each song. With the addition of drummer Becca Blumen, the first version of Throwing Muses was born. (Over time, the lineup evolved to include male members as well as female, with Hersh still at the helm to this day.)

Despite being only fifteen years old when Throwing Muses began, Donelly and Hersh took it very seriously. It helped that their parents encouraged them, too: "Our parents were super supportive of the band and drove us to gigs before we could drive."

The band quickly gained a local following, though "I wouldn't say we were proficient," Donelly says of those early years. "I think we had the great luck of having this little group of incredibly supportive friends and being inspired by each other's songs."

By the time Donelly and Hersh were seniors in high school, Throwing Muses were regularly playing shows in Providence and Newport, and occasionally in Boston. "We would walk into a club and the staff would be startled by us. There'd be a lot of confusion about, '*You're* the band?'—[as if] giraffes just walked in the door. But then we'd start to play, and it overcame the fact that it was three young women and a man on drums. I think that the music immediately overwhelmed the gender conversation because people ended up focusing on what they were hearing.

"On the flip side of that, there were also plenty of people waiting to exploit it, too—happy to have that as an angle for marketing. That was also an issue because that was something that we felt that we had to address, just as equally as being discriminated against. It's a form of inverted discrimination to use that, in a way."

Even those gender-focused experiences didn't make Donelly and the rest of Throwing Muses think much about the fact that they had young women in the band, however. "It sounds implausible, but it really didn't occur to us," Donelly says. They simply didn't think they were doing anything unusual, as evidenced by the artists who'd inspired them. "There were many, many women involved in the music we loved. Such as X, the Slits, the Velvet Underground, Joni Mitchell, Linda Ronstadt, and Siouxsie Sioux. A lot of the music that I loved was very inclusive on many levels—gender, sexuality, identity—so we never felt left out. Or, more accurately, we never left ourselves out with that kind of doubt."

The band moved to Boston, got a deal with the influential UK record label 4AD, and released their self-titled debut album in 1986. Their mix of punk and folk rock immediately created a buzz. By the 1990s, they had established themselves as a highly original, successful, and influential alternative rock band.

* * *

As Throwing Muses got bigger, though, Donelly felt her role got smaller. For example, she had written only one song, "Green," that made it onto the *Throwing Muses* album; Hersh had written the rest. "Kristin was just bringing in so much music," Donelly recalls. "Elaine and I were more supplemental as songwriters. That was the formula of the Muses until I left." She quit the band after their fourth album, 1991's *The Real Ramona*.

"There was so much going on in [Hersh's] guitar playing that there was already a melody there to respond to, there was already something fertile happening to latch onto," Donelly says, "and so I feel like it was a really fortunate school for me, musically. It was almost like she would come in with something and you're already mid-conversation when you started playing with her. So it was just a lot of response as a guitar player, for me, when she would bring a song in."

Two years before departing Throwing Muses, Donelly had already begun working with Kim Deal, who was then the bassist and co-vocalist in the alternative rock band Pixies. Donelly and Deal called their new band the Breeders. Donelly hoped that this could be a place where she would have more space for her songwriting, but admits the circumstances were muddled from the start.

"Initially, the Breeders fluctuated a lot, between Kim and myself, around what we wanted for it. What our goals were for it, what we were looking to get out of it, what we wanted the future of that band to be," she says. "Within the space of a year, we had so many ideas around where it was going to go. It went from being purely a side project, to then we were going to leave our [other] bands and focus on that entirely, to then becoming a side project again."

Still, Donelly felt pleased about being in another female-fronted band. "I think at that point, it was a little more conscientious, the decision to seek out women [bandmates]. And it felt good. It was something that I had been comfortable with, and I guess Kim had been yearning to be in a primarily female band. Kim had grown up playing with her sister, Kelley [Deal, the Breeders' guitarist], so that was a comfort area for her, too, that feeling of sisterhood."

Soon, though, Donelly realized that this, like Throwing Muses, would be another case where she couldn't contribute as much as she wanted. After the band released their debut album,

Pod (1990), and an EP, *Safari* (1992), she departed. (The Breeders would go on to have a hit with the song "Cannonball" in 1993.)

"That was sort of a pragmatic choice," she says of her departure. "Kim committed to a year-long tour with the Pixies, and I had the songs that we had just demoed. At that point, I called her and had a slightly sad and uncomfortable conversation about starting my own thing. At the time, it was a bummer for both of us. We were disappointed."

But thirty years later, as she reflects on her experience with the Breeders, it makes Donelly feel good. "It's one of those things where it's a real gift of hindsight," she says. "I can look back on that and say that we ended up being each other's portal out of our first bands. Not that there was an S.O.S. going on in either situation, but we had both started to write more, Kim and myself, separately and together, and [our main bands] started to feel a little tight. Like the Muses for me—things got tighter and tighter. It was time for both of us to move on, and I think we provided that service for each other."

*   *   *

It was clear that Donelly was ready to front her own band, and she already had songs ready to go. "The first Belly record [*Star*, 1993], the demos for those songs say 'Breeders' on it. That was supposed to be the second Breeders album, for a minute. And Kim actually plays on the demos for those songs," she says.

Forming Belly was also easy because she brought along another former Throwing Muses member, bassist Fred Abong, as well as brothers Thomas Gorman (guitar) and Chris Gorman (drums), who she'd first met when they were all starting out in the Rhode Island music scene. "So it was like, 'Let's just make an album and see where that goes.'"

It was the first time where Donelly would be the only female member. "I felt like, 'I don't want to always have to have another woman in the band—let's try without.'" Unfortunately, she soon found that this arrangement didn't suit her. "I was a very uncomfortable frontperson for a while. I did suddenly feel this weird isolation onstage."

That feeling was compounded when Belly's debut single, "Feed the Tree," shot up the charts around the world. The video, focusing heavily on Donelly, made her a poster girl for the alternative rock scene. By then, Donelly knew she wanted to bring another female into the band, realizing "that I do like to have that energy beside me." Abong had left the group, so Gail Greenwood joined as their new bassist. "We really only auditioned women and fell in love with Gail right out of the gate," Donelly says.

Besides their lineup switch, the band's musical style also changed, growing more hard-edged for their second album, 1995's *King*. The album wasn't as successful as their debut, and Donelly decided to pull the plug on Belly in 1996.

This time, instead of forming another band, she launched a solo career and largely scaled back to her folk rock roots. "I think it was because at that time in my life, I was feeling like I didn't want to commit to anyone on that level," she says of her decision not to join another group. "More importantly, I didn't want to have anyone have to commit to my very erratic and quirky schedule, [working] around what I'm able and willing to do." Her first solo album, *Lovesongs for Underdogs*, came out in 1997. So far, in this capacity, she has released four full-length albums and eleven EPs.

Over time, Donelly also began collaborating with others, to varying degrees. Sometimes she'll work alongside an established band, as she did with the Parkington Sisters for a 2020 album of cover songs. Other times, she forms a band but keeps the time frame amorphous, as she's currently doing with the Loyal Seas, a duo she created with Dylan in the Movies leader Brian Sullivan; their debut album, *Strange Mornings in the Garden* (2022), debuted at number 1 on *Billboard*'s Alternative New Artist chart.

In this phase of her career, Donelly has finally found the flexibility that works best for her, enabling her to get material out into the world entirely on her own terms.

*   *   *

As she got her solo and collaborative career underway, things were also getting settled in Donelly's personal life. She married and had her daughters. She also worked as a doula, providing practical help and emotional support to women who had just given birth.

Looking back, she is fine with her decision to shift her focus more onto her personal life, especially when it came to bringing up her daughters. "I made choices that were very personal to what I wanted to do around that—I wanted to bring my children on the road. I wanted to have them with me. [My husband] Dean could have, and would have, happily taken that off my plate, [but] I wanted my children strapped to me, basically. I didn't take any significant hiatuses after they were born, but I did tailor everything around being able to be with them. I have to be really clear that that was not done to me. *I* did that. That was my choice.

"I know plenty of women who either completely stop playing for a while, or don't break stride for a second. And no judgment on anybody, either, because everybody's doing the thing they have to do at the time. But yeah, anything that I did postbirth was a series of decisions and dances and finesses by me."

The key to balancing a family life with being a working musician is, she says, "Absolutely about logistics, definitely. But really, the thing that I found the most difficult to navigate was my attention split and my emotional split. I started to realize that my focus is going to be split, always."

Now that her older daughter is grown and moved out, and her younger one is an independent teenager, Donelly is figuring out what the next phase of her career, and her life overall, will be. "It's more just seeing what comes. Nothing is predictable in my life at all right now, so I just manage it as it comes," she says.

With what she's already accomplished, though, Donelly has cemented her place as a trailblazing woman in rock, and she believes that she's helped lead the way for the next generation of aspiring female artists. "Mainly the reason that I [know that] is because I have been told that by young women. So I'm going to believe them when they tell me," she says. "The most gratifying thing for me is when a young woman has come up and said, 'I started playing because of you. I'm in a band because of you. I started writing because of some band that you were in, or this song that you wrote.' Having someone say that to you is a huge gift."

12

Paula Cole

With one phone call in 1993, Peter Gabriel changed Paula Cole's life. Nearly thirty years later, she still sounds thrilled as she recalls picking up the voice message he left asking her to join his "Secret World" tour as a featured singer. At the time, he was one of the most successful musicians on the planet—and she was a singer-songwriter who hadn't even released her first album yet.

"I died, because I *love* him," Cole says. "His music was profoundly influential to me: the Jungian psychology behind the lyrics, the seeking of individuation through the poetry, the cinematic quality of prog rock. I used to walk around Boston listening to [Gabriel's 1986 album] *So* on repeat. I can't tell you how much I loved his music and how important it was to me."

So that she could begin learning what she was supposed to sing, she was sent "board tapes" (recordings done through the soundboard) from previous shows. It helped that she was such a fan of Gabriel's that she'd already seen this particular show—twice.

She jumped on a plane, leaving her life in San Francisco behind. "They flew me to Mannheim, Germany, on Halloween," she recalls. It was only two days before her debut performance with the show. "I literally had one rehearsal. We didn't even do all of the songs, but the first one we did was "Don't Give Up." But I knew the music and I loved it with reverence, so I was ready."

"Don't Give Up" had particular significance for Cole because she also admired Kate Bush, the artist who dueted with Gabriel on the studio version of that heartrending ballad. Suddenly, she found herself taking over Bush's part in front of sold-out arena audiences.

It was also an intimidating situation because Cole didn't personally know any of the other performers or crew members. "I was quiet and terribly introverted and shy. At times, it was lonely," she says. "I'm twenty-five years old, and everybody's older and English, mostly." Also, she estimates that there were about sixty people working for the tour, yet she was one of only four women in the group (the other three worked in wardrobe, as assistant tour director, and as Gabriel's personal assistant).

For someone who was an up-and-comer, it was a heady experience, though. "I'd never been on a tour operation like that," she says. "I was flown all around Europe and Hong Kong and Japan. It was so brilliant. It was such an education. It was an important thing to be part of. A few days after I joined the tour, they shot the [*Peter Gabriel:*] *Secret World Live* [concert] video in Modena, Italy. God, what a beautiful experience. And what a beautiful video it was. People still learn about me from that video. It's incredible."

But some of what she learned was distressing. "I found out that I was getting paid one-fourth of what the whole band was getting paid," which she thinks happened because "I was young, I was female, and I was a singer. It's like the bottom of the totem pole on three counts. But it's still not right or just. People should be paid equally." She spoke with Gabriel and got a raise, but "I never did get equal pay."

She sighs. "Welcome to the music business. That's been my experience throughout."

*   *   *

Cole came into the world during a turbulent time: she was born in Manchester, Connecticut, in 1968, the day after Martin Luther King Jr. was assassinated. Still, she recalls feeling optimistic as she grew up. "As a child of the '70s, I remember Jimmy Carter being president and feeling hope about my lifespan on planet Earth, that it amounted to something," she says.

She seemed destined to become a professional musician because her entire family was musically inclined. "I thought it was perfectly normal that everyone would break out into three-part harmonies and be able to play instruments," she says. Her father was an avid semiprofessional musician who played bass in the popular polka band Johnny Prytko and the Connecticut Hi-Tones, performing on their albums and touring on weekends.

"I started whimsically writing my own songs in my head when I was an infant: my mom says I had a song to sing myself to sleep to," Cole says. "It was just a very primal language for me."

In some of her earliest memories, she remembers listening to both of her parents playing the piano. "It gave me this really profound foundation, musically," she says. At fourteen years old, she seriously hurt her foot, which turned out to be a blessing in disguise because the enforced downtime as she recovered prompted her to take piano playing more seriously. "That accident proved to be a catalyst in my life, directing me to music with deep purpose. I started coming to the piano to express my troubles, to express my soul." She tried to emulate her sister, who was five years older and could play much better. "But I could sing, so that set me apart."

Her father was also an entomologist, so the family went to live in Ithaca, New York, while he finished his studies at Cornell University, and then they moved to Rockport, Massachusetts, where he accepted a teaching position at Salem State College. Her mother became an art teacher at a public grade school.

Rockport had once been a major granite mining town, but the quarries had shut down during the Depression. By the time the Cole family arrived there, it felt "really like the end of the Earth. So I grew up in this geologically beautiful place, [but] I think the boredom of it had me relying on myself for music and imagination."

This relatively isolated setting also meant that there were no distractions as Cole went through school. "I was a good student. I was earnest. I wasn't popular with boys, but I was respected," she says. "I was class president for three years. It's weird because I really didn't want to be the leader, but I knew that I could help look out for my classmates." It's always been a pattern for her to put others' needs ahead of her own: "That happens to me all the time. I'll set the table and I'll forget to make a place setting for myself. It's that New England sense of duty."

This outlook came about, Cole says, because her parents' salaries, while respectable, didn't allow for extravagances. "We were frugal. We were hardworking. We were smart. And I wasn't going to be baggage to anybody. I had to be good and keep our life as streamlined and positive as possible. And that's reflected in the songs on my first album [*Harbinger*, 1994]. If you listen to a song like "Bethlehem," you can really hear how I was striving to be that person."

Cole felt much more at ease when she focused on music. She won awards and scholarships while attending local music camps, and often landed starring roles in her school's musical productions. Toward the end of her high school years, she discovered jazz and quickly became obsessed with it.

By the time she graduated, it was clear what she needed to do next. "I considered [going into] academia, but the force of music was just so strong," she says. She accepted a scholarship to study jazz singing at the prestigious Berklee College of Music in Boston, but "My parents, who were natural musicians themselves, were wary about letting me go into the music business. It's really one of the seats of the patriarchy. So bad, and so damaging to women."

The inequity became evident the moment she arrived at Berklee. "The [student] ratio was something like thirteen to one, men to women. That's when I first started understanding just how male [the music business] was," she says.

But a few of those male classmates have become some of the most important people in her life. "I made beautiful friends," Cole says. "I met my future band there. Like my drummer, Jay Bellerose, who's still one of my best friends. We came up in the music business together, along with Kevin Berry, my guitar player since forever."

Still, this very masculine environment eventually took its toll. "Somewhere at the three-quarter mark of college, I hit a wall—I didn't want to be singing these songs that were written by men in the '50s that didn't really understand a woman's point of view.

"In [jazz] standards, there were very few women [songwriters]—Ann Ronell wrote "Willow Weep for Me"; that's the only one I can think of," she continues, referring to the song recorded by Nina Simone and released in 1959. She also revered Billie Holiday, who cowrote some songs, but even those "revealed a lot of [domestic] abuse, like the lyrics to "My Man (Mon Homme)." So they were songs that were very depressing to me because of violence towards women, or just written by men, and it's too sad, sad, sad. So I'm singing the songs, and I'm like, 'What the fuck?'"

She had an epiphany: she would write her own more modern singer-songwriter style of music instead. Her first songs "came exploding out of me." Even though she'd wanted to distance herself from downbeat jazz standards, her own lyrics turned out to be confessional and melancholic, as well—but they spoke her truth. This catharsis caused some of the people closest to her to worry. "My mom was very concerned. She asked me if I was depressed."

Cole recorded these first songs in the Berklee College of Music studios. Eventually, after cassette tapes of these sessions were passed around, a small record label in New York offered her a deal.

"That struck me. I thought, 'That was easy.'" And then she politely told them no. "Although I appreciate them profoundly,

I just felt that it wasn't the right fit. That if it could happen that quickly, then I should write more songs and really have a more respectable catalog and understand myself, and [then] sign to the right label. People told me I was crazy for turning it down. I went back to singing jingles and waitressing at the MIT Faculty Club."

* * *

Cole graduated from Berklee and moved to San Francisco. That city, still bohemian before the 1990s tech boom made it a prohibitively expensive place to live, seemed perfect for a young, ambitious aspiring artist such as herself. Even so, she ended up enduring three years of very lean living.

She worked at Tassajara Bakery in the Cole Valley neighborhood, "making cappuccinos and baking and washing pots." When not there, she wrote a lot of music, which she recorded in the bedroom of her apartment at the corner of 17th Street and South Van Ness, in the city's then-edgy Mission District. "I was extremely prolific. I wrote most of my first and a lot of my second album at that time," she says.

Once again, cassette tapes of her music were passed around in music business offices. "A publisher, Famous Music—they're now Sony/ATV [Music Publishing]—offered me a writer's deal. It was something like $15,000. It was a total deal for them to have a chunk of my publishing forever, but it allowed me to stay alive just enough. I would exist on a burrito a day. I would eat half for lunch and half for dinner, because all those amazing taquerias were around."

She got a break when she signed with a good manager. "His name was John Carter, but everybody called him Carter. He totally believed in me. Oh, I loved him." Carter was already a legendary figure in the music business. He'd written the classic song "Incense and Peppermints," which became a hit for Strawberry Alarm Clock in 1967. He was also responsible for getting Tina Turner signed to Capitol Records, where she released her

1984 comeback album, *Private Dancer*. Carter passed away in 2011. "I miss him so much," Cole says.

With Carter's help, Cole shopped her songs to record labels. Several expressed interest, but there was one that stood out. "There was this funky label called Imago. I liked that they were musically diverse." Imago's A&R person, Kate Hyman, had already signed former 'Til Tuesday frontwoman Aimee Mann to the label. Punk rock pioneer Henry Rollins was also on the roster. "Kate just got me. And they didn't want me to change anything. Other labels were very heavy-handed, telling me, 'Change this, change that.' I felt like I could just be me at Imago. So I signed with them."

She recorded her first album in 1992 and 1993, with Kevin Killen as the producer. He had made his name engineering U2's *The Unforgettable Fire* (1984) and Peter Gabriel's *So* (1986), as well as coproducing the soundtrack to the 1991 hit film *The Commitments*, among his many other credits. "Then my album sat in the coffers for a year because I was touring around America in coffeehouses to build up a fan base," Cole says.

That same year, Peter Gabriel was on his "Secret World Live" tour. Sinéad O'Connor was singing with him, but her time with the show was almost finished. Unbeknownst to Cole, Killen played Cole's unreleased album for his friend David Rhodes, Gabriel's longtime guitar player, and suggested her as O'Connor's replacement. Rhodes loved what he heard and gave her songs to Gabriel, who then made that fateful call offering her the job.

As grateful as Cole is for that opportunity, it also showed her what she *didn't* want. "It made me really understand that I didn't want to be a backup singer. I really wanted to be my own artist, even though in some ways I was more successful on Peter's tour—it was arenas, and five-star everything. And I'd go back to my clubs and uncomfortable van tours—but it's mine, and it's my truth."

Working with Gabriel did, however, set Cole up perfectly, in terms of raising her profile in time for her first album's release.

* * *

"*Harbinger* came out in '94, and it was met really warmly and got critical acclaim. I'd only had my first single out, which was called "I Am So Ordinary," and it did really well on AAA ["Adult Album Alternative" radio stations]," Cole says.

Then, just as swiftly, disaster struck: "We were setting up for the second single, and that's when Imago went under. Suddenly, my album disappeared." She quickly signed with Warner Records (then Warner Bros. Records), but it was too late: "*Harbinger* didn't do anything more. It's too bad because it had momentum."

Cole spent the rest of 1994 and 1995 on tours opening for Counting Crows, Sarah McLachlan, and Melissa Etheridge. "So I'm there with these fabulous opportunities, being championed by these wonderful artists, opening for them on their tours, gaining fans—and people can't find my album. *Can't find it.*"

But Cole refused to let this setback derail her for long. "I got back to my piano and started writing more songs that would be on *This Fire*. That was the second album, and that was released in the fall of '96. And out of the gate, "Where Have All the Cowboys Gone?" became a big hit." That track, featuring distinctive spoken word verses and soaring choruses, tells the story of a woman daydreaming of a better life after becoming stuck in an unsatisfactory romantic relationship.

The song grew out of Cole's admiration for the English alternative rock band XTC. "I just loved their humor and wit. And I thought, 'Wouldn't it be nice to hear something from a woman's point of view in pop that's actually humorous and clever and ironic?' It made me think that there's really not very much of that in music, so I wanted to try and write something to add to that vacancy."

When she sat down to write in her San Francisco apartment, "The phrase 'where have all the cowboys gone' just flowed out onto the page. Then the lyrics came very quickly." She notes, however, that her words have been "misinterpreted so much.

People thought I was being earnest, like I pined for my John Wayne. They didn't get the irony or the sarcasm. And I'm like, 'Oh my gosh—this is like a gender role examination!'"

Cole had originally given the song a rumba rhythm, but "Nobody really liked the song because of that off-putting beat. So the song just sat there, left abandoned for a couple of years. Later, when I was gathering songs for the second album, I thought, 'That's a good song, and I'm not going to give up on it. It just needs a little renovating.'"

For inspiration, she turned to the Beatles album *Sgt. Pepper's Lonely Hearts Club Band* (1967). "On the last song, Ringo Starr counts off, 'One, two, three, four,' and then he plays this drum groove. I *love* that beat. So for the home demo, I sampled Ringo and looped that drum in. Everyone responded to that rhythm." (Later, Jay Bellerose emulated it on the version of "Where Have All the Cowboys Gone?" that appeared on *This Fire*.)

This marked the moment "when I stepped into my power as a producer, because I was having realizations like, 'I don't need to explain this to a man. I want my ideas to go straight to tape.' So I started taking the reins of my life through my music."

She told executives at Warner that she wanted to self-produce her next album, so she only needed a recording engineer to help her. "I took a bunch of meetings, set up as, 'I'm interested in a prospective engineer.' All but one started talking like they were a producer. Because I'm a young woman, I think. I couldn't believe it."

The only one who didn't act that way was Roger Mountenot, and he got the job. "He was kind. He understood that he was engineering, and he supported me to be self-producing. That was really rare at the time."

Still, even her own record label tried to dissuade Cole from producing the album herself. "How they try to beat you down is money: 'I'm going to give you half of a budget.' So I was making phone calls for discount tape, discount [studio] time, just to make it be able to fit." She believes this is another instance of unfair treatment that happened because she was young and female.

"The only example I found of a female artist that produced herself was Kate Bush," Cole says. "I remember thinking, 'This music is so fascinating. It's so different.' I would turn over the cassette tape and it would say 'Produced by Kate.' I could just feel her hands all over that [soundboard] console, and it makes the music much more interesting and original."

But in the 1980s and early 1990s, "We were in a very patronizing culture of star male producers. You would hire them, and they were expensive. I'm sure they were brilliant, but their sound was very identifiable. It was like their sound laminated over your music, and I didn't want that. I wanted the music to come from my mind and my heart and go onto the tape. So I had to stand there and say, 'I want to do this.' And say it over and over again. I just stood my ground."

Cole was vindicated when, in 1998, *This Fire* was nominated for seven Grammy awards, including "Producer of the Year." That award went to R&B artist Babyface, but Cole still felt that she'd accomplished a breakthrough for women. "I found out that I was the first woman to solely be nominated as best producer," she says. "I realized that's why it was so hard: it was like I was going against culture, and people's thought process. It just needed to be reexamined." (Since then, she says, "I've been happy to see more women self-producing. And now, with the advent of digitization and [music production software] Pro Tools and Logic, even more artists, regardless of gender, are self-producing, and that's beautiful.")

Cole did win the "Best New Artist" Grammy that year. Unfortunately, she found that even after that, she wasn't granted the respect she feels a male artist in the same position would be given. "You have to still keep proving yourself. And assholes will always be assholes. There'll be the photographers who pinch you, even though you've just made this beautiful work of art."

This was clear even at the Grammy awards ceremony itself, where "I remember being treated in such an infantilized way and thinking, 'Gosh, I'm here and I'm still experiencing this patronizing affectation by male producers that are my senior.' It just doesn't stop."

She recalls facing particular criticism because the outfit she wore to the ceremony revealed that she chose not to shave her armpit hair. "People were really kind of fucked up and cruel about that," she says. "Like, Jay Leno on *The Tonight Show*, he made a Paula Cole doll, and he would shine his shoes with the doll's furry armpits. It's funny, but it's not funny. Making fun of somebody's hair or body part, that's really fucked up. I'm so happy to see the fourth wave of feminism understanding that more."

After that, "I definitely went off the rails. I felt like I hated the thing I loved. I made a very different third album as a follow-up [*Amen*, 1999] and it just wasn't what people were expecting at all." *Amen* didn't perform nearly as well as its predecessors, only making it into the far upper reaches of the *Billboard* Top 100 chart.

"I think I was existentially tired of the music business, and I wanted off the hamster wheel. I felt like there was less meaning in it at that time. I needed to regroup. And I wanted a child," Cole says.

So from 2000 to 2007, Cole put her music career on hiatus and focused instead on her personal life. Her daughter, Sky, was born in 2001. Sky's father, Hassan Hakmoun, is a Moroccan musician whom Cole had met when they both worked on the Peter Gabriel tour; they married in 2002 but divorced in 2006.

By this point, Cole was living in New York City—a place she loved, but which she found difficult to navigate as a single mother. "It was really hard. I was paying for everything. I was doing everything. It was impossible." But she adds, "Thank God for my hits that allowed me to take that time [off from work]."

She moved back to Massachusetts with her daughter, where her family helped her get her equilibrium back. Eventually, she felt ready to resume her music career. "I came back in 2007 with [the album] *Courage*," she says. "I've [released] seven or eight albums since that time—it's like a new era for me. I am more of a self-realized adult, and I'm more prolific."

These days, Cole releases her albums through her own label, 675 Records, which gives her complete artistic control over her new music. This arrangement also means she doesn't have to share her profits with another company—which, unfortunately, continues to be a problem with her earlier work. "I'm still trying to get free from that Imago contract—*still* dealing with that," she says. "It's terrible. It's like a sharecropper's contract."

She tries not to dwell on the past, though, preferring to focus on the positives in her life. She's been with her current partner, David (an "awesome, gentle, good man"), since 2007, helping to raise his two children—one of whom now attends Berklee, as she once did. Cole herself is also back at that school, teaching song-writing and voice lessons as a Visiting Scholar. "I learn through my students. It keeps me more connected. It's beautiful."

Still, she says she's gradually scaling back on her teaching so she can make her music career her main emphasis again. "I refuse to let my gift to create songs fall by the wayside. I'm not going to lose my joy. I'm going to keep loving the music and keep writing, and leave a fantastic catalog of music. That's the victory." She describes her current fanbase as "Small and tight and loyal and loving. I'm not huge and it's kind of niche and you have to find me now, so I'm grateful when people do."

Beyond her singer-songwriter work, Cole also recently started writing songs for a musical. "Talk about full circle. I started sing-ing in musicals; now I'm writing one," she says. "It's about the second wave of feminism. I feel like I'm the right person to do that because I care so much about empowering women.

"I think they've tarred and feathered the word *feminist*. I think it has become a dirty word, and that's wrong. Let's reclaim [it]. It's about equality. It's about being treated with dignity and being an equal human citizen."

Motherhood has been one of the main reasons why Cole feels compelled to push for progress in this regard. "I want a better world for my daughter. I don't know if it's happening. Sometimes I fear it's worse." But this relationship also gives her hope: "I've learned a lot from Sky, because she is in the fourth wave of feminism. She has educated me."

Even as Cole continues to evolve, both personally and professionally, she hasn't lost sight of what she's already learned. "It's interesting to ride these waves of life: motherhood, sexism in the [music] business, ageism. And it's interesting to look back and see your body of work reflecting your life like an autobiography. I'm aware of my mortality. I just want to leave really, really good art behind."

13

Tobi Vail (Bikini Kill)

During the 1990s, Tobi Vail rose to fame as the drummer for pioneering punk band Bikini Kill. Their outspoken feminist-focused music and activism helped foster the "riot grrrl" movement, which sought to seamlessly blend music and politics in order to promote women's rights. It was an unapologetically aggressive approach that is widely credited for sparking the "third wave" of feminism and, thirty years later, still seems to inform the debate about gender equality.

Vail's early years gave little indication that she would become an influential musician, however. For much of her childhood in the 1970s, her family lived in Naselle, Washington, in the remote southwestern corner of the state. She estimates that the population was only a couple hundred people.

"It was really depressing," she says. "In an isolated logging town, you really saw the violence. There was a lot of domestic violence. There was child abuse. I mean, not in my family, but that was around. That was the climate."

She was also highly conscious of the dangers inherent in the logging industry. "I think there was only, at most, twenty kids in my grade. When a kid would get called to the [principal's] office, a lot of times it would be because their dads were in a logging accident—and they often died. That trade was very violent," she says. She isn't being melodramatic: the US Occupational Safety and Health Administration states, "By many measures, logging is the most dangerous occupation in the United States."[1]

Fortunately, Vail's father was not a logger; his job was at Naselle's only other major place of employment, Naselle Youth Camp, a detention facility for juvenile offenders. (The Washington State Department of Children, Youth and Families closed the facility in September 2022.) He worked as a counselor, though he wasn't much older than his charges.

Vail's parents had been born and raised in the Seattle metropolitan area, so they were quite different, politically and culturally, than most of their Naselle neighbors. To get along in such a small community, they kept their opinions to themselves. Vail followed suit, but this often left her seething inwardly—especially when she was expected to acquiesce to discrimination.

"I was very aware of sexism and unequal treatment of girls from living in Naselle because it had a public school, but it was not run like a public school," she says. "For example, we had to pray in school. And girls didn't get as much recess as boys—girls would have to just read or something. The whole point of that town really was their basketball team, and they were grooming the boys at a very young age to win the championship. But girls were not encouraged to be athletic. It wasn't fair."

Topping off Vail's dreary experience in Naselle, there was also the remarkably gloomy weather: she remembers that it rained almost every day. Small wonder, then, that the nearby town of Aberdeen, Washington, became the birthplace of the depressive grunge music scene during the 1990s.

"When people talk about grunge and how bleak that part of the state that Nirvana and the Melvins come from, Naselle was actually bleaker," Vail says. Later, when she befriended members of those bands, even they were horrified by her background: "Those guys were like, 'Wait, you lived in *Naselle?* Fuuuuck.'"

*   *   *

In 1979, when Vail was ten years old, her father was transferred to a job in Washington's capital city, Olympia, and her family left Naselle behind.

In another happy development at that time, Vail started play-ing the drums. Her father, a drummer who'd long been active in the Northwest music scene, was her teacher. He encouraged her to smack a footstool with drumsticks until she learned to keep a beat, then gradually eased her into using his full drum kit.

"My dad was all focused on playing music," Vail says. "Sometimes the drum set was in the living room, sometimes it was in the bedroom. The house was very small. But it did have an outside shed, too, so eventually we moved the drums out there and that became a practice space and recording studio."

Her mother approved of this father-daughter bonding activ-ity. "She was really into music and had seen the Beatles and the Rolling Stones on their first tours. She saw my dad's band at their eighth-grade dance," Vail says.

Vail's parents welcomed her into the world when they were still teenagers, which meant that they were still young enough to enthusiastically embrace punk music when that scene erupted in the 1970s. "They found out about it through *Rolling Stone* and *Saturday Night Live*. They went to see the Clash in 1979," Vail says, recalling that they also frequently played a wide range of punk records.

Vail liked punk, but when the all-female pop rock group the Go-Go's became famous in the early 1980s, she became a major fan. She has fond memories of her parents taking her and her younger sister to see that band in concert.

The Go-Go's influenced Vail's budding musicianship. She enrolled in guitar lessons at school, and while she got an A+ in the course, "It *definitely* did not sound like the Go-Go's," she says with a laugh. "They taught us one Beatles song, 'Rocky Raccoon.' I could play it perfectly, but I didn't really know how to play the music that I liked on guitar. It was way easier to play drums and have it sound like rock and roll."

She tried to emulate the Go-Go's drummer Gina Schock, whom she met years later. "I was like, 'Obviously, I'm influ-enced by you.' And she was like, 'Really? I can't tell at all.' She wasn't being mean or anything; she was genuinely surprised. And I was like, 'I guess my style is a lot different at this point.'

But when I first started playing, that's what I was going for, a surf-y kind of Gina Schock thing."

Vail soon found out that not everyone shared her enthusiasm for the Go-Go's and other female musicians, though. "It was very clear to me that people who thought the Go-Go's sucked were often just very sexist," she says. "You would read something about a band of girls, like the Runaways, and the media coverage would often be very sexist." Vail took note of the way those women faced double standards and unfair barriers.

This didn't discourage her from playing music herself—if anything, it made her even more determined to show that girls could rock as hard as any boy. She started inviting girlfriends over to her house for jam sessions. During high school, she formed her own all-female band, Doris.

At sixteen years old, she began hosting her own local radio show, on which she made a point of showcasing relatively obscure bands that had women in them, such as the Pandoras, Shonen Knife, the Calamities, and the Shop Assistants.

But when she started venturing out into Olympia's hardcore punk music scene, she realized that women still had a long way to go to reach equality. "There were a lot of girls involved in hardcore punk—the idea that there wasn't is not true," she says, "but at the same time, it was very male-dominated. You'd go to see a show, and it was not uncommon for there to be zero women onstage the whole night. Maybe you'd get a female bass player, drummer, singer—but very rarely would you have a band of all girls on the stage."

To her frustration, Vail realized that this gender-related obstacle seemed self-imposed. "All of the boys who were in bands would practice once and they'd play a show. And I'd try to get my female friends to come over and jam and write a song and play a show, and nobody wanted to get on a stage. So I was like, 'What is that about?' It was just a question in my head. It wasn't like somebody wasn't going to let us play—the culture just wasn't in place."

Vail wanted to change this, but her ambitions were sidelined by practical considerations. After graduating from high school, she'd received a small scholarship to a liberal arts college in

Olympia, the Evergreen State College, but when that funding ran out after only a few months, she found herself at loose ends.

This was not an entirely unexpected situation. Her father had sat her down when she was seven years old and explained that her working-class background meant that she would need to be self-sufficient. She remembers that he told her, "You've got to start saving your money now because you will be paying for your own college. And when you're eighteen, you'll be paying your own way. So you've got to figure out how to do that." Heeding his advice, she'd worked hard at paper routes and babysitting—but now, she wasn't sure that she wanted to spend everything she'd earned on continuing her college education.

Instead, she decided to move to Eugene, Oregon, and get a job. She chose that city because it seemed similar to Olympia but would give her a chance to try living outside of Washington. But it wasn't a good experience, and she only stayed there for six months before coming home and reenrolling at Evergreen.

This time, she decided to simply learn as much as possible about a wide array of topics, including science, film, and feminist theories. It was interesting, but aimless. Adding to the disjointed nature of her studies, she had to keep dropping out to work various jobs so she could earn enough money to pay for rent and more classes.

She was also stretched thin by playing in two bands, as well as continuing her radio show. Even with all that, she somehow found time to squeeze in one more activity: starting a fanzine, *Jigsaw*—which would have ramifications that radically changed her life.

*   *   *

In 1989, Vail published the first issue of *Jigsaw*, using it as a forum to put forth her feminist views. Her fanzine fit in perfectly with Olympia's countercultural scene, where women were taking a highly outspoken and activism-oriented approach to disrupting the status quo. In *Jigsaw*, Vail wrote about this "riot grrrl" movement, and she is often credited with coining the growling "grrr" spelling within "girl."

Like-minded Olympia musicians Kathleen Hanna and Kathi Wilcox began contributing to *Jigsaw*. They also decided to form a band together, with Vail on drums, Hanna on vocals, Wilcox on bass, and Billy Kaaren joining on guitar. Naming themselves Bikini Kill, they set about channeling their rage via politicized lyrics and a ferocious stage presence. Finally, Vail's dream of being in a female-forward music scene was coming true.

Jigsaw and other feminist fanzines became popular, spreading across the United States. "I think a big strength of 'riot grrrl' was the network that happened through the mail, where women could talk to each other outside of the mainstream media," Vail says. At the same time, Bikini Kill and other Washington bands were quickly gaining a broader audience for their music. It wasn't long before major media outlets took notice—but, Vail says, they often misinterpreted what was happening, conflating the movement with the music.

"At the time, we didn't consider 'riot grrrl' to be a genre of music—it was more of an activist network. And we didn't consider ourselves to be a riot grrrl band," Vail says. Nevertheless, when Bikini Kill released their first two albums, 1991's *Revolution Girl Style Now!* and 1993's *Pussy Whipped*, they were branded as the foremost riot grrrl group, a label that has stuck with them ever since.

They used their platform to profess a "girls to the front" message, encouraging females to come up to the edge of the stage during shows (reclaiming a space that had often become hazardous for women at punk and rock shows when male audience members instituted mosh pits and other aggressive behavior). They also intended to use their message to urge women to get involved, both in the music industry and as activists in the wider world.

Some people were taken aback by Bikini Kill's forceful approach, but others—including Vail herself—thought it was cathartic to use music to express things in such an unfiltered way. She admired how Hanna skillfully delivered this bold female empowerment message: "She was really powerful, and she was talking a lot about sexual violence and that kind of stuff."

This resonated with Vail because of a horrifying incident that had happened to her in Oregon. "I don't really talk about this very often, but when I moved to Eugene, I was assaulted in my apartment by a stranger. I got away, but it was very terrifying," she says, her voice shaking. "It was also retraumatizing when I called the police, because they were like, 'Was your door locked? Did you tell him to leave?' I was like, 'Well, no, the door wasn't locked, and I don't remember what I said.' It was really messed up."

That wasn't the only disturbing thing that happened in Eugene, either. "There was a lot of creepiness there," she says. "One of my bandmates had a guy masturbating outside of her window every night. A lot of people that I knew had had these experiences. And Kathleen was someone who was talking about them publicly."

Still, Vail wants to clarify that Hanna shouldn't be given *all* the credit. "Kathleen was perceived as the leader of Bikini Kill because she was the singer and she was the most extroverted, but we actually functioned as a collective. We all had equal say and an equal share in songwriting. So basically, the media seized [on] 'Kathleen is the leader, and riot grrrl and Bikini Kill are one and the same.' But that's not how we saw it as a band."

This team mentality became imperative as Bikini Kill's fame grew, and Vail and her bandmates found they had to look out for each other's safety because their ultra-feminist stance rankled some people to the point of violence.

Vail remembers one night in Boston where a man who had been arrested on a domestic violence charge came directly to their show after being released from jail. "He went to the front [of the stage] and spit at Kathleen. Our friend Laura was our roadie, so she got in the middle. He punched her, knocked her out, gave her a black eye. She was on the ground. The guy didn't get thrown out because he actually worked security at the club, but he wasn't working that night. So we had to leave. People were telling us he had a gun. Not long after that, he went to his girlfriend's work, shot and killed her, and then shot and killed himself."

Vail and her bandmates put up a defiant front, but privately, they were worried because there was only so much they could do to protect themselves. "We had a very intense experience because we had limited material means," Vail says. "We didn't have a manager. We were trying to do everything ourselves, which meant booking tours. A lot of times there would be no backstage [area], there would be no security." When a male audience member hurled sexist remarks at them, they could only hope that it wouldn't escalate into something much worse.

"On the other side, our fans kept getting younger and younger and younger. So there'd be these very young kids, super freaking out at the intensity of the live show," Vail says. "You'd also have people who were experiencing domestic violence, sexual abuse at home, abuse from their parents for being queer, runaways. They would try to have a conversation with Kathleen, who was the only person they knew of who had experienced something similar or talked about it. So she would be in rape crisis counselor mode to these teens who were not safe."

Meanwhile, a backlash against the riot grrrl movement was brewing, fueled by people who felt that it was too centered on middle-class white women's experiences. Much of the vitriol was aimed at Bikini Kill. "You had people criticizing us for stuff that was happening at riot grrrl conventions," Vail says. "I'm sorry, but we've never even played a riot grrrl convention. We definitely didn't organize this thing where you faced discrimination or felt not included. All of those criticisms of riot grrrl are entirely valid, but we were really just trying to survive at that point. People were like, 'You aren't feminist enough.' It was really hard."

She sighs. "It was a lot of stress just to put on a rock and roll band," she says wryly.

*   *   *

Bikini Kill have also been accused of being man haters—a charge that overlooks the fact that their lineup has included a male guitarist. This claim also fails to give credit to their many male allies. In fact, Bikini Kill's earliest studio sessions were made possible by Ian MacKaye, the influential leader of the Washington, D.C.-based punk band Fugazi and cofounder of indie label Dischord Records.

"Ian MacKaye was one of our biggest supporters from the very first time that he saw us," Vail says. Bikini Kill even relocated to D.C. for two years in order to be in a better position to take MacKaye up on his offer of assistance. "He was very helpful in recording us for free and getting people to hear our demo tape. Fugazi was the way that we were able to get our music to Joan Jett. She ended up producing our [1993] 'Rebel Girl' single."

Even before that, Vail's own connections had led to significant support from certain male musicians. "As far as the Olympia punk scene goes, for sure the guys in Nirvana were our biggest cheerleaders," she says. "Definitely, Nirvana was crucial to our first year. Kurt [Cobain, Nirvana singer/guitarist] was at all our early shows and was very encouraging. And I was also playing in a band with him at the time. Obviously, I would never say that I had the same talent or ability as someone that gifted, but he was a collaborator, and I felt like an equal in that collaboration."

She and Cobain were also romantically involved for a brief time, though they remained good friends even after their split. She was happy to watch him lead Nirvana on to major international success, though she admits it felt surreal.

"Nirvana is probably one of the most famous rock and roll bands in the history of the world, but it's really weird when you see your friends get famous and you actually come from the same community," she says.

Vail was supposedly the inspiration for the Nirvana track "Aneurysm," and it's also been reported that Cobain wrote their breakthrough hit "Smells Like Teen Spirit" because Kathleen Hanna spraypainted that phrase on his wall to tease him about smelling like Vail's deodorant. But while Vail admits these stories are "probably true," she doesn't think this is an entirely fair assessment of the situation.

"I hesitate to even say this publicly, but Nirvana were actually influenced by our band, too," she says. "I think Kurt was influenced by some of our band's music and presentation, and certainly by some of my songwriting at times. And he would have been the first to admit that. Maybe we weren't just 'the muse.' Maybe we were actually, at some point, equals with these people.

"The way that these stories get told is also a part of the sexism because women are always taught to give credit to other people. The idea that there could have been an influential woman in Kurt Cobain's artistic life, it's like, 'Well, she must have just been a girlfriend or a muse or not had a voice.' Actually, we had a lot of conversations about what we wanted to do with our bands. We spent hours playing guitar together and all kinds of stuff."

Vail remains protective of Cobain, who passed away from suicide in 1994, so she declines to say more. "There's a lot to that story that doesn't get told, but I'm not going to be the first one to really put my effort towards that," she says. "And it's a sad story with a sad ending, too, so people who were around [then] don't really want to talk about it."

* * *

Though she's gone through many ups and downs in her life, Vail has arrived at a happy place these days. She's calling from Olympia, where she still lives, and has remained extremely active in that music scene, playing with numerous bands. "I never quit playing music. I've been in bands since I was sixteen years old, and now I'm fifty-three. And I probably will do it my whole life," she says. Most recently, she's been active with the "feminist collective" band girlSperm (a.k.a. gSp).

Bikini Kill reformed in 2017 after a twenty-year hiatus, and they continue to perform sold-out shows worldwide. Nowadays, they play mainstream venues (with proper backstage areas), but other aspects of their touring experience haven't changed. "Some of the security issues do still persist," she says. "We spend a lot of our tour budget on extra security, to make sure that things are safe. Not just for us, but also for the crowd. We actually have metal detectors in our budget. Do other punk bands have to deal with this kind of security shit? I don't know."

The band are still intent on encouraging women to get involved—but Vail admits it can be a challenge to put that into practice. "It's been hard for me to find a drum tech that is not a guy. It's still not very common to go into a recording studio and have there be a female producer or [recording] engineer. And you realize that women still don't really headline festivals very often."

Even so, she's optimistic because she sees that progress is being made on some fronts: "It's still not equal, but within the D.I.Y. hardcore punk realm, definitely things have shifted incredibly to be way more inclusive. Not just in terms of girls in bands, but more people of color, more queer people, more trans people—everything is more inclusive."

She's pleased with the role the riot grrrl movement had in effecting this change, though she also believes it's important to learn from that experience: "I think one of the mistakes that riot grrrl made was putting the emphasis on 'girl,' rather than on 'riot.' If we had created some kind of template for action, rather than an identity category, that might have been more useful."

With that method in mind, Vail helped to organize Ladyfest, a festival that was first held in 2000 in Olympia and featured women-centered bands, with proceeds donated to female-focused nonprofit organizations. This was intended as a model that others could follow to put on similar shows, tailoring it to fit their particular community's needs and interests. So far, there have been nearly two hundred Ladyfests held around the world.

Vail's current approach to activism has also been informed by the liberal arts degree that she earned when she returned to The Evergreen State College when she was in her late thirties. With her studies, she focused on feminist theory, politics, and history, which gave her further insight into what still needs to be done to ensure that women (and other marginalized groups) attain the equality they deserve.

"If you look at history, you can see that progress is not linear; it goes back and forth," she says. "You never know when it's going to go backwards, so you always have to be fighting. You have to be aware that rights we do have were achieved through political struggle. You can't take them for granted."

14

Laura Veirs

"I was surprised that bringing a baby on tour is really pretty easy," says Laura Veirs. "I mean, it's never *easy* to be traveling with a child, but babies are really portable."

The Portland, Oregon-based singer-songwriter has released twelve critically acclaimed albums—half of which have come out since she became a mother to sons Tennessee and Oz, born in 2010 and 2013, respectively. To effectively promote her work, she learned how to tour the world through her pregnancies, and then while keeping her children by her side. The early days of doing so were, she says, quite an eye-opening experience.

"The thing that I didn't know is that babies don't really cry that much at all if they're right next to mom and they can nurse," she says. "Because a lot of times, all they want is food, rest, or attention. And if you're right there—and most of the time when you're on tour with your baby, you *are* right there—then the baby is happy. So it was really cool to tour with both babies."

She also found it interesting to watch how elated her backing band members were to have an infant in their midst. "They would always be cooing and helping and playing with the baby," she says. "Being on the road is really boring. There's this liminal space between waiting for the gig, and then you're done, and then packing, and then you've got to get to the next place.

The baby can offset the boredom of that with the bright smiles and giggles and cute stuff. So that was a really cool surprise."

Veirs feels so strongly about showing other musicians how to balance their careers with motherhood that she did a 2018 podcast series, *Midnight Lightning*, about this topic. In the fifteen episodes, she interviewed female artists about how they handled this situation, "because I was feeling a lack of community around this." Her diverse guest lineup included stars such as Rosanne Cash and Meshell Ndegeocello, as well as local Portland artists. "It was really great because I got to hear the ways that they hack it, because you kind of have to hack the system to be able to pull it off because it is very complicated to be a working musician and mom," she says.

By checking out these episodes, Veirs says, "I would hope that more women would see ways to be moms and musicians, because a lot of times, people feel like you can't do both. I think if they see more people like me, and listen to the podcast, they'll be like, 'It's hard, but you can do it.'"

She knows what happens when women can't make this balancing act work out. "I've heard of musicians, women, and I won't name names, but they've gone off and left their kids for months and months at a time with grandparents, to build their career. Which, maybe they needed to do, for finances. But also, it could be construed as narcissistic to just go away like that. But of course, men do that constantly and no one says that's narcissistic, right? There's no stories that I heard of where the woman left for several months at a time and left the kids with the dad."

This seeming gender inequity motivates her to keep trying to help other female artists. "I guess there's this part of me that just wants women to be free to be able to do what you want to do *and* be a mom," she says. "Of course you're going to have constraints on your life when you choose to be a parent; that's just part of the job. But I would like to see a world where women didn't feel that there were certain jobs that were off-limits because they wanted to be a mom, also. And I think that will be one of the things people can take away from my career, is how I did do both, and I feel like I'm doing well with both."

That doesn't mean that it's always easy, though—especially now that Veirs is doing it as a single parent since her divorce in 2019. "When I go on tour, it's super complex. Like, I have this Excel spreadsheet that's deeply logistical, getting everything in order for me to have care for my kids, because I [typically] have them 85 percent of the time."

For instance, she outlines how she'll handle her 2022 tour to promote her latest album, *Found Light*: "My brother is helping, and my parents are helping, and my ex [husband, Tucker Martine] is helping, because I'm going without the kids. And then my nanny is bringing them over for a week to the UK next month. Planning all that is a headache. Without the village—my friends, my kids' teachers, my parents, my brother, my ex—I would literally not be able to do it. I would have to get a normal job."

When she isn't on the road, though, Veirs finds that being a musician actually makes life much easier for her than if she had a regular nine-to-five job. She cites the royalties she gets from her recorded work as being a huge factor in this. "Right now, because I do have this passive income, I can really be available to my kids. I don't have to work long hours. I can pick them up from school, and I can take them to soccer practice and be a really engaged parent, in a way that I think people who are working full-time can't."

Now that her sons are twelve and nine years old, they're becoming aware of what Veirs is juggling. "They're seeing a woman—me—doing everything. They're also seeing me ask for help and getting help. So it's not like I'm this Superwoman that does it all. I'm leaning on people constantly. I'm just doing my best, and I think they're seeing that."

This is part of her bigger plan for how she wants her sons to view the world. "I'm raising feminist sons the best I can," she says. "We talk about patriarchy all the time. We also talk about white supremacy, homophobia, and transphobia. It's very much in the culture of their public school, too, to be talking about all these issues and trying to move the needle in the right direction.

"Sometimes they've brought up feeling guilty that they're white men, privileged men. But I said, 'You don't need to feel guilty. You need to use your power to be good allies to all these people who are less privileged than you.'

"We also talk about how, traditionally, women did the work of the house, but that's not equitable, and we need to share in the work." To make this really sink in, "I get them to help me in real ways around the house every day. We call it 'family work,' where we work together. Whether that's cooking, cleaning, laundry, yard work, walking the dogs—they are learning everything. A lot of parents—especially women, because women are in charge of the house, typically—haven't traditionally taught their sons how to do that stuff."

She's hopeful that all this will result in her sons turning into conscientious and productive adults. "You can never predict what your kids are going to do, but I'm doing my best to raise good sons. And I think they're going to be great people. It makes me happy."

*   *   *

This progressive and engaged parenting approach is reflective of the way in which Veirs herself was raised. "I feel like my parents helped me see strong women a lot growing up—they are feminists," she says. "I mean, they weren't perfect in terms of the way that they did things, but no parent is. But they were way ahead of their time. My parents always made me feel like I could do anything I wanted to do, and there weren't gender barriers."

Born in 1973 in Colorado Springs, Colorado, where she was also raised, Veirs grew up in an environment where education was especially important. "My family is pretty academic," she says. "My dad was a physics professor. My mom was an elementary schoolteacher." Her brother, older than her by three years, went to Stanford University, where he earned a PhD in oceanography.

Through her childhood, it seemed as if she'd follow their lead into academia—there was little indication, at this time, that she was destined instead for a professional music career. "My parents tried to get me to do piano lessons, but I never took to it," she says.

Her father was what she calls "a casual guitar player," though, and her brother also picked up that instrument and joined bands when he was in high school. When she was eighteen years old, her brother taught her some guitar chords, but she didn't warm to these music lessons, either.

Instead, after a childhood spent doing a lot of camping and other outdoors activities with her family, she felt more drawn to the natural sciences. To that end, she went to college at Carleton College in Northfield, Minnesota, just south of Minneapolis, where she majored in geology.

"I went to Carleton because I wanted to get out of my hometown, and I couldn't get into a place like Stanford," she says, "but I wanted to go to a smaller liberal arts school, and I knew that that was a good one."

But then things took an unexpected turn. In 1992, during her early days at Carleton, "a friend introduced me to the riot grrrl scene," she says. "I was like, 'Wow, this is a whole 'nother thing I've never even heard of.' That was basically pre-internet—we had email, but we didn't have websites or anything—so it was very much like an underground network of passing along tapes and buying CDs."

The riot grrrl movement was a new brand of feminism that emerged in the early 1990s from the Pacific Northwest punk rock scene. Those roots gave it a more overtly aggressive edge than any feminist wave had displayed before, and it quickly became a cultural phenomenon. At the same time, musical acts such as Bikini Kill and Sleater-Kinney blended assertive, edgy music and outspoken activism as a vehicle to spread their defiant message of female equality and individualism.

"I think part of what attracted me to the feminist riot grrrl scene was that it was allowing women to be angry in public," Veirs says. "Women are encouraged so much to be nice all the time, from when we're tiny until forever. And sometimes the situations we're in don't make us feel nice. Like, we *shouldn't* be nice; we should be pissed off, because life is unfair, and we live in a patriarchy. So sometimes we want to express that. And I found that to be a liberating way to do that. I'm really grateful I discovered that community."

For the first time, she started thinking seriously about music, "because I think, at that time, I was unaware that women were doing this, and they were doing it on their own terms. Like, I knew there were women pop stars. I just didn't know there were people driving around in cars selling shit from their trunk and managing themselves and making their own artwork. It took me actually meeting people who were playing in the bands, doing riot grrrl stuff, to believe that *I* could do it. So when I started figuring all that out, I was like, 'Damn, I can do this without formal infrastructure, and I can find my way on my own.'"

Remembering the chords her brother taught her, she picked up the guitar again. "I started thinking it was really a fun puzzle-solving thing to write songs on my acoustic guitar," she says.

Unsure how to move from writing songs to performing them with others, she sent a letter to the punk band Bikini Kill. "I wrote, 'How do you start a band?' And [drummer] Tobi Vail wrote back. I don't have the letter anymore, which I'm sad about. But I remember she said, 'Play with as many people as you can, and have fun.' I thought that those were two really cool things to say."

Following that advice, Veirs formed a band, Rair Kx!, with some girlfriends. "I really wanted to collaborate with women because I did feel this sense of annoyance that so many of the bands in my brother's scene were all boys. I was like, 'Where are the girls?' So once I got to college, I was like, 'Oh, you can make your own girl group; you don't need to be with boys in this way.'" (She notes that she and her bandmates bonded so tightly that, more than a quarter century later, they're all still close friends.)

Though she had only recently picked up her instrument and started composing, those became her primary duties within Rair Kx!: "I was the songwriter and the guitar player, which I think really is my happy place."

Rair Kx! played some shows and made a split seven-inch single with another local group, but as the members moved on from college, things fell apart. "I wanted to keep the band together, but they didn't want to do it," she says.

Veirs graduated with a degree in geology—but by then, she knew that she wanted to pursue a music career instead. She'd had this epiphany as she neared the end of her college days, when she was in China doing a geological field research project. "On that trip, I had brought my guitar with me, which was very weird. I was playing a lot and writing a lot of songs. I came to the realization, 'I just want to be a writer.' I identify more, I guess, as a writer than as a musician sometimes, because I put so much effort into the craft of the songs."

*   *   *

After graduating from college, Veirs was unsure of how to make her professional musician dream become reality, so she set her artistic ambitions aside and took a job at the Pacific Science Center in Seattle.

Before long, though, fate seemed to steer her back into music when she began working with Tucker Martine, a well-established record producer and engineer. "We met when I was such a young person, without having done any [solo] recording," Veirs says. "I was mostly interested in the songwriting, and then the rest I guess I just left to him [because] he was already an accomplished producer."

Veirs threw herself into truly mastering the guitar, taking weekly lessons for about a year from John Miller, an expert in advanced picking techniques. "I learned really complicated fingerstyle stuff, like "Freight Train" by Elizabeth Cotten, Mississippi John Hurt, all those old-time folk people."

This, along with her previous punk band experience, has informed her music ever since, resulting in a distinctive alternative folk style. "Basically, my pendulum swings between complicated folk guitar and punk rock. I like both," she says.

Though she longed for the camaraderie that a band would provide, Veirs opted to embark on a solo career. In making that decision, "I think probably there was a practical side that was like, 'This is a really hard business. If I can do it on my own, just solo, then I'll be able to survive more. I can bring a band with me if I have the budget.'"

She credits her friends in the D.I.Y. scene for helping her learn how to think her choices through in this way: "They encouraged me to be very careful about my career, in terms of maintaining control and ownership of my stuff, which I have done. That's really served me well." This is why she has always been vigilant about retaining the rights to her own songs (and why she also created her own record label, Raven Marching Band Records). "I had models of people doing that early on that set me up for paying attention to that," she says.

With everything seeming conducive to pursuing a music career, Veirs took the plunge and quit her day job. The gamble paid off: her self-titled debut, released in 1999, earned critical praise. The same has been true for all twelve studio albums she has released so far. However, with hindsight, Veirs wonders if she let Martine (who she started dating in 2006) take the reins a little too much.

"With our lives as complicated as they were with kids and [recording] studio and just trying to keep our heads up, I didn't assert myself enough to say, 'I'm going to work with another producer.' We were married for eight years, and together for fifteen romantically, so it was a really long collaboration with one person."

Veirs and Martine divorced in 2019, though they worked on one last album together, *My Echo* (2020), in which she chronicles the disintegration of their relationship. Two years later, she is able to take a more objective overview of their partnership: "I know we made some beautiful records and some great music, and I'm proud of the work that we did."

In 2022, she released her first album without Martine's input. Its title, *Found Light*, represents the happiness she's discovered after going through such a dark time prior to making it. It also marks a major step forward in her creative accomplishments, as it is the first album where she served as a coproducer.

"When I made the new record, I thought I might try to produce it on my own at home or with a friend. But it was in the pandemic, and I was single parenting—it was overwhelming," she says. Then she remembered multi-instrumentalist / producer Shahzad Ismaily. "He has a studio in Brooklyn. We had actually gone on tour together fifteen years prior, in Italy. So I had spent some time with Shahzad, and I had loved hanging out with him; he's super friendly. He came to Portland, and we did half of it here and then half in Brooklyn.

"It was really different because my ex was more like a jeweler, in terms of making sure everything was really perfect. He would make me do things over and over, and there was a ton of editing and making it perfect. I started to feel like I wasn't any good at recording or playing in the studio."

In contrast, with Ismaily, "We played live and recorded live and did everything in one or two takes with hardly any edits. I was like, 'Damn, I'm good—I can play these things without needing to do it multiple times.' And it was really liberating to be like, 'Yeah, you *should* be this good after this long—it's been almost thirty years [in the music business].' So that was a really big eye-opening, fresh, liberating experience. It's actually improved my confidence."

This newfound self-assurance is, she says, quite vindicating. "Somebody had told me once, 'You're not very good live,' which sucks. So you get these comments, and they get in your head. I think that is part of being female in the culture, is absorbing that more than men do. I think they're more like, 'Whatever, man. I'm good.' And then women are like, 'Are they right? Am I not good?' We doubt ourselves more.

"Now that I saw, with clarity, how well I could do in the studio, I realized, 'That's you playing live. You *don't* suck—you're great live.' I think it just takes these experiences over time to release that baggage and these messages that tell you to be small, tell you to stop or slow down, or you're too bossy, or whatever the message is that women often get. It's our work to dig deep and push away that negativity and rise above and say, 'Well, I disagree, and I'm going to keep doing this because I'm good at it and I like it.'"

*   *   *

After going through her own transformations, both professionally and personally, Veirs hopes that others will get the same chance to find fulfillment. "I do think that women are often overlooked, as queer people and people of color are, because they're not really in the scene," she says. "They're not the dominant group. White men are the dominant group in the music scene. So sometimes I feel like they overlook people who are outside of them. Not all of them, but some of them overlook people. I don't want to sound sour, like, 'I've been overlooked,' because I don't feel that way. But I do think that the genius of women and outsiders is often overlooked."

She also believes that it's a crucial time for women, in terms of their place in society overall. "I feel like it's a fraught time for women's rights in general right now, and it's maddening," she says, adding that it especially rankles her when she sees another woman rejecting being called a feminist: "I really don't get it when someone minds that. It frustrates me."

But at the same time, she also feels that there is much reason for hope. "You can see this next generation coming and their true open-mindedness—especially around gender. Their fluidity around gender and their nonbinary thinking around that is so refreshing. I see the next generation acting in a really cool and new way that will disrupt what's going on right now."

She can already tell that there are significant changes happening within the music business. "I like seeing the fresh energy of women coming up, recording themselves and hiring lots of women in their bands. I feel like there's a more conscious acknowledgment of how we need to include women, and people of color and queer people, in the inner circles of our creativity—being in the band, being behind the mixing board, mastering, doing videos, styling, tour managing—all of it. And I see that more and more as the next generation comes up, and that makes me happy. I think it shows a lot of hope."

15

Catherine Popper

For the past thirty years, Catherine Popper has been a highly in-demand bass player, admired for her expert musicianship and striking stage presence. Her impressive résumé spans multiple genres and includes recording and touring with artists such as Jack White, Gaslight Anthem's Brian Fallon, Grace Potter and the Nocturnals, the Band's Levon Helm, Jesse Malin, and Ryan Adams. She's a member of the acclaimed alt-country group Puss n Boots, which also includes Norah Jones and Sasha Dobson. She has contributed to numerous hit film and television soundtracks and worked in the orchestra pit for several Broadway musicals.

It's a career that anyone should be proud to claim. But as Popper relaxes in the summer sun at a New York City sidewalk café not far from the apartment she shares with her husband, theater actor Jeffries Thaiss, she recalls a time when she was distinctly disrespected despite her undeniable talent: "When I was in high school, we had the All-State Symphony in North Carolina. Everybody from all over North Carolina auditions for this orchestra. I got in every year. The bass section in an orchestra, it's the chuckle patch, we're a good hang—but when I won the principal bass position, everything changed. The guys started to treat me differently. And these were guys who had been my friends."

She won this distinction twice, and this negative reaction from her male peers happened both times. On one of those occasions, hoping to salvage her relationship with one bass player who'd been an especially close buddy of hers, she gave her "first chair" position to him. "I was so willing to sacrifice what I had earned, but didn't think I deserved," she says. The conductor, irate, made them change back to their rightful places.

"It's not that often that I say, 'I think this happened because I'm a woman.' But that, in particular, was a time when that was true," she says. "I was so terrified of taking up that space, I had a panic attack in the middle of the concert and had to put my bass down and leave the stage. My orchestra teacher found me in the bathroom, shivering, not wanting to go back out onstage."

She doesn't want to make it sound like men are the only ones to blame for misogyny, though. "Women aren't always the most supportive either," she says. She recounts another memory, this one from her college years, when her bass playing skills earned her an invitation to audition for a respected all-female jazz band in New York. "I thought, 'I'm not going to wear makeup onstage because if I wear makeup, people are going to take me less seriously,'" she says. So she was startled when, as soon as she walked in the door, "They took a look at me and they said, 'You know what? We've changed our minds.'"

She begged them to let her play something for them before they made their decision, at least. "They were really pissy about it. They said *fine*. And they let me play half a song." Then they gave her a final no. She felt certain this happened because she looked so young.

"It wasn't a gig that was beyond my capacity; I could have easily done it," she says, "but there was a lot of cliquey-ness with the women. I think the women's scene was very insular as a necessity, but I was collateral damage from that, too."

Now, more than three decades later, Popper's extensive experience in the music business has given her even more insight into why this type of thing happens. "A lot of women, they shut down. They get hard. They don't know it, but they become really bristly around young women. Because that's how they were treated. And I don't ever want to do that."

These days, she tries to take a charitable view of her oppressors in both of those eye-opening situations. "This stuff can be hard. It's hard to be people," she says. "Let's talk about your humanity, and that it's hard to feel like you don't belong. Everybody assumes that what they're insecure about is why things are happening to them."

*   *   *

In 1993, Popper moved to New York City to study jazz bass at the prestigious Manhattan School of Music. Upon arrival, she discovered that she was one of only a few women enrolled there, which made her uncomfortable—but she shrugged it off and dove into her classes. She started dating a successful saxophone player who had previously also attended that school. It seemed like her personal and professional lives were off to a promising start.

So she was dismayed when she once again encountered discrimination based on her gender. "We had to write a twenty-page paper on one Duke Ellington piece. I worked so hard—I bled over it," she says. "And somebody said, 'Yeah, [the male professor] said your boyfriend probably wrote that for you.' That was the first time that's happened to me where somebody accused me of having a guy do it for me."

Not long after, another male teacher told her, "'You are really hung up about the fact that you are a woman.' Which was right and not right. Because I was really self-conscious, having a professor say that somebody wrote my paper for me, and having people definitely treat me a certain way because I was a woman playing jazz. So I was pissed about what he said. He was right—but he didn't understand that I had to frame everything with my gender for a long time."

For one thing, there was the safety factor, which women often must consider more than men do. Beyond her studies, Popper had thrown herself into the New York music scene—and because the bass is such a versatile instrument, she would play anything from bluegrass to Irish music. The problem was that all this work meant that she often had to put herself in a precarious position as she made her way home after gigs.

"The New York I moved to, you didn't want anybody to no-tice you on the subway—but having an upright bass is definitely an idiot magnet," she says. "Everybody wants to talk to you. Later at night, I definitely was threatened a few times. Some-body smashed a bottle once and was going to cut me with the jagged neck." Another time, as she was walking home in the wee hours, a city bus pulled up beside her, its driver insisting she get on board so he could go off-route and drive her directly home.

Still, she was doing what she loved, so she was happy. She was hired to play two sets a week with an all-female trio at Au-gie's, a dive bar on the Upper West Side. That, in turn, led her to meeting many other accomplished musicians, who began offer-ing her work—especially in rock, so she had to quickly master playing the electric bass, as well.

Making the leap to becoming a full-time professional musi-cian wasn't entirely smooth, however. At one gig, she met Chip Taylor, who wrote the classic hit "Wild Thing." He told her that he was looking to hire a bass player, "But he said, 'I'm just curious, are you married?' And I said, in a joking tone, 'Are ya askin'?' And he said, 'No, I just want to make sure that I'm not going to hire somebody who's on a baby train.'" She sighs. "First of all, I wasn't really interested in going on tour with him. But I said, 'You do realize that a large part of my career is subbing for guys who have newborns, right?'"

A similar incident happened soon after: "A guy from a rock band that I have no interest in playing with said, 'Too bad you're not a dude, because you would be so great in the band.' I remember thinking, 'He's assuming that I would *want* to be in his band.'"

In both cases, Popper made the effort to walk away from the conversation on friendly terms. "If I took on every inappropri-ate remark or come-on, I wouldn't be able to sleep at night," she says. (It is an attitude that she still holds to this day.)

Finally, in 2001, she became the bassist for the folk band Hem, who were signed to DreamWorks, a major record label. This enabled her to check off some career milestones: her debut international tour, and her first studio recording experiences for the group's albums *Rabbit Songs* (2001) and *Eveningland* (2004).

An even bigger break came later in 2004, when Popper joined the Cardinals, the backing band for Ryan Adams, who had been the leader of the popular alt-country band Whiskeytown from 1994 until 2000. As a solo artist, Adams had continued his prolific and critically acclaimed trajectory. Working with him changed Popper's life—for better and for worse.

*　*　*

From 2004 through 2007, Popper toured extensively with Ryan Adams and the Cardinals, and recorded two albums with them in 2005, *Cold Roses* and *Jacksonville City Nights*. It was the first work that brought widespread recognition to her bass playing. Looking back on those years, she has fond and painful memories in equal measure.

"Ryan is so charming. He's so creative. But it was such a codependent experience—and it was that way with everybody in his life," she says. "I was ripe at the time to fall into something like that because of my addiction: I was a very active alcoholic at the time—and gleefully so, because I had spent a lifetime teetotaling and not letting myself go. That era was when I finally did. Oh my God, we had so much fun. Honestly, it was some of the most fun I've ever had in my life. But it almost killed me."

In 2007, Popper finally recognized that she *had* to quit Adams's band or she could die—not only from substance abuse, but also because she was barely eating. But even then, she wasn't ready to get sober. "I had a therapist who was like, 'I can't see you anymore unless you stop drinking.' Back in New York, I was living the same way, in terms of drug and alcohol use, that I was when I was on the road. It doesn't work at home. I was afraid to leave the house. It got so sad."

Finally, she got the help she needed, and has been clean ever since. "I survived it, I came out of it, and I'm a stronger person. Not everybody does. So this is where it gets complicated, because I want to consider the more vulnerable people."

She knows talking about her experiences with Adams will inevitably lead to questions about the controversy that engulfed him in 2019, when an article in the *New York Times*[1] detailed how several women (including his then-wife, actress Mandy Moore, and singer-songwriter Phoebe Bridgers) had accused him of sexual misconduct, including harassing and retaliatory behavior. Adams initially denied the claims, though in 2020, he published an apology in London's *Daily Mail* newspaper.[2]

"When the allegations against him came up, I had a heads up from him that some bad shit was getting ready to go down," Popper says. After reading the *New York Times* article, she had mixed feelings: "I think there's a difference between older women learning a really hard life lesson and taking advantage of younger women." And given her complicated history with Adams, she didn't feel she could defend or decry his supposed behavior, so she decided to keep quiet on the matter. "He's a pain in my ass. But I do still feel like we shared a very special experience in that band."

Her silence soon led some people to make *her* a target, too, condemning her for not being supportive of other women. This still rankles her: "Don't fucking come for me on Twitter and *demand* my experience because I'm a woman."

She knows she will probably also face blowback for her belief that Adams should be allowed to resurrect his career. "I do think that it was good for Ryan to learn a lesson, but to exile someone from life is inhumane. And it doesn't mean the people who have had an experience with him can't exile him from their lives. But I'm learning to embrace the humanity of others, and that's what a big part of my growing up is."

This is, in fact, the first time she has publicly opened up about her perspective on the situation. "It's weird, actually, to talk about this for this book," she says, "but I feel like, I'm talking about *my* experience, which is just as valid. I think what's most upsetting to me is that I'm not allowed to really have that conversation.

"I know that the broader picture is that I've been really encouraged by men, but I definitely have wounds from the sharper things that have happened to me. But I think it's really important for me to not be forced to reframe some things that have happened to me as traumatic experiences that weren't. Women can get very angry when you don't jump on a bandwagon. But I think it's important for me to be allowed to have my experience as a person."

*   *   *

Popper learned early on how to stay true to herself, even if it wasn't what everyone else seemed to expect from her. Born in Charlotte, North Carolina, in 1973, she was showing a keen interest in music by the time she was seven years old, making up songs on her family's piano—but then stubbornly refusing to get on board when her parents sent her to formal lessons.

"I remember my piano teacher's house stank, and she had these two huge sheepdogs that would sit under the piano so I couldn't really reach the pedals, and she had the loudest clock in the world," Popper says. "I remember not having practiced. So I had my hands on the keys, hearing *tick tock tick tock*, and saying, 'I did really well on my science project!'—and her not really caring about that."

When she was in the fifth grade, she joined her school orchestra, choosing to play the violin because that was what all the popular girls were doing—but she soon abandoned this, too. "I hated the sound, and it was very close to my face," she says.

But then, when she was nine years old, she saw a woman playing an upright bass in a local symphony, and she immediately knew that was what she wanted to do. Her desire to play bass was reinforced around that same time when Sting, lead singer and bassist for the Police, appeared in music videos playing that instrument.

Her parents and teachers clearly thought this was an odd thing for a young girl to want to pursue, but they allowed her to give it a try. This time, she was so successful at her lessons that she ended up attending a prestigious performing arts high school, North Carolina School of the Arts. There, she studied classical bass playing—at which she excelled, even though that style was not to her taste. "Being raised by a perfectionist father, I was pretty much constantly seeking to find things that were wrong, and would vigilantly attend to them and get better, so I was a really good classical player," she says.

As a teenager, she found other ways to rebel: "I was hanging out with the local punks. We'd go to the mall and smoke cigarettes and look tough and steal from [fashion accessory boutique] Claire's."

By the time she graduated from high school, Popper had quit the criminal mischief—but she was also on the verge of quitting music. "I didn't want to be in an orchestra. You spend ten hours a day practicing. You play the same five or six excerpts for auditions. And then you go to work in an orchestra. It's like having a job in a bank or something. No offense to people who work in banks, but I didn't think that was going to be my trajectory."

Instead, when she enrolled at the University of North Carolina at Chapel Hill, she intended to pursue a geology major. "But they said, 'We'll give you a scholarship if you play in the orchestra.'" Reluctantly, she accepted that offer, but started playing in the school's jazz band as a compromise. To her surprise, she discovered that she adored playing this kind of music. It was the fortunate twist of fate she needed to rekindle her joy for music and put her back on the path to becoming a professional bassist.

*   *   *

Years later, Popper once again found herself rediscovering her love for music when, after getting sober, she joined the band Grace Potter and the Nocturnals in 2009. She had felt some uncertainty as she reentered her career full force, but her bandmates were "Such a good group of people. Grace was so supportive."

Besides finding joy in playing again, Popper also has fond memories of Grace Potter encouraging her to have fun with her onstage image. "So there's all these pictures of me on the internet in a short skirt and heels. It was so fun to play dress-up for the first time in my life. I was thirty-five years old, putting on makeup for the first time."

This more glamorous image came in handy when, in 2012, she performed with Jack White, the influential former leader of the White Stripes. As a solo artist, White has continued to be highly regarded as an innovative musician. When he hired Popper, White had undertaken the unusual move of touring with two different bands simultaneously: one featuring all women ("The Peacocks"), the other with all men ("The Buzzards").

"Jack is such a great guy," Popper says. "I asked him, 'Why are you doing an all women thing?' And he said, 'I just really wanted to make a clear difference between the band from one night to the next, and it was the best way I could think of doing it.' And both bands were terrific." She went on to play bass on four songs on White's 2014 album *Lazaretto*.

Also in 2014, she worked with Rock and Roll Hall of Fame inductee Levon Helm, who was the former drummer and co-vocalist for the Band. With this gig, she reverted to a more casual style, despite Helms's occasional good-natured encouragement to get her to reconsider that move. "He did used to say, 'Lord, you need to get you a dress. You'd look so great.' At the time, I thought, 'That is the cutest thing. Here's a seventy-year-old man telling me how great I'd look in a dress.' I was so charmed. He was just excited at the prospect of me wearing the dress; it was very sweet. He was like a granddaddy to me. But the last fuckin' thing I wanted to do was wear a dress on that gig—or any other. He had a sister who played upright bass, and she wore a dress, so that was his point of reference."

Interwoven with these shorter-run jobs, Popper has also done long-term work with certain artists, such as her 2015 to 2020 stint in singer-songwriter Jesse Malin's backing band. She had met Malin years before, when he was first establishing himself as a solo artist by opening for Ryan Adams and the Cardinals on an extensive tour.

She went on to work with Malin and his band on four studio albums and numerous world tours. This was another healthy experience for her. "I always felt so safe and so respected—I loved touring with those guys," she says. "It was such a fun and very familial thing. They let me be me. Everybody knew that I was going to mess with them; I was playing pranks on people." She only quit because their tour schedule got too intense for her, but she and Malin remain close friends.

Another long-standing project for Popper has been Puss n Boots, an alt-country band that also includes Grammy-winning artist Norah Jones and Sasha Dobson. They created this group in 2008 because all three women have solid roots in jazz but wanted to do something different and more experimental. So far, they've released two albums and an EP.

In one way, Popper says their gender isn't a factor: "When we're playing together, we're not thinking about it." But in another way, she admits that it can be more relaxed than when she plays with men. "I remember one time, we baked cookies during rehearsal, wearing our bras or whatever. It's not like I'm shy or I don't feel safe being that way around men; it's just not appropriate for me to be in my underwear around them. They may have wives, or it may make them uncomfortable."

Popper's ease with her Puss n Boots bandmates made her trust them when they encouraged her to take on lead vocals and songwriting duties for the first time. This, in turn, led her to release her debut single as a solo artist, "Maybe It's All Right," in 2020. The next year, she put out a cover of the Pere Ubu song "Breath." On both of those tracks, she played most of the instruments herself, proving that her musical prowess extends well beyond bass playing. She plans to continue releasing singles as the inspiration strikes.

*   *   *

"I feel, sometimes, like a novelty, or that I'm making someone else money," Popper says of the way her career stands currently. "People will call me and blatantly say, 'We want a woman because we want a woman's energy in the band.' What the fuck does that mean? At the same time, I do understand, in a way.

"I guess, if you want that, just don't tell me. Because I went to music school. I studied. I can write big band charts. I can write horn arrangements. I'm really, really good at my job. And to reduce me to just being a woman when I can clearly do the job better than a lot of men, it's uncomfortable."

On the other hand, some of the gender-related exiling she'd encountered early in her career still lingers: "There was somebody recently, a big artist, who told some friends of mine that he was going to hire me, but he already has a woman in the band. He thought it would be a weird thing to have two women."

Fortunately, even with all this confusion over hiring a female musician, Popper continues to find plenty of work. In 2018, she played on *Painkillers*, a solo album by Gaslight Anthem singer / guitarist Brian Fallon, followed by an extensive tour with him. She continues to pick up tours, one-off gigs, and recording work with a wide array of musicians.

She also frequently contributes to hit soundtracks, such as the film *The Irishman* and television series *Marvelous Miss Maisel*, both in 2019. (Her previous contributions in this capacity include work on 2006's *Short Bus*, 2016's *Vinyl: Music from the HBO Original Series—Vol. 1*, and 2017's *The Only Living Boy in New York*.)

In recent years, she has begun playing bass in the orchestra for Broadway musicals, such as *Head Over Heels* (2018) and *Diana* (2020). She notices that the same questions surrounding gender equity are arising in this arena, too. "It's constant now in the Broadway world: 'We're looking for an all-female [orchestra] pit for this gig.' Somebody called me and said that. And they said, 'We can't find anybody.' And I said, 'Well, I hope your musical director comes to his senses, then.' Because why do this to yourself?" But she concedes, "On the other hand, you're giving women an opportunity who might not [otherwise] have one."

Ultimately, regardless of the type of work Popper is doing, "I feel like there's so much more representation in hiring a mixed, diverse band," she says. "There's just something about seeing and hearing different genders playing together that is appealing."

But if someone does want to hire her because she's a woman? "I don't write it off right away, as long as I feel like my musicality is respected."

PHOTO BY ALLAN AMATO, ASSISTED BY XINE TREVINO

16

Amanda Palmer

Singer-songwriter/performance artist Amanda Palmer has never shied away from creating songs about taboo subjects such as violence and abortion. While the mainstream shuns artists who sing about these things, this approach has earned Palmer a highly devoted cult following—and she makes a point to be equally supportive of her fans in return.

"From the very beginning, I was writing songs, playing those songs for people, and then reading all of the letters and [online] comments. And doing long [autograph] signing lines after every show, listening to all of the rape stories and the abortion stories and the incest stories and the abuse stories and on and on and on," she says. She often hears, "You have finally expressed what I have been feeling. Thank God."

Palmer says she writes these ultra-honest songs, and forges this unusually personal bond with her fans, because "I wanted what so many women coming to my show wanted, which was a sense of connection, and not being alone—I wanted recognition that my experience as a woman wasn't crazy."

Receiving such positive feedback from thousands of fans for the past two decades has, she says, "changed the direction of my art making. I don't take for granted that it turned me into the kind of artist and the kind of songwriter and the kind of person that I am."

* * *

Palmer has been unafraid to court controversy right from the very first time she ever performed one of her own songs for an audience when she was seventeen years old.

She was attending high school in Lexington, Massachusetts, a suburb of Boston, where she adored her drama teacher, Steven Bogart. "He was a massive inspiration and mentor to me," she says. During her senior year, Bogart was tasked with directing a production of the musical *Carousel*, and she joined the cast. "I was only in the chorus. I didn't have one of the lead parts because the musical director thought that I couldn't sing, and she might have been right about that. But, ha ha ha, look at me now," she says, amused.

Though *Carousel* is regarded as one of the most beloved classic musicals, Palmer quickly became disenchanted with it as she attended rehearsals. "I remember reading the lyrics to "What's the Use of Wond'rin'?" And I was horrified. I was like, 'This is a song sung by a woman to another woman about the complete okayness of domestic abuse. This is *fucked up*.'"

She pointed out the problem to Steven Bogart. He agreed with her—but also told her that the school administration had made it clear that *Carousel* must be the musical that year. "So I went home and, in a rage, wrote the song called "June Is Busting Out All Over," which was also the title of a song from *Carousel*—a really very Amanda Palmer-y minor-key ballad, with my tongue fully in my cheek, about domestic abuse and commercialism."

She showed her song to Bogart, who told her she could perform it onstage during the play's intermission. So, along with two of her female castmates and the orchestra, she sang her defiant song in front of a thousand people over the course of three nights.

It was a highly memorable way to begin her performing career. "I stood there gazing into the eyes of the anodyne, suburban, sweet Lexington parents, who were just showing up for *Carousel* the musical, and sang this song that really bubbled out of the bottom of my dark soul. I meant every word of it," she says. "I think people did not know what fuckin' hit them. They were shocked and impressed.

"I didn't realize it at the time, and I think it isn't even really fully occurring to me until now, that that was a life-changing moment because a male ally with power handed me the mic, literally," Palmer says. "Steven Bogart had the balls to let a seventeen-year-old girl insert her super feminist, super anti-commercial, anti-patriarchy anarchist song into the intermission of *Carousel* at a public high school. What a punk rock thing to do. It's because he didn't have to do it, and he did it anyway, that it was such a powerful moment in my life. That this guy, this older teacher who had everything to lose and nothing to gain, was willing to ally with me."

*   *   *

Palmer had actually dreamed of becoming some kind of performer, like a rock star or an actress, for many years before she hit the stage in *Carousel*. "The minute I fully intellectually grasped that it wasn't just a fantasy but a real job that you could have, I wanted that job—and I wanted it with a kind of single-minded clarity," she says, "which of course made it very frustrating when the adults around me thought that it was a silly idea. But I *knew*."

She began writing songs as a very young child. By her mid-teens, she felt she was writing good material, so she recorded it onto cassette tapes—but she didn't dare show her work to anyone. "I think it was probably to my advantage that I incubated out of the public eye, because I know my ego at age fifteen could not have taken the kind of criticism that I see being hurled at anybody and everybody [online]. I was ready to write, but I wasn't ready to be torn apart yet." (She adds with a laugh, "I'm ready now. Bring it on.")

Songwriting was a good emotional outlet for Palmer, who recalls a happy but sometimes complicated childhood. Her parents divorced less than a year after she was born in New York City in 1976. Her mother moved to the Boston area while her father remained in New York, and both of them soon remarried.

"I was exposed to two realities," Palmer says of that time in her life. "There was the reality of my dad and his new wife living on the Upper West Side in Manhattan. And then there was the reality of my mom and my stepdad's world in bucolic Lexington, Massachusetts, which might as well have been another planet."

She was the youngest of four children (two much older step-siblings and an older full sister), which also deeply affected her worldview. "I always desperately wanted to hang out with the older kids. As the youngest, I felt like I was constantly being left out of the fun and not allowed to go to the party. Watching all my older siblings get dolled up at 10 p.m. to go off to *The Rocky Horror Picture Show* while I had to go to bed."

This constant uncertainty about where she belonged ultimately led Palmer to make a pivotal decision: "It seems too cinematic to be true, but there really was a single moment in my life where I felt total clarity: it was the night before the first day of school in eighth grade. I was trying to decide what to wear, and I was looking at all of my very hard-won color-coordinated clothes from Express and The Gap from the mall, because I desperately wanted to fit in and have the right designer clothes and be friends with the popular girls. And I was always failing. And I made this sharp left turn overnight and decided to forsake that particular rat race and embrace my inner weirdo, which had always been kicking around.

"I threw away all of my colored clothing or dyed it black. Dyed my hair black. Bought a cheap black lipstick from CVS, pronounced myself goth, and detached myself from my sister and her friends and all of the popular kids at school, and went off in my own direction. I discovered punk and goth and anything countercultural I could get my hands on. And that was that. I was done with the world of the straight, normal people."

She went on to attend Wesleyan University in Connecticut, where she stayed on her own atypical path, majoring in German Studies while also writing and directing plays. Combining the two interests, she spent a year as an exchange student in Germany, completing an internship at an experimental theater. Through it all, she continued writing edgy, introspective songs.

Even though she was doing well creatively and academically, Palmer also remembers this was a particularly difficult era for her personally. "I really struggled through college. That was a dark time for me. I lost a brother, a boyfriend, and two grandparents, all within six months of each other. And discovered alcohol at the same time. So it was a gnarly cocktail.

"But I look at those years as a very necessary and painful period that I had to survive to wind up where I wound up. Wesleyan was a really progressive university, and I look back at that and do not take it for granted. At Wesleyan, I fully wrapped my head around the possibilities in performance art and the avant-garde.

"I remember in my early twenties going, 'I'm either going to start a band and be a touring rock musician, or I'm going to start a weird experimental theater. And I don't even care [which one], because one will serve the other. If I start a weird experimental theater, I'll probably have a band on the side that plays in the theater. And if I start a band, I'll probably do weird theater stuff onstage that nobody understands.'"

After graduation, Palmer moved to Boston, where she "went through a freewheeling early twenties where I did a billion jobs and really learned how to hustle for money." Her employment ran the gamut: working in a coffee shop, coming up with names for dot-com companies, stripping, and being a dominatrix and nude art model. "I would basically do anything for fifteen bucks an hour or more. Preferably more," she says.

A turning point came when she was twenty-five years old, when she moved into an art collective and began throwing outrageous parties. At one of those gatherings, on Halloween in 2000, she met Brian Viglione, a drummer who had just moved to Boston from New Hampshire the year before. "I played some songs for the guests at the party that night—these really aggressive, strange songs that didn't really resemble anything else—and Brian's jaw dropped to the floor," she says.

Viglione's reaction was distinctly different from the way other musicians had responded to her work, where she could tell they didn't understand what she was trying to do. "And what I really wanted as an artist and a songwriter was to get to the emotional heart of the matter and to play these songs for someone and move them—including the people I was playing the songs with," she says. "I couldn't handle a dispassionate session musician. I was looking for emotional punk rock brothers and sisters."

Feeling hopeful, she asked Viglione to rehearse with her to see what happened. Her instinct proved correct: "The minute Brian and I first played music together, I looked at him and he looked at me and we both practically burst into tears. And I was like, '*I have found you.*'"

Palmer also thought Viglione was a good match for her because of his attitude. "The thing about Brian and my songwriting that was alchemically, unbelievably perfect, was that Brian had feminist values. Brian had an incredibly non-patronizing love and respect for strong women. Brian was the first human being who shook me by the shoulders and said, 'This is incredible. You're a *great* songwriter. I cannot wait to play music with you. Our band is going to be amazing.' His confidence in me was unlike anything I had ever been allowed to experience. Brian absolutely believed in the music and the message of my lyrics and in my rage.

"And I also had the same kind of unreserved belief in Brian's musical abilities. I could not believe that I got to play music with this guy every night. I still believe to this day Brian is ten times the musician that I am. But he wasn't a songwriter. So we were two parts of a whole."

Forming the Dresden Dolls with Viglione, Palmer finally had the esoteric rock band/experimental theater hybrid that she'd dreamed about during her college years. This came across on the duo's albums (2003's *The Dresden Dolls* and 2006's *Yes, Virginia . . .*), but it was especially evident in their imaginative, wide-ranging live shows.

"I was really focused on the entire traveling performance art circus of the Dresden Dolls," she says. "The band was the highlight, but also, I was deeply invested in working with every community and finding the buskers and street performers and performance artists and convincing some local wide-eyed fan who couldn't afford a ticket that if she could bring a typewriter and put it in the bathroom and wear some Christmas lights on her head, that was a fair trade."

But Palmer soon learned that not everyone appreciated the Dresden Dolls' avant-garde ways—and it felt like much of the derision was aimed at her, not Viglione, though he tried to shield her from it. "When Brian sensed that there was a sexist vibe in the room, he spoke up. He was one of the good guys. Brian had zero tolerance for stupid dude shit—and it happened constantly."

It wasn't just audience members being chauvinistic, either. She remembers that all of the sound and light technicians they encountered were men, as well as most of the venue managers. "And it was really fucking uncomfortable. Had I been solo, I think my spirit might have broken."

Still, she knows she fared better than a lot of her female peers in this regard. "Because Brian and I acted as a team, I always walked through the door with a dude, and I was afforded a lot more respect. So I wasn't ever really on the receiving end of the sorts of comments that I hear from a lot from women about, 'Hey, little lady, do you need me to plug in your guitar? Do you know how that amplifier works?'"

She also thinks her own attitude discouraged blatant sexism. "I learned quickly to have a really aggressive exterior to fend off anyone who might question my professionalism. I was afraid of appearing weak. And that meant comporting myself in a really masculine manner, with a really masculine, low tone of voice that people would absolutely take seriously."

In retrospect, Palmer has mixed feelings about the way she handled things. "It was defensive, and it was necessary," she says. "I would argue that I did the right thing because the alternative probably would have been getting squished. But it's still a bummer. I look back with some regret because I think, like a lot of women in a lot of professions, I made my exterior so hard that I calcified. And I did that at the expense of what might have also been on offer on the soft and vulnerable side, which can also have its own value."

Still, the Dresden Dolls gave Palmer the kind of support system that she needed to come into her own as an artist. By 2008, though, she and Viglione were burnt out, and they amicably agreed to put the band on hiatus. "We toured ourselves into the ground," she says. "Basically, we veered off the road while going at 110 miles an hour."

*   *   *

Buoyed by the Dresden Dolls' success, Palmer felt confident enough to strike out on her own. She released her debut solo album, *Who Killed Amanda Palmer*, in 2008. Her 2012 follow-up, *Theatre Is Evil*, reached the Top 10 on the US "*Billboard* 200" album chart.

During this time, her personal life was also evolving. In 2011, she married famed novelist Neil Gaiman. That raised her profile—but this experience could be unpleasant. "One of the things that I took away from my relationship with Neil was just how deeply sexist the world is—and Neil would be the first one to point it out," she says. "Neil and I could literally say and do the same thing, and I would be painted as the hysterical, crazy woman, and he would be painted as the delightful genius.

"Even though my career and my success way predated my relationship with Neil, I would see, and Neil would see, people on the internet saying, 'Of course Neil Gaiman must have done that for her.' Including the book that I wrote that became a best-seller," she says, referencing *The Art of Asking: How I Learned to Stop Worrying and Let People Help* (2015), which marked her debut as an author. "Oh, it was so infuriating."

On the other hand, Palmer can see why she and Gaiman spark such differing responses. "Neil is a much more private person than I am," she says. "He does not blog about his trauma, his experiences, his childhood, his feelings, his relationships. And I do. And people find it very threatening. They always have. From the early days of my blog in 2001, I encountered a lot of hostility, just because I was a woman chatting about my feelings. There are times when I am very tempted to say, 'Man, I wish I could go back thirty years and make it all fictional. People wouldn't have yelled at me if I had just written fiction.'

"And yet, I wouldn't change a thing, because I know that I did it because I *needed* to do it. And I know that I've passed that torch on to [the next] generation of women who are going to be a little less afraid to speak the truth in their art."

Palmer took the confessional nature of her work to a whole new level in 2015. That year, she and Gaiman welcomed their son, Ash, and she wrote and released the song "A Mother's Confession" soon after, detailing how harrowing parenting can be.

"[Motherhood is] a messy undertaking," she says. "The patriarchy has a lot of reasons to want to paint motherhood as a soft, delightful thing. And it is *not* a soft, delightful thing. It surely has soft, delightful moments in it, but it's a brutal, agonizing, bloody job being a mother."

Her lyrics reflect that reality, including describing a terrifying near-accident that happened when she was caring for Ash on her own. "It was the first song that I wrote as a mother. I went to visit my friend Jason Webley when Ash was three or four months old. Jason and I are both songwriters, and we challenged one another to see if we could both write a song really quickly while Ash took a nap.

"What was in my head that day was this collage of really painful experiences that had happened the day before, and the week before, that presented a pretty good messy finger painting of what having a baby feels like—which is utter annihilation and confusion, but also a kind of vulnerability and awe as you walk through the world with this little baby in your arms."

Knowing that this song, as she puts it, "had no fucking commercial appeal," she released it to her followers on Patreon, the online crowdfunding platform she joined in 2015. Listeners' response was immediate and intense. Even Palmer was surprised to find out how her lyrics were interpreted.

"It resonated with anyone who's ever taken care of a baby. It resonated, shockingly, with people who have lost children. The chorus says, 'At least the baby didn't die.' And in some cases, the baby *does* die. It dredged up all of the darkness for the people on my Patreon—and in the audience of my shows—whose sons and daughters had committed suicide, and that song took on an entirely new meaning. But this is what happens when you're an artist who dabbles in the emotional cauldron. You don't think of these things. And then you take your songs out into the world, and you find out what they mean as you are singing them to your people."

In 2019, she tackled another taboo topic with "Voicemail for Jill," in which she offers comfort to a woman who is about to have an abortion. It is a subject she understands well, having gone through three abortions of her own.

"I had been trying to write a good abortion song since I was seventeen, [when] I had my first abortion. I just thought, 'I need this song to exist. I didn't have a song like this to listen to when I went through my abortion. I can't retroactively go back and give it to myself, but I can give it to somebody else.'

"Just like motherhood, people have ideas about what abortion is and what the experience of an abortion may or may not feel like. It's complicated. There are plenty of abortions that happen where there isn't a huge, complex emotion that goes along with them. Then there are abortions that are absolutely heartbreaking. And everything in between. It really does feel like if we're going to try and untie this nine-foot knot, you've got to start with being honest about what the thing in itself is. So I wrote that song as my bid to normalize not just the experience of having an abortion, but the experience of writing a song about an abortion."

Once again, listeners let Palmer know that she was speaking their truth. "Nobody on Instagram, Twitter, or Facebook is going to say, 'Hey, your song about abortion really got me through a rough day yesterday.' But everybody comes to me privately. They come to me through my Patreon messages or through DM's or backstage at a show."

Inspiring this kind of reaction lets Palmer know that she has succeeded in creating a deep connection with her audience, just as she'd aspired to do when she first began her career. For her, it is therapy—and activism. "I feel like, as with rape and incest and all sorts of things, one of the most powerful things we can do as artists is take a teeny, little Shawshank nail file to the taboo and keep chipping away at the silence around it," she says.

*　　*　　*

As Palmer nears twenty-five years of being in the public eye, she continues her unapologetically confessional, nonconformist output. In 2019, she released her third solo album, *There Will Be No Intermission*. The next year, she began a podcast, *The Art of Asking Everything*. And, in 2022, she announced that she's resurrecting the Dresden Dolls with Brian Viglione.

"We're finally coming full circle," she says. "It feels really poetic that this would be the moment in history where the Dresden Dolls finally get back together to ying and yang onstage because we are a powerful force, but everything needed to be worked through and aligned for us to get back together. And I think we are both much more compassionate and powerful people than we were in our totally lost and flailing—and beautiful—first chapter."

She credits her Patreon followers for giving her the freedom to continue her artistic endeavors without the constraints that would come with signing to a traditional record label. "I think that crowdfunding and patronage is one of the most powerful feminist tools that exist in the music industry," she says. "I'm a working mother who does not want to do brand sponsorships or sit around a boardroom with fucking old white men telling me that every decision they're about to make on my behalf is for my own good and that I am a silly little girl who doesn't really understand how the real world works.

"The most obvious door out of that kind of hell is doing business directly with the people who want my art. And that group of people, which right now stands at about eleven thousand patrons, are directly making it possible for me to do motherhood and make art on my own schedule, as my own boss. On Patreon, I am allowed to say, 'This is what I think has value this month. This poem. This video. This podcast. This essay.' It's a huge step for feminism, given how deeply controlled women's fates, destinies, and careers in the arts have become."

She fully expects that her art—and her perspectives—will keep evolving, just as she can see has happened through the past two decades. "I look back at the story I was telling myself and the story I was telling the world in 2002 and 2008 and 2012 and even 2019," she says, "and I find myself cocking my head and thinking, 'Oh, you poor girl. You didn't quite understand everything back then.' It's progress and also devolution, both going at the speed of light, and you find yourself trapped in a rabbit hole of your own recontextualization as you look at the choices you made. And it's frustrating because hindsight is always 20/20."

Still, Palmer is satisfied with what she has achieved. "When I do the giant career retrospective when I'm eighty-five, I think the songwriting will be a big part of it, and my piano and vocal abilities will be a big part of it, but I sometimes feel like the biggest thing that I will have accomplished is creating space for women to feel a bit less alone and a bit less crazy."

17

Bonnie Bloomgarden (Death Valley Girls)

"Almost every club we go into, you are treated like a girl," says Death Valley Girls leader Bonnie Bloomgarden. "You are treated like someone that doesn't know their own equipment, that doesn't know how to use the venue's equipment, that maybe has never even seen a mic stand before. They'll adjust your amp, and they'll look at you like you're some two-year-old. And you're like, 'Oh, boy—thank you *so much!*' You have to be so thankful. Then after seeing you play, those same people are buying you shots because they're like, 'Whoa, that was amazing!' They're shocked. It's crazy." She sighs, exasperated. "This is my job—I know how to do it."

Bloomgarden is certainly no amateur. Death Valley Girls—playing what Bloomgarden describes as "cosmic rock and roll space gospel"—have crisscrossed the world building up a reputation as a stellar live band since their formation in Los Angeles in 2013. They've also released five critically acclaimed studio albums and numerous standalone singles.

Despite those accomplishments, Bloomgarden says she feels compelled to thank the men who treat her like a know-nothing instead of setting them straight "because we're at work. You can't tell people off at work. That's not professional. What they're doing is not professional, but combating their rudeness with rudeness doesn't work. The best thing you can do is just play a really good show and blow their minds."

Unfortunately, Bloomgarden is familiar with being treated differently because of her gender when she's not at work, too. "The way society is structured is to size up all these different aspects of each female—or non-male—we come across," she says.

"There is not a person that walks by that doesn't completely judge all the aspects of me—and with men that doesn't happen," she continues. "You look at them and there's one or two words [to describe them], like 'sports fan.' For me, people notice lipstick, makeup, type of shoe. Am I dressed slutty? Am I dressed frumpy? Am I skinny, am I fat? Am I pretty? Am I old? There's a million things, and all of those things go into how they judge you.

"And the reason I know that—and the reason probably every woman knows that—is because when you do one thing to dress up, it changes your whole day, as far as how you're treated. When you tour around the country and you're wearing your sweats going into the gas station because you've been waiting five hours to pee and you don't smile, you're treated a whole different way."

Her experiences have caused her to rethink her approach. "For a while I was like, 'I'm not a feminist because there shouldn't have to be that.' I don't like that that label has to exist. But I totally am [a feminist], and I totally want to be. I believe in equality for all, and I believe that no one is any less important than anybody else. And I simply cannot believe that anybody disagrees with that."

Bloomgarden admits that until the pandemic began in 2020, she resisted talking about the types of challenges that women routinely face. "Before COVID-19, I liked to point out positives," she says, adding that she did this to perpetuate a more optimistic view. "But I think now we need to talk about all of it. All of it matters."

* * *

Bloomgarden knows from firsthand experience what happens when negativity is suppressed for too long.

"I got super sick from storing emotions," she says. "I got a fever for five months in 2021. I went to a bunch of doctors. Some recommended surgery, all these different things. But honestly, it was just emotions. You hear, 'You're going to worry yourself to death,' and I was doing that. It was because I didn't ever have the time to stop and feel the emotions I was having. I just locked them away, and it's because we're not really taught that being an emotional being is good."

She thinks this is true for everybody, but especially for females. "Something that's different about women than men is that we've been really taught to just shut up and keep pushing on. That what our bodies are telling us is not important: 'Push past the pain.' We've been taught to not really listen to ourselves. And because of that, if COVID didn't happen and I didn't get a break, I think I was about to crack."

She explains that this was because, much as she loves being in Death Valley Girls, their success has hinged on an intense amount of effort. For instance, for the years between the band's formation up until the pandemic resulted in widespread lockdowns in March 2020, "We went on tour every other month. What you do on tour is you forgo all of your earthly desires and food needs and restroom needs and every kind of need you can imagine to be a perfect team member. Where you're easy to be around and you're going with the flow. And when you practice that for a month straight every other month, you stop being in touch with yourself and your physical nature. It's not good for your mental health, either."

Bloomgarden was growing up in the West L.A. neighborhood of Los Angeles, California, when she first learned how society seems to want to ignore people's emotions and slot them into easy categories, even if it's at the expense of that person's well-being. Born in 1981, she calls herself "an '80s and '90s kid." Back then, "There were just two boxes you could fit into: Barbie or G.I. Joe," she says. "That was how you were defined, as either one thing or the other."

The problem was, as a tomboy, she didn't neatly fit into that idealized feminine stereotype. "I'm not sure why, but the most important thing for me is that I've always wanted to be the toughest person. I don't like girly stuff." As a result, within the wider culture, "I always felt out of place. I've always felt like I was doing something wrong."

While still a child, she sensed that this seemed unfair. "It occurred to me that society is trying to have this duality, instead of encouraging everyone's individuality." She feels this is true for everyone, not just women: "It's not always easy for every man to be a man either. It's not fair or healthy or right for anyone—male, female, or anyone in between—to be told how to be themselves, or to be directed to be someone else. It's this societal thing, this idea that there's two different things and you are just one, and that if you don't fit into that, there's something wrong with you. Having to fit into either box is the biggest problem in the world, as I see it."

But she also found a silver lining to her outsider status: "I think by being forced into two boxes and not fitting in either of them, you have to find something outside of society, which is why I found music. People in the art and music scene aren't as judgmental and want to see what makes you special. It's kind of the only safe place to do it in our culture."

Even here, though, she took an unusual path. Instead of following the music that was currently popular, she chose to listen to artists who'd become famous in previous decades: soul and R&B legends such as Otis Redding and Sam Cooke, or rock bands from the 1960s. Then, when she got to high school, she became obsessed with jazz.

"I didn't learn about music that was going on currently," Bloomgarden remembers about those years. "I didn't know about punk or anything. At that time, everyone was into hip-hop, or I don't know what else. I was trying to be like a rebel and be into jazz. I didn't want to listen to what anyone else listened to. I wanted to be *so* unique," she says with a laugh.

As she began thinking about becoming a singer herself, it never occurred to her that most of her musical idols were male. "I didn't really ever think about gender. I didn't realize that there were fewer women, ever. I would see the Rolling Stones and I would just think, 'That's a job I want.'"

Her feelings about music were reinforced when she was going through a particularly rough time. "I went to the looney bin when I was fifteen because I was super depressed," she says, "and one of the psych nurses that worked there was really cool. He was [also] a musician, and we talked about music."

That nurse encouraged Bloomgarden's dream of seriously pursuing music. Feeling inspired as she left the psychiatric hospital, she enrolled in a jazz program when she returned to school. That, in turn, led her to move to New York City after graduation so that she could continue studying jazz singing at Hunter College.

Once there, though, her insecurities resurfaced. "I was too scared to sing," she says. "I would ditch every time we had a test or I had to perform. The teacher was like, 'You can't be a singer if you can't sing!'"

Despite being too petrified to perform, she still knew that singing was what she was destined to do. "Spiritually, I've been told a few times from healers that I used to be a channeler—like a medium," she says. "I also have been a jazz singer in past lives. And I believe that to be true. I feel very compelled to channel energy and readminister it to a large group of people. I think that's what I'm meant to do, in the purest of ways: that's just who you are, what you do, what pulls you. Nothing could stop you."

As a result, she says, "I kept forcing myself to sing." To stretch herself beyond what she was learning at school, she also joined a rock band, the Witnesses, as a keyboard player and backup singer. She was the only female member, but "that was my first band, so that seemed normal."

She doesn't remember any fuss being made over her gender within the wider New York music community, either. "No one asked me what it was like to be a girl then," she says, even though she only recalls there being four or five women who were active in that the city's rock scene at the time (including Yeah Yeah Yeahs singer Karen O). "It's so weird, but there really were so few, and nobody ever talked about it. It was like a secret or something."

Being in a supportive band within an equally supportive music community helped draw Bloomgarden out of her shell. Too shy to sing without covering her face when she first joined the Witnesses, she gradually grew confident enough to perform without fear in front of an audience.

Although she was personally blossoming within the Witnesses, being in the band was a difficult experience overall. "It was a strange time in this country," she recalls. "Our first show was a week after 9/11, and the world just changed so much." As the band traveled from city to city for gigs, she noticed a heightened suspicion of anyone who seemed different, and this seemed especially evident when they played shows in the South. "We looked funny, and everyone harassed us."

Still, the Witnesses toured relentlessly, building up a following in the United States. They became successful enough that Bloomgarden dropped out of college so she could work with the band on a full-time basis. Between 2002 and 2006, they released two EPs and two full-length studio albums.

Eventually, though, the band seemed to run out of steam, and the members agreed to call it quits. Bloomgarden moved back to Los Angeles, where she reinvented herself. "I got off drugs and worked really, really hard at a job," she says. She initiated the creation of a food truck and ran it herself for Canter's Deli, the much-beloved California restaurant chain that was founded in 1931 by Ben Canter, her great-grandfather. Determined to stay clean and succeed in her family's business, she estimates that she routinely put in eighty-hour work weeks.

Adding to the stress, "I found myself in an abusive relationship," she says. "I didn't even realize what was happening. I basically lost my whole self over that time. I had gotten [physically] healthy, but not mentally."

After two years of this, she realized that things had to dramatically change. She started by quitting both the food truck and the relationship. Then, deciding that her happiness depended on getting back into music, she set herself a deadline: she had one month to form a rock band. If that didn't work, she would return to New York and try to start over again in the music scene there.

She knew that she was on the right track when, only one week later, her sister introduced her to Patty Schemel, who had been the drummer for the seminal alternative rock band Hole from 1992 to 1998. Schemel was, like Bloomgarden, a recovering addict, so they could support each other in their sobriety. They decided to form Death Valley Girls along with Schemel's brother, Larry (guitar), and Rachel Orosco (bass).

For Bloomgarden, Death Valley Girls immediately felt perfect. She had found bandmates who were interested in playing their own original material, not cover songs. Like her, they also wanted to use music as a means to escape from the stresses of the real world. And they were all sober, so she didn't have to worry about anyone pressuring her to return to bad habits. It was as if she had found a family that she hadn't known existed before.

She thinks that Larry Schemel has been equally content, despite his unusual position of being the only male in the band lineup: "He grew up with two older sisters. I think it would be hard for a boy that hasn't had sisters to be in this dynamic, but he understands all that we go through. We always have girl tour managers, too. I think he likes it. No bro energy! He's a good guy."

Death Valley Girls practiced for a year before playing a gig, perfecting a distinctive euphoric, off-kilter blend of garage rock and punk—though Bloomgarden admits with a laugh that this was not at all what she'd originally had in mind: "It started out that I was just trying to rip off Tina Turner. We unsuccessfully channeled Tina Turner, but successfully found our own sound."

In 2014, the band released their debut album, *Street Venom*, and received much critical praise. Soon after, Patty Schemel amicably left the group to pursue other creative endeavors. Many others have joined the band for their subsequent album releases: *Glow in the Dark* (2016), *Darkness Rains* (2018), *Under the Spell of Joy* (2020), and *Islands in the Sky* (2023). Through it all, Bloomgarden and Larry Schemel have remained the band's constant members.

Bloomgarden was, for the first two albums, the band's only vocalist, but since then, they've included backing vocals from other members—a move she believes has had "a huge positive effect on the music." There have also been notable guest vocal groups, as with the children's chorus that was featured prominently on *Under the Spell of Joy*. Though she had worked so hard to become comfortable as a vocalist, Bloomgarden says she decided to share that role with others so Death Valley Girls would become more "like a choir, or like [pioneering funk/soul group] Sly and the Family Stone." This multi-voice sound has become one of Death Valley Girls' most distinctive features.

The band's image is equally imaginative. Bloomgarden says she puts a lot of thought into her onstage outfits, feeling that this is an important part of the way performers convey their message to the audience. "Some [performers] dress super, super sexy, which I think is good, so that people can see that and know that it's okay," she says, "but I just went through a phase where I was like, 'I'm going to dress like a Puritan to show that that can be sexy, too.'"

While the band's profile has steadily risen through their decade of existence, they got a significant boost in 2018 when legendary rocker Iggy Pop starred in their video for the single "Disaster (Is What We're After)." The clip simply features Pop (nattily dressed in a suit and tie) eating a hamburger, in a sendup of a 1982 film in which the artist Andy Warhol did the same. The director, Kansas Bowling, had worked with Death Valley Girls on several previous videos; Bloomgarden credits her for coming up with the concept and convincing Pop to do it.

Though Bloomgarden and her bandmates don't appear in the video, they were present for the filming near Pop's home in Miami, Florida. It was, she says, a "magical, magical experience. It seems like it would be scary, but it wasn't. It felt like I imagine it would feel like to be in front of the Dalai Lama. Just super chill. I hate to say this because it sounds so pompous, but he did say we are a gift to the world." She pauses, then adds, "It still feels funny to say a compliment about yourself."

*　　*　　*

Though she's still working on comfortably claiming the praise that she's earned, Bloomgarden knows she's become far more self-assured since she joined Death Valley Girls. She believes that this has been possible because this band allowed her to finally figure out her true self and have the freedom to express it.

"I've had a really hard time being in a human body," she says, "but every year, I feel a little bit stronger. I get more confident that I'm helping other people and not hurting them. I think that us being up there onstage is so helpful because we're pursuing our dreams, and everyone needs to know that they should pursue their dreams."

She often sees evidence that she and her bandmates are inspiring others to achieve self-discovery, especially their female fans: "At every show, a kid will come up and go, 'I didn't know that I could be in a band.' Or, 'You guys inspired me to learn how to play bass.' I think it's because so many girls are playing now that people are like, 'I can do that? I didn't know that.' Everyone can have an example of a female musical hero, where maybe not everyone had one before."

This is Bloomgarden's way of fighting back against the societal expectations surrounding gender that had so confused her as a child. "Everyone is being told how they're supposed to be in their body: 'You're supposed to be more manly. You're supposed to be more girly.' All these 'supposed to's' are keeping people from being who they are."

She also points to the current high-profile media attention surrounding transgender matters as an important example of progress in this regard. "You hear people say things like, 'Why are there so many gender-fluid people now?' It's because they see it in popular culture, and they see that what they're feeling is real and they see it represented. They know that it's okay to have those feelings.

"I think, in a lot of ways, the people that are outside of the two [gender] boxes are the ones that are helping women get recognized. It's like, no one's equal until we're *all* equal. I think things are getting better and better because they're getting talked about. That's what has to happen now for change."

She hopes that this transformation will extend to the way female musicians are regarded, too, so she'll no longer have to endure sexism as she and Death Valley Girls continue their career. She feels like there is still a long way to go in this area, though. "'Women in music' definitely seems like a genre. You would never be like, 'Let's look at music in the male singer section.' And even though it seems like there's so many [female artists] now, it still is a genre of music, which is weird."

But in music—and in society overall—Bloomgarden sees reason for hope: "There's still work to do, but I think the pendulum is swinging," she says. "I feel like if people have a positive, healthy, physical way to express their emotions, the world will definitely be a better place."

18

Orianthi

Orianthi, amused, recalls her mindset when she was a kid: "I knew exactly what I wanted: 'I'm moving to America. I'm going to have a hit single. I'm going to drive a Cadillac.'"

It's unknown whether the celebrated guitarist has that Caddy yet. But she not only accomplished those first two goals, she has far exceeded them. She did, in fact, relocate from her native Australia to Los Angeles. Then her debut single, "According to You" (2009), charted in a half dozen countries, including making the Top 10 in the United States, Japan, and Australia. As a hard rock guitarist/vocalist, she's released five studio albums (her latest, *Rock Candy*, came out in 2022). Equally adept across a wide range of styles, she's also been handpicked by Michael Jackson, Carrie Underwood, and Alice Cooper, among other major music stars, to play guitar for their bands.

By any reasonable measure, she is a highly successful musician. Yet she has been startled to find that she is often singled out for being "the *female* guitarist," not simply "the guitarist." She initially encountered this when, at fourteen years old, she watched venues use "girl guitarist" as a marketing gimmick for her shows. This made her feel "like I'm a strange animal at the zoo. I felt like a circus act or something."

Now in her thirties, she still sometimes encounters this type of attitude—and she's no more used to it than she was two decades ago. "It honestly has been a really strange thing to me because I just never think about it," she says of her gender.

This is why she hesitates to call herself a feminist. She is, instead, an advocate for all humankind: "Honestly, for me, I'm about equality for everybody on this planet, especially when it comes to being a guitar player and musician," she says. "If it's good and you're singing and playing with conviction and it's coming from the heart, [and] as long as you make people feel something, then that's what should matter. It's just putting your art out there. That should speak for itself, whether it's coming from a man or a woman. I just wish that this world was more about people and character and not that divide of male-female. But hey, it is what it is, right? I just try to let that go."

But even as she tries not to dwell on gender, Orianthi still admits that the music business is what she terms "an environment where there is a sense of 'boys club,'" so she has some advice for female aspiring artists: "Be you. And don't let anyone tell you that it's not possible, because that's so hindering. Fear, I think, comes in as you get older because people tell you, 'Oh, you can't do that; you're crazy.' That's just so bad. Never dim your light. Always stand in it and always try to inspire other people with what you do."

* * *

Orianthi herself has never had a problem with defying anyone she believes is trying to diminish her dreams. Even as a kid, she recalls, "I didn't like authority figures. I didn't like rules. I just thought, 'Be a good person, but do your own thing. Create your own path.'"

Born Orianthi Panagaris, she grew up in Adelaide, South Australia. She wasn't concerned with fitting in with other girls her own age. "I was a bit of a tomboy, I guess," she says. "I had more guy friends than girlfriends."

She was also unusual when it came to musical taste. "Everyone else is listening to New Kids on the Block at that point. I always felt like an outsider in that sense, just because of the fact that I was brought up in this time warp, listening to my dad's vinyl collection. He would always be playing records: Elvis Presley, Jimi Hendrix, Santana. So all these wild sounds are coming out of the living room, and I was like, 'What is that?'"

Even then, she didn't favor one gender over the other: "I listened to Bonnie Raitt. I listened to Eric Clapton. I like both. I don't say, 'That's a female singer; that's a male singer.' They're both awesome and they make me feel something. Art is art, right?"

Besides sharing his record collection with her, Orianthi's father also inspired her with his own musicianship. "My dad's a guitar player. I'm half Greek, so he played in a Greek band," she says. Though she'd taken piano lessons since she was three years old, the guitar seemed far more appealing to her. Watching him play, she remembers thinking, "That's so cool. I want to do that!"

When she was six years old, her father taught her a few guitar chords, and she knew she had found what she was meant to do. "I'm like, 'Well, this is who I am. I'm an artist.' After that, I was completely addicted to playing guitar."

She'd stay in her bedroom and practice for seven hours at a stretch, "trying to learn every Santana song, every [Jimi] Hendrix track. I was like, 'I've got to learn every solo.' I would play along and pretend I was sitting in with them. It was an obsession, just wanting to be better, and feeling like this instrument is magical. Endless possibilities."

This established a pattern that she has repeated throughout her life. "I guess with my personality, if I want to do something, I just do it. I lock myself away and don't speak to people for months. I'm weird like that."

With her skills rapidly improving, the urge to perform soon kicked in. "When I was seven or eight, I was opening school assemblies with my friends as backup dancers. It was really weird. I had a Beatles haircut, and I was obnoxious. My mother was worried."

Her mother's concern only grew as this music obsession began affecting Orianthi's education. "I kept wanting to change schools because I didn't like the teachers. I didn't like to deal with them." Every time she'd switch, "I'd be like, 'I have to meet the headmaster before I decide if I'm going to this school.'

At eight years old, nine years old, I would be interviewing the headmaster to see if he would allow my music, because I wanted to play guitar and open [school] assemblies with my band. I was making sure the headmaster was cool with that. I was really kind of full of myself as a kid. I was very bossy. I was like, 'This is what I want to do.'"

She didn't mind studying if it was something that would improve her guitar playing, though. At ten years old, she took lessons in classical guitar and how to sight read written music. She also enrolled in music theory courses at a local university. "I was the youngest [enrolled] there ever, I think," she says, "and they thought I was really weird."

She ignored the skeptics and soon made significant progress in her music career. At only ten years old, she got her first professional performing job when she joined the orchestra, as the sole guitar player, for a local theatrical production of the musical *Oklahoma!* "I got a lot of dust kicked on me from all the stage stuff going on. I thought it was fun," she says of that experience.

But rock music was what she really wanted to play—so she started writing her own songs. At fourteen years old, she signed her first management deal, which led to an opening slot for American guitar virtuoso Steve Vai when he came to Adelaide.

"I was so nervous," she says of that show. "Steve was at the side of the stage, watching me. [Afterward], he was like, 'Let's keep in contact. Send me your demos. I really like what you're doing.'

"We stayed in contact. I would send Steve songs. He would write to me and say, 'Hey, that sounds good, but maybe try this'—constructive criticism that really helped me as a player and writer. That, I will forever be grateful for—the fact that he took the time and listened to this fourteen-year-old crazy hippie kid from Australia. It was like, 'Wow, this is awesome.'"

She quit school when she was fifteen years old and joined three cover bands. "The freedom in music was more appealing to me than school," she says, "so I wanted to follow my heart and that freedom." To her, it seemed like she was emulating the musical innovators she admired: "Prince, [Jimi] Hendrix, Santana, all these different influences—there was a sense of freedom and joy in their music and playing that really resonated with me."

By her late teens, Orianthi was ready for her biggest challenge yet: recording her debut album—and doing it entirely by herself. "I'm going to play every instrument. I'm going to write every song. I went down to a [recording] studio in Adelaide and learned how to engineer and how to mic things. Produced it myself. Played drums, everything. I would practice drums for hours and hours—and then bass, and then keys."

She remembers her routine during this time: drinking copious amounts of coffee and Diet Coke so she could stay awake and keep working, "I'd be up until 7 a.m. My parents would be going to work, and I'd be going to bed." When they got home that evening, she'd show them what she'd created that day. Then she'd wolf down some food that her sister had brought from her job at a Subway sandwich shop, sleep for a few hours, and repeat the whole cycle. This went on until she finished the album. The entire process took seven months.

During those months, her motivation never faltered. "I became like a crazy scientist. No drugs involved. It was literally just feeling like, *'I'm going to do this.'*" If anyone tried to discourage her, she shook it off. "No one can change my mind—I'm really stubborn."

Finally, *Violet Journey* was finished, and she released the album herself in 2005. "I sent it out to everybody"—including Carlos Santana's management—"and Santana's brother wrote back an email and said, 'We've been playing your record in our offices, and we all love it.' I was blown away by that."

Word spread about *Violet Journey*, until all her hard work was finally rewarded: "I got a record deal with Jimmy Iovine at Interscope with that record." Iovine is one of the most legendary figures in the music business; he'd started out as a recording engineer, and later became the cofounder and head of Interscope Records (now Interscope Geffen A&M Records under the Universal Music Group). Iovine has worked with a slew of significant artists, such as John Lennon, Bruce Springsteen, U2, Stevie Nicks, Tom Petty and the Heartbreakers, the Pretenders, Tupac

Shakur, and many more. Signing a deal with him was the big break Orianthi needed.

With this success under her belt, she was able to achieve her goal of moving to America.

*   *   *

Orianthi left Adelaide for Los Angeles in 2006. Though her mother and sister flew with her to the United States and helped her settle in, their work obligations meant they couldn't stay for long, so she soon found herself alone in a foreign city.

She quickly found her footing, though. "The people at the [record] label made me feel pretty good. I made pretty fast friends. I got my band together, so they became friends," she says.

She also found acceptance within the L.A. nightlife scene. "I was across from [shopping and entertainment complex] The Grove, which is a celebrity-filled environment. So my place was pretty much party central for a while."

Still, she never lost sight of the fact that she was there to carve out a music career. Word spread about her guitar-playing abilities, and she was hired to play in the backing band for the popular country singer Carrie Underwood. In that capacity, Orianthi performed at the 2009 Grammy Awards.

Soon after that, pop superstar Michael Jackson gave her the coveted position of lead guitarist in his band for "This Is It," his much-anticipated concert residency of fifty shows that was meant to occur in 2009 and 2010 at London's O2 Arena.

"Michael saw me on the Grammy Awards with Carrie Underwood. That's how I got chosen, because he saw me on that and then he asked around, and [Carlos] Santana actually recommended me to Michael. I'll be forever grateful for that."

That residency never happened, though—instead, it turned out to be Jackson's final project before his death from an accidental drug overdose on June 25, 2009, when he was only fifty years old. Though they never got to do shows in front of a live audience, footage from rehearsals (released as part of the 2009 documentary film *Michael Jackson's "This Is It"*) shows the ease with which Orianthi and Jackson performed together. More than a dozen years later, she still sounds somber when she reflects on that time. "I think everyone that went through that experience with Michael is bonded for life—we hang out every other week, basically."

It was a harsh lesson in how unpredictable a music career can be, but she refused to let it break her. "It's never easy sailing. You make it look that way on social media and all of that, but you don't post the photos of you in the corner crying. But you have to get yourself up again, and that's life.

"We are all energy fields, and whatever we emit, that's what we attract. It's really easy with this industry to be weighed down by a lot of fear and uncertainty. Once that creeps in too much, you've got to replace it with positivity and reprogram your thoughts. Love is the highest frequency."

*   *   *

Even as Orianthi became known as a well-respected guitarist-for-hire for some of the world's biggest stars, she never stopped pursuing her own solo career. In the gap left by the ill-fated "This Is It" shows, she released *Believe*, her second album, in October 2009. It reached number 77 on the US "*Billboard* 200" chart.

Unlike *Violet Journey*, where Orianthi had been in charge of everything, *Believe* was a team effort—and it was a team mostly comprised of men. Still, she didn't find this problematic, for that album recording process or any of them since: "I make sure I'm heard," she says.

To do that, "I tend to stay quiet, and then they get concerned," she says. "Silence is more powerful than arguing, I find. Silence does speak volumes. Then they're like, 'What's going on?'" That is the point, she says, when it's okay to voice your dissent with what's being suggested. "As an artist, I get very emotional about things—but I've learned over the years, it doesn't serve yourself or the situation or other people. The best thing to do is remain calm and centered. [So] you just say, 'Hey, I'm really not feeling that.' And you say it in a really truthful way.

"If you have control over your emotions and how you're really feeling, that speaks louder than you going irrational like,

'Oh my God, this is terrible!' I've seen that so many times, where people get really upset: 'They made me do this!' It's like, no—no one can *make* you do anything. You can do whatever you want to do. But you have to take control of the situation yourself."

The first single from *Believe*, "According to You," made the charts in several countries, and achieved platinum sales status in the United States and Australia. In it, Orianthi sings to a former flame, telling him all the ways in which her new boyfriend loves everything about her that the ex never appreciated.

"That song is such an empowering message about not staying in a situation where you don't feel valued, and knowing your self-worth," she says. "I got so many messages going, 'I heard that song and it made me want to break up with my boyfriend, so I did, and thank you for that.' You put on that song and it's like, 'I'm beautiful, I'm incredible'—everyone is, in their own way. And that's why that song did well, because it connected with people, in a sense of celebrating your self-worth. It can get beaten out of you, that's for sure, especially in relationships. When your heart's involved, you become very vulnerable."

She knows this from personal experience. "I take things to heart. I'm a very all-in person—with my friends, and especially [romantic] relationships. And after you go through a few of those where it's really bad heartbreak, you really get the blues. You give everything, and they don't value [it]. It's mortifying."

For someone so committed to her career, Orianthi admits that she's still working on integrating her personal life. "I haven't found that right balance yet, that's for sure," she says. "I've chosen right now to be alone. I date, of course, but right now I'm more about my career and happiness, as opposed to being in a serious relationship."

But she has a long-term plan for herself in this regard: "I want to tour a lot more and put out a few more records. Then I think I want to have a ranch in Nashville with chickens, and definitely have a family. That's probably my next thing. I see it being a really good balance, actually. I've seen people make it work. I would love to have that. So I'm going to really focus on my career for a minute, and [then] I want to be settled down in a healthy environment, surrounded by a lot of animals, and focus on a home life, too."

*   *   *

For now, though, Orianthi remains firmly focused on her career. While her guitar playing and singing skills are at the heart of what she does, she also thoroughly enjoys the image aspect of being in show business. This is another way in which she feels she's following the tradition that her musical idols established.

"My favorite artists when I was six years old were Elvis Presley, Roy Orbison, and the Beatles. Then it was Santana, Eric Clapton, and Jimi Hendrix. And they all had an image," she says. "I mean, that's part of your brand. And that, to me, was really strong. As a kid, I always thought Elvis Presley had a really strong sense of himself. It's iconic. He wore the suits; his hair was perfect. Everything was a certain way. And Dolly Parton, Cher, all these people, I love their style. I love that whole aspect of this business. It's exciting."

As a result, her own onstage image is quite striking. "It's all show business, so your outfit should go with the music. I'm kind of like a peacock: I wear the colorful shit—it's a whole situation. Because life's too short to be boring." She makes sure that her guitars are equally glitzy and memorable.

Her love for blending music with a theatrical image came in handy when, in 2011, she became the lead guitarist for legendary shock rocker Alice Cooper. She was the first female member of his band, but "I didn't think too much about it, to be honest with you," she says. "I just wanted to serve the song and performance and bring entertainment value to the show. That was my concern: that, ultimately, Alice—the boss—was happy."

She first met Cooper when she was hired to appear with him on a season finale episode of the hit television show *American Idol*, playing his 1972 hit "School's Out." For that occasion, she dressed as a schoolgirl, put her hair in pigtails, and adopted a bratty persona as she played the song's iconic riffs.

"Then Alice and I and Bob Ezrin, his producer, ended up hanging out after the show and chatting. It felt really comfortable to me. They just seemed like really great people. Alice and I got on really well. Bob then called me to do a session with him and Fefe Dobson, this great singer from Canada. Love her. We did the song "Can't Breathe"—I played all the guitars on that, which was a big single for her [in 2010], and Bob produced that."

When Cooper later called to invite her to join his band, she agreed—but there was a catch: she had only one week to learn twenty-five songs before the first show of an extensive world tour. Reminiscent of her obsessive youth, she sequestered herself, working feverishly until she had mastered every lick.

She loved the horror-themed theatrics that are a key part of Cooper's show. "I covered myself in blood and I was an irritable zombie for three months. [It was] Halloween every night. It was really fun, and a great experience."

Although she quit Cooper's band in 2014 so she could focus on her solo career again, she and Cooper and his team remain on excellent terms: "They're family forever," she says. Since leaving his band, she's played guitar on a cover version of the Led Zeppelin classic "Whole Lotta Love" with Cooper's other group, Hollywood Vampires (which also includes Aerosmith guitarist Joe Perry and actor/musician Johnny Depp). And she has routinely played Cooper's annual "Christmas Pudding Fundraiser," an all-star concert in his hometown of Phoenix, Arizona (with proceeds benefitting the "Alice Cooper's Solid Rock" teen centers that Cooper and his wife, Sheryl, opened in Phoenix and Mesa, Arizona).

When Cooper replaced Orianthi with Nita Strauss, some fans took sides, implying that there was animosity between the guitarists. In reality, though, the two of them are friends. "She's awesome," Orianthi says of Strauss, adding that she takes a dim view of some people's attempts to instigate a rivalry. "Music is *never* a competition to me. It's such a huge field. If you want to get into competition, then get into sports. Become a runner or swimmer, do something like that, that's cool. But with music, it should be about freedom, love, and supporting each other as musicians."

She has simple advice for other performers wanting to avoid getting caught up in toxic situations in general: "Never read [online] forums," she says wryly. "I did that a couple of times. I was like, 'Holy shit, wow!' Guys or girls just going on about how much they hate me. It's quite weird to me to read that, because if you don't like something, don't listen to it, don't watch it.

"People can say their opinions, and that's great and all, [but] whatever is going on in your head and your heart and how you feel about what you've done, that matters the most. That's it, at the end of the day—you live with yourself and your thoughts. So for me, it's just doing the best job possible."

*   *   *

"I'm surrounded with guitars right now in my living room," Orianthi says. "I feel that they're all different characters. They've got different personalities, and they speak to you differently."

It's clear that she's still as in love with the guitar as she was when she was learning her first chords at six years old. Her skill with that instrument—and the drive and self-belief that it inspired in her—have brought her around the world, gained her admiration from many of her favorite artists, and earned her legions of fans. It is everything she'd dreamed of accomplishing, and more.

"Honestly, for me, it's really been a roller coaster," she says, "and it's going to continue to be this wild journey. I'm in for the ride!"

19

Fefe Dobson

"Love, for me, has always come with some sort of a price," says pop-punk singer-songwriter Fefe Dobson. "Be it love from a mother or from a significant other or from the [music] industry. I don't know what keeps me this way. But I've never been jaded by love. It still really pushes me and inspires me."

Her complicated feelings come as a direct result of an equally complicated childhood in Scarborough, a district in Toronto, Ontario. She is the second-oldest of four children born to a single mother who, according to Dobson, never received child support, so they lived a frugal life in government-run public housing. "My mom is a very strong woman," Dobson says. "Put food on our table every day and gave us Christmases. Which was a beautiful thing—but with every toy came a tear."

Her relationship with her older sister and younger brothers was also complex. "We were under the same roof but very, very different," she says, "and we were all separated at some point with foster care, on my brothers' side. And we all have different fathers. My dad is Black and my mom is white. The rest of my siblings are white."

As a result, "Identity has always been a funny thing because I've never been one to follow trends, and I've never been one to be like, 'Oh my God, I have to be like *this* person,'" Dobson says. Years later, she would reference this attitude with humor-tinged sarcasm in the lyrics to her songs "As a Blonde" and "If I Was a Guy."

As an adolescent, though, she recalls "a maze of emotions, and a maze of trying to get out. I grew up in a family where it was solely up to me to get out and to be something. And so that's what I worked on since I was twelve years old."

The problem, she discovered, was that "I couldn't be seen visually because I dressed in my uncle's hand-me-down clothes. I felt like an ugly duckling. I wasn't popular. I wasn't a girl that boys looked at. I was a girl boys hung out with because I would beat them up and they could keep up with me and I could keep up with them. But I was made fun of all the time."

But Dobson knew she had a gift that could be her ticket out of Scarborough. From the time she was in elementary school, teachers and other adults had routinely commented on her singing talent. Finally, she had an epiphany: "I was not seen until I sang—so I tried to sing everywhere."

She became determined to use her singing to land a record deal. She also began composing songs, though it took a traumatic experience to set her down that path. "I had kind of a mini breakdown when I was twelve years old," she says. "I was chased home by a couple of kids, and it broke me down. I started writing [songs] at that point. I needed to get a lot out."

*　　*　　*

A turning point came at the end of that year. Dobson remembers how, leading up to the holiday, her mother had become even more careful with money than usual. "Literally, we'd eat Kraft Dinner [macaroni and cheese], and we'd live on that," she says. She also recalls seemingly endless amounts of mashed potatoes and cabbage rolls—anything that could feed the family while stretching a dollar.

That frugality paid off on Christmas, when Dobson's mother surprised her with a high-end karaoke machine. "It was huge, heavy, but it was cool. The technology was new, and it was that you could put any CD or tape in—didn't have to be a karaoke CD—and it would mute the main vocal and you could karaoke over it."

Dobson eagerly made the most of the contraption. "I would lock myself in my bedroom and sing," she says. "I did Celine Dion's "If You Asked Me To." Celine Dion was like my vocal teacher. She doesn't realize. Her and Mariah Carey. I love Mariah Carey, absolutely. I would practice their songs every night in my room, and push and push and push to see what my range was. Kids would be outside my window, laughing, because I was so loud, but I was determined to get my vocals where they needed to be."

She soon realized that she could use the karaoke machine to create demo tapes of her singing, then send them to record companies. She recorded her own cover versions of songs by Paula Abdul, Shania Twain, Britney Spears, Janet Jackson, Mariah Carey, and Celine Dion. She chose these artists because they were women that she strongly admired, and she thought that emulating them would show that she had vocal chops.

Dobson's mother found a magazine that listed every record label's address and helped her mail the demo tapes to them. Then they anxiously awaited the results. "And my goodness, it was like 'no' replies every five seconds. 'No, no, no.' Anybody that doesn't have a manager or a lawyer, they'd call it 'unsolicited material' and they would send it back. It was heartbreaking."

But Dobson was undaunted. Her mother also continued to believe in her talent, accompanying her to auditions in downtown Toronto—even though that necessitated a city bus ride that often took an hour or more each way. After a couple of years, nothing significant had come of the demo tapes or the tryouts, but Dobson remained optimistic.

"I would go to high school and try to be a normal teenager, but I was absolutely out of my mind," she says. "I would be like, 'I'm going to get out of here. Justin Timberlake is going to know me.'" (Timberlake, a singer in the boy band NSYNC at the time, even inspired her to write "Take Me Away," a song in which she fantasizes about having him whisk her away from her current situation. She later recorded it for her debut album.) Her classmates were distinctly unimpressed by her assertions. "People would be like, 'She's crazy. She can barely afford to come to school.'"

A year later, after sending out even more demo tapes, she finally got the break she needed. A Canadian record label that was affiliated with Jive Records in the United States reached out to her. "They were like, 'Hey, we don't know what's going on with this tape. There's a lot of songs you're singing where you sound great, but we don't really know what your style is. But we'd like to do a development deal and get you in with some writers.' I was like, 'Heck, yeah!' I was *ecstatic*."

*   *   *

Dobson's joy soon turned to confusion when her record label steered her in a direction she didn't understand. "I started going in with the writers and producers, but I felt like I wasn't finding my voice or my energy; I wasn't really finding that connection," she says. "The writers and producers were amazing, and the label was really gracious—but something felt wrong."

Then she found out what the label executives had been telling producers to make them interested in working with her: "I'll never forget. I forget a lot, but I don't forget this because it was a pivotal moment for me. They called me 'Brandy Spears.' And that really bothered me. I didn't know why at that point, but now, looking back, it was because I felt like I was being penned into something that, to me, made no sense.

"I hadn't even really scratched the surface of what I was trying to do musically. But it was like, 'Well, she's Black, so it's like [R&B superstar] Brandy. But she's got a pop voice'—which, I guess to them was like a white girl voice, like Britney Spears. So it was just an easy way to get people involved, to explain to them what I was. But it affected me."

Dobson felt her work had more depth to it than that. Lyrically, she was inspired by her love for the 1996 film *William Shakespeare's Romeo + Juliet*. "I was obsessed with the poetry and how romantic it was," she says. She also wanted to emulate

Daniel Johns, the leader and main composer for the Australian alternative rock band Silverchair.

Still, she wanted the development deal to work out, so she continued showing up at Wellesley Sound Studio in Toronto, where she continued to be paired with producers and writers that her label had selected. After they came up with a song idea, Dobson would dutifully sing a demo version of it, but nothing seemed to click.

It wasn't all for nothing, though. A pair of producers working in the room next door heard Dobson's vocals through the wall. "They came in and were like, 'Hey, sorry to bother you, but we need a demo singer on a pop-punk song. We heard your voice. We think it's powerful.'" Those producers were Jay Levine and James Bryan McCollum, who were already famous for their pop band Prozzäk, then one of the top-selling acts in Canada.

"So I go over, I learn the song, and I sing it. It's called "Get a Clue." After it was done, Jay Levine was like, 'Hey, you really shine with pop rock.' I was like, 'Yes, this is what I'm trying to tell people—I want guitars!' They're like, 'We agree, this is you.' So all the sudden, I had this synergy and amazing connection with Jay and James."

Levine and McCollum offered to work with her on an album—but there was a problem: her record label didn't want her to go into pop-punk. If she defied them, she'd lose the label deal she'd worked so hard to obtain—and all the potential profits from it, which she had hoped would help her family's financial circumstances.

Collaborating with Levine and McCollum could be a risk, too. "I remember Jay saying, 'Look, we'll make the album of your dreams—but I can't promise you anything. You might just make a record of your dreams and that's it,'" she recalls.

In the end, she went with what made her happier. "I remember going out for lunch with the label executive that was developing me and telling her, 'Hey, I'm really thankful for this. I'm so appreciative. But I have to go with Jay and James.' And then I left. I walked away from the label situation."

Without a record deal, Dobson began writing and recording with Levine and McCollum. "I think 'Bye Bye Boyfriend' was the first song we wrote. We knew then that we had something," she says.

Levine and McCollum were so confident in Dobson's abilities that they invested their own money in the project, renting studio and soundstage facilities in Toronto at Sony Music (the label behind Prozzäk). In return, Dobson had to work tirelessly. "I was basically put through performance camp every day," she says. "I would be onstage practicing the music we were writing and learning how to put on a show. Every day was a hustle. I would go to school, and then I would go to Sony and work on my album. And then go home and start all over again. It was pretty crazy."

Despite being run ragged, Dobson was happy because she was finally working with people who respected her: "They heard me. And I was an open book to them about how I felt." Her confessional lyrics were especially evident in songs such as "Kiss Me Fool," where she sang about not being pretty or special enough to make someone love her, and "We Went for a Ride," in which she begs a driver to continue cruising around so she wouldn't have to go home.

Pleased with the songs, Prozzäk's manager took Dobson on as a client. In a bid to get her a record deal, he lined up private showcase performances for various label executives. At one such show—at 9 a.m. in a small Toronto music club—she performed for Island Def Jam co-president Lyor Cohen and Head of A&R Jeff Fenster, who had flown in from New York for the occasion. "Literally thirty seconds into the song "Stupid Little Love Song," Lyor was ready to sign [me]," Dobson says.

Inking a deal with Island Def Jam, Dobson relocated to New York—where she immediately felt overwhelmed after her sheltered upbringing. "I'd never even gone to a party. And then all the sudden, I was in New York making an album, having a completely free life to do whatever I wanted. So I wasn't prepared for that at all," she says.

She credits her Toronto roots for preventing her from going totally off the rails, though. "I wasn't in the craziness all the time. I could go home, and I had some really good friends in Toronto that kept me very humble. At least, I hope. They might say something else. But I felt like they were grounding me, which was very important to me. But I still was out of control at times. Boys started seeing me for the first time. I was like, 'Yes! I'll take him, I'll take him, I'll take him.'"

Things got even more intense when her self-titled album was released in December 2003, when she was eighteen years old. "It was a whirlwind," she says. The album eventually achieved platinum sales status in Canada and earned her "New Artist of the Year" and "Pop Album of the Year" Juno Award nominations (the Canadian equivalent of the Grammy Awards).

Another triumph came when she embarked on her first international tour—as the opening act for Justin Timberlake, who had gone from NSYNC to a highly successful solo career. Her high school bravado had become reality: Timberlake did, indeed, know who she was.

She became a star in her country: "Bye Bye Boyfriend," her debut single, shot to number 8 on the Canadian Singles Chart. Another single, "Don't Go (Girls and Boys)," also reached the Canadian Top 10, and it was used in a 2004 commercial (starring Dobson) for fashion designer Tommy Hilfiger.

But for someone who had grown up wearing secondhand clothes, she found her newfound fashionista status challenging. It was, she says, "Competing and looking beautiful and trying to feel beautiful, even though I was going through all this crazy shit in my mind."

She believes this is a particular pitfall for female performers. "Of course men have insecurities. But if we [women] stand on a red carpet, I feel like there's still pressure [to look glamorous]. I try to find my balance with that. When I get too glammed up, I don't feel like myself. So I have to find middle ground."

Musically, she also felt like her male peers had it easier, simply because they far outnumbered female artists. "When I came out, there were moments where I was competing with dudes. Rock bands, it was mostly dudes." In response, she tried to fit in with them. "My whole goal was to rock just as hard, or harder. I always wanted to be that girl that walked onstage and the guys would be like, 'Whoa!' And high five me."

Her life got even more disorienting when her father, who had not been around during her childhood, suddenly reappeared just as her album gained traction. It is a connection that remains complicated twenty years later. "We're still trying to figure out our relationship," she says, adding that a big issue stems from the fact that she "grew up so fast. So all the things that he now, in retrospect, wants to teach me, he can't really teach me because I've already went through life. I have fallen and gotten up so many times, and I never had him put a Band-Aid on it.

"It's one of my goals to always be able to do what I need to do and not feel like I have to rely on a man or whoever. I mean, there's nothing wrong with that, at all. Sometimes we need help. But I just have a personal goal of always being able to provide for myself."

* * *

This determination not to lean on anyone could have a down-side, as Dobson discovered when she began contemplating how she was going to match the success she'd had with her debut album. "At that point, I was going through a darker period," she says. "I was going through a really tough relationship. I think that's when my childhood shit kind of rose to a head a lot."

As a result, she relocated to Los Angeles and revamped her image. She adopted a punk fashion sensibility that she says was heavily inspired by Nancy Spungen, the girlfriend of Sex Pistols bassist Sid Vicious (whom he stabbed to death in 1978).

Her new musical output was equally edgy. This time, she collaborated with a wide range of songwriters (but not Jay Levine and James Bryan McCollum). "I really wanted to make it an authentic rock album," she says. "I wanted it to sound like Hollywood. I wanted it to sound like a burning palm tree. That's how I felt. Inside, I was broken."

She titled the album *Sunday Love*, after a name her mother had used. "That was her alias, let's just say, 'after hours,'" Dobson says, "so I wanted to name it that in honor of her. "'Sunday Love,' for her, meant something else—but for me it was a character that existed. And Sunday Love's voice was a very dark voice."

Initially, it seemed like her record company was behind this new direction. "Everyone seemed totally into it. I never heard anything negative," Dobson recalls. "The first single came out, "Don't Let It Go to Your Head," and we did a video." After that, however, "There was word in the label building that it was a little bit too hard musically, and that I didn't really know who I was, and they didn't know what to do with me.

"Unfortunately, they decided to part ways [with me], and that was that. My album got shelved at that point. Of course, I was very, very bummed." (Island Records did end up releasing *Sunday Love*—but not until 2012, and only as a digital download.)

"Looking back, it really was the moment of change. It was like a real 'choose your adventure' moment: 'There's Door A and there's Door B. You take Door A, you can continue [in music], but it's going to be really difficult and you're still going to go through some shit. Door B is give up.' And I do not give up. That's not who I am. Again, this is survival for me.

"And my choice was, I'm going to go back to Toronto. I don't have a label. I don't know what I'm going to do. I'm going to drink myself to sleep a few nights. And I'm going to cry and cry and cry. And then at some point I'm going to be like, 'Fefe, get your shit together,' and go through almost like a re-birth, in a way."

That rebirth began when Dobson saw pop superstar Miley Cyrus's video for "Start All Over" on MuchMusic, a Canadian music television channel. It was a stunning moment: Dobson had cowritten that song for *Sunday Love*, and she hadn't even known that anyone was covering it. Suddenly, there it was on national television, apparently a hit for someone else. "I remember seeing the video, and all the background vocals were me. It re-inspired me. It was instant. I felt good," she says.

More high-profile covers of songs from the still-unreleased *Sunday Love* album followed: Selena Gomez did "As a Blonde." Jordin Sparks did "Don't Let It Go to Your Head." For Dobson, it was vindicating.

She began writing songs for a new album, once more collaborating with a variety of songwriters. The results were so good that she ended up re-signing to Island Records, who released the album in 2010. "I'm always very careful with my titles now," she says. "I named it *Joy* because I was in a joyful place."

Joy returned Dobson to stardom in Canada, where the album charted. But, once again, success was followed by a severe bout of self-doubt, thwarting her attempts to write new songs. "Something felt wrong. I wasn't happy," she says. "I felt like there was more pressure for me coming off of *Joy* than off my first album, to be honest.

"I decided, 'I can't do this.' I ended up leaving management and kind of running away and coming to Nashville and started making another record." This time, she was determined to take charge of the situation. "I wanted to write a record fully by myself. No cowriters. I wanted to see what I was capable of. And I wanted to make a different genre of music. So I made an album that was inspired by surf rock and a romantic, kinda psychedelic, Quentin Tarantino vibe. Didn't put it out. I did it for myself."

*   *   *

"I'm such a believer in manifestation. I've seen it happen. It's so real," Dobson says.

She's referring to her career overall—but it also applies to her latest reinvention of herself as she prepares to release a new album in 2023 (the title is still undetermined, as of this writing).

"I feel like this album is way more whole. I can't say *I'm* fully whole yet, but I'm getting closer. And I feel like this album is going to show that," she says. "It's back to my roots: pop rock. I feel like it's a little bit of the first album, and *Sunday Love*, all of it. I think it's every piece. It's the puzzle coming together."

This time, she's certain she's on the right track because she's finally been able to figure out who she really is: "I came to realize, I need to stand onstage and be me and not try anything else. This is who I am, and I get it. As human beings, we all go through it, you know. Shedding skin, trying new things. It's important. How do you really become whole if you don't try out different things?"

Much of Dobson's newfound clarity and inner peace also emerged out of her happy personal life: in 2019, she married American rapper Yelawolf; they live in Nashville. "There's a lot of equality in our relationship," she says. "We both do the same thing [music], so we understand the addiction of our career. And understand that it's a unique lifestyle."

Dobson is excited to rejoin the music business, which she sees becoming much more inclusive for women than it was when she first debuted, or even when she released *Joy* in 2010. "I feel like women are supporting each other way more, which is amazing," she says. "And also, there's a lot more women in production, and a lot of female songwriters."

She is doing her part to try to continue this positive outcome: "Whenever I do a session, I always request another female, because as a woman, I want to work off of another woman. We have similar struggles, and they can understand my emotions, my feminine qualities, so the writing becomes a little more feminine. And for my band, I'm all about an all-girl band, because we have to support female guitarists and drummers and bassists and show that women can kick ass, too."

In this way, she feels she has led by example as she has navigated the many ups and downs in her career. "I identify myself as a strong woman," she says. "A feminist? Some people say I am, but I don't know. I don't like putting myself in any category, really."

Instead, she offers an empowering message for everyone, regardless of gender: "A lot of times, there's beautiful things about to rise from the ground. Like a flower. Being positive is so important because when you start beating yourself up, it's like you're making that flower go back into the ground. You've got to keep watering yourself with positivity. It's a hard thing to do. Life can be quite difficult at times. Life's crazy. There's so much pain, and there are so many questions. But there's so much beauty, too. We've got to remember beauty, and we've got to continue to give beauty. We've got to be mindful as humans."

20

Sade Sanchez (L.A. Witch)

During the past decade, L.A. Witch became one of the most buzzed-about bands to emerge from the Los Angeles music scene. The all-female trio's distinctive sound—retro garage/surf rock mixed with punk swagger—has earned them international fame, as they proved when the COVID-19 pandemic eased up enough in late spring 2022 for them to undertake a triumphant string of headlining shows across Europe.

As on previous tours, the band's vocalist and guitarist, Sade Sanchez, ran the merchandise booth herself after the shows. "It's been a way for me to be able to communicate," she says, during a phone call just a few days after her return to Los Angeles. "You can really gauge what you mean to people. A lot of them are like, 'I've been waiting two years to see this show.' Or, 'I've seen you five times.' Or, 'I drove from Spain for this show.' There are people that bring gifts. There are people that have our names tattooed on them. It really blows my mind. I'm glad to be able to see that and know what an impact we have."

Even so, Sanchez admits that it can also be difficult for her to interact with fans because it requires her to continue being outgoing like she is with her onstage persona. In reality, though, "It's hard for me to socialize with people. I'm super shy," she says.

Working the merch booth has also exposed Sanchez to rude or downright bizarre treatment. "Oh yes, there's been a ton of that, unfortunately," she says. "A lot of people are drunk, and people get really touchy. People want to take photos and hold on to you and not let go. People get really close to your face. It's scary. That's why we always have a guy tour manager. It's fucked up that that's how it is, but you feel like you need some sort of protection."

Striking the right balance between openness and guardedness, Sanchez says, is "something that I'm still trying to figure out how to navigate because you're like, 'Okay, these are the fans.' But where do you draw the lines? How do you go about communicating and protecting yourself and standing up for yourself? It's kind of weird to be in that position. You don't really know what to do sometimes—at least, I don't. I don't want to be mean to people. At the same time, I don't want to be disrespected, either."

*   *   *

Sanchez first encountered this problem of reconciling opposing facets of her life when she was growing up in the San Fernando Valley area of Los Angeles. "Half of my childhood was really happy, and the rest was me feeling alienated and just really different," she says.

Born in 1989, Sanchez is a first-generation Mexican American. Her parents left Mexico for L.A. in the mid-1980s, arriving soon before her older sister was born. "They left everything behind—not that they had much," Sanchez says. "They came to this country not really knowing English or having money or knowing anybody. I always think about that when I have any weird little problems. I'm like, 'That ain't shit compared to what your parents went through.' So I definitely have a lot to be grateful for."

Still, coming from an immigrant family meant that Sanchez faced certain challenges. She grew up speaking Spanish and didn't really begin learning English until she reached the second grade. This set Sanchez apart from her classmates, and the impact of that language barrier still affects her to this day. "I feel like I've always struggled with my communication," she says.

"Sometimes I'm like, 'Am I just not smart enough? Do I need to read more? Am I a really weird, awkward person, or am I just misunderstood?'" This, combined with her naturally reserved personality, made her feel isolated.

Her family's economic status also made her feel like an outsider. Her father apprenticed as a machinist (eventually mastering it enough to open his own business), and her mother worked as a caretaker for children and the elderly. While her parents' jobs were respectable, their incomes were not lucrative.

"My parents gave us everything they could," Sanchez says. "I had a really hard time, having a lot of insecurities due to the things that I didn't have. I think that when you're a little kid, you don't really know what you don't have. It's not until you're at school and you see other children that you start to realize that you don't have certain clothes, certain toys, certain things. You know, kids can be really mean."

Fortunately, Sanchez found a refuge in music. "For me, music was a great way to escape," she says. Early in her life, her parents instilled a love for rock and roll in her: "They were very artistic and open-minded, and they always had music playing around the house. My dad was really into rock and roll, like the Rolling Stones, Black Sabbath, or any classic rock. And my mom really liked the Beatles, the Mamas and the Papas, stuff like that."

Sanchez's initial experience with actually playing music was decidedly non-rock, though. "My first instrument was the cello," she says. She started lessons when she was in the third grade. "The school I was going to had a music program. I ended up kind of regretting it because the cello was the size of me, so carrying that thing around was a pain in the ass! And I was awful at it, but I enjoyed it. But once I got out of elementary school, that program didn't exist anymore, so I had to give back my instrument.

"But that's around the time, when I was twelve or thirteen, where I picked up the guitar," Sanchez continues. Her dad had a couple of guitars, so it seemed natural for her to follow in his footsteps. Also, she admired many of the male rock guitarists she'd grown up hearing. Despite the lead guitarist role being held mainly by men, her tomboy tendencies made her feel comfortable emulating them.

There were female role models, too. "I was also watching a lot of MTV," Sanchez says. "I know a lot of people say that there wasn't a lot of women in music at the time, but to me, there was. I remember seeing Gwen Stefani, Shirley Manson, Courtney Love, PJ Harvey—all these women."

Sanchez especially admired Exene Cervenka, co-vocalist for the pioneering punk band X; one of their CDs was among the first Sanchez bought for herself. "Hearing Exene was a huge thing for me because punk was so new to me, and it was cool to see someone like her. There was this whole other world of women in that genre." Having X hail from Los Angeles, Sanchez's own hometown, fired her ambitions. "It makes you feel like, 'Well, *I* can do that.'"

When Sanchez began attending John Burroughs High School in Burbank, she started jamming in a few punk bands with some friends. "It was nothing that ever got that serious," she says, though she adds that all this practice dramatically improved her playing abilities.

A turning point came when she joined an arts club at her school. It was "for photographers, poets, or anything art related—you would come and showcase whatever it was that you did. At that time, I was writing my own songs, so that was the first time that I started playing those to people."

That club put together a CD featuring members' songs, including Sanchez's. "That was passed around school, and somehow it made it over to our rival high school, which is where Ellie [English, L.A. Witch's current drummer] was going to school. She got ahold of that CD, so she had known about me. And the funny thing is, I had known about her because I had seen her band play at my school at lunch. I thought she was super rad. At that time, there weren't a lot of female musicians, so when there was one, you would know about it, especially in high school. Your world is so small."

Sanchez and English met in person at a party a short time later. Their admiration for each other's work prompted them to start jamming together. They soon started writing songs, which they felt were good enough for them to enter their duo in a "Battle of the Bands" competition at English's high school.

As they prepared for that contest, they found out that not everyone was ready to take them seriously, however. "We went to Guitar Center to get guitar strings and drumsticks," Sanchez says, "and I remember the employee there was this older rocker dude, and he was being *such* a dick to us. He was so annoyed with us."

Vindication came when Sanchez and English ended up winning that Battle of the Bands. Their prize? A gift card to Guitar Center—which they promptly took to the store to redeem. To their delight, their previous nemesis was again working there that day. "We were all stoked to tell him, 'Yeah, dude, we *won!*'"

Encouraged by their success, Sanchez and English continued their band after they graduated from high school. "We were still underage, so we would have to leave the bars after we played. We were booking our own shows all by ourselves. We didn't know what the hell we were doing. We recorded our songs onto an MP3 player and put them up on MySpace. It was fun."

But then, suddenly, things weren't fun anymore. "Ellie and I ended up splitting up," Sanchez says. She takes the blame for this. "I was going through my weird dark time, so we weren't friends for a few years. We didn't talk for a long time."

A few years later, Sanchez says, "I had gotten sober, and I wanted to start a band." But there was a problem: "I was in this really abusive relationship, and my boyfriend said that if I wanted to be in a band, I had to find girls. That he would not allow me to be in a band if there was a guy [bandmate]."

Eventually, Sanchez came to understand that that relationship "was really abusive, really manipulative," and she was able to end it. But things weren't so clear to her in the moment, when she was in such a vulnerable and fragile state: "I was newly sober. I was young. He was ten years older than I was." So she obeyed his ultimatum and started a hunt for band members— female ones only.

But it wasn't easy. "I was going crazy because there were not a lot of girls that were playing, like how they are today," Sanchez says. "And the girls who were playing were already in bands that were established." It started to seem like forming an all-female band would prove impossible.

By now, Sanchez was working a demanding job, managing multiple stores for the clothing retailer American Apparel, including the L.A. flagship store on Melrose Avenue. There, through a mutual friend, she met Irita Pai, who was in charge of the store's vintage department.

Pai and a couple of other friends were aspiring musicians, but as Sanchez recalls, "They didn't know how to play—they had just picked up their instruments. But they had a rehearsal space. And I was so desperate—I had been searching for such a long time that I didn't even care that they couldn't play. I was so, 'If they want to start a band, I'll do it, just because this is my only chance.'"

Naming themselves L.A. Witch, the quartet began jamming, becoming good enough to play at house parties. Finally, their first "real" show happened on September 4, 2011, at Little Joy, a hip dive bar in L.A.'s trendy Echo Park neighborhood. But just as things seemed like they were going well, disaster threatened to befall the band.

"Our drummer went to New York and ended up not coming back," Sanchez says. "She had booked this residency for us at The Silverlake Lounge. She only played one of those shows, out of four, so we had to find a replacement drummer because we didn't want to back out of [the rest]. So we found a drummer for one of the shows. Then, coincidentally, I had bumped into Ellie, and we were kind of cool again. So I hit her up: 'Hey, do you want to fill in on these shows?'"

English agreed, played the remaining residency gigs—and has stayed on with the band ever since. "We ended up keeping Ellie because it just made sense," Sanchez says. "She's one of the best drummers that I know to this day."

When they pared the lineup down to a trio of Sanchez, Pai, and English, L.A. Witch in its current form came to life. Sanchez is grateful that things worked out, even if it came out of such a dark and abusive time in her life. "It's really unfortunate that that's the reason, but at the same time, I'm so glad that it happened that way," she says. "These girls, they're my family."

*   *   *

"If you don't think of yourself as 'a girl in rock music,' you can become more than that," Sanchez says. "I'm not saying being a girl in rock isn't enough, but I think sometimes our minds can limit us. I always try to avoid putting myself in any genre or any category, and I think that's really worked out for me."

Sanchez's refusal to submit to the status quo led L.A. Witch to take an unusual route to stardom: instead of rushing into the studio to record an album as soon as possible, they took their time, releasing a few stand-alone singles starting in 2013.

In the end, it would be a six-year wait between the band's formation and the release of their self-titled debut full-length album in 2017. They'd spent those years perfecting their woozy, haunting lo-fi sound as they toured relentlessly across the United States. This meant that *L.A. Witch* came across as an exceptionally confident and cohesive album, and it earned them critical praise and fans around the world.

"That was a really amazing feeling," Sanchez says about releasing *L.A. Witch*. "Once we actually had a record, it was like this physical thing that showed what we were working for. It made everything feel more real. And of course it definitely did help take us to the next level. It was really exciting for us."

With a record label and a manager in place, the band members were able to stop doing so much of the business end of things themselves. Finally, they could focus mainly on their music—meaning it was a much shorter wait for their sophomore album, *Play with Fire*, which came out in 2020.

Looking back at L.A. Witch's trajectory, Sanchez gives credit to a couple of key supporters: "There have been some women that really helped us out early in our career," she says. "Paige Stark from the band Tashaki Miyaki was one of the first women to reach out to us and want to help produce and record us. Another one was Julie Edwards of Deap Valley. She's someone who took us aside and was like, 'Hey, I've been doing this for a while. Let me help you. Let me share what I know with you.' We'll never forget that. It's always something that really sticks out in our minds."

Sanchez says she also felt this kind of helpful, welcoming attitude within her hometown's music scene at large, right from the start of L.A. Witch. "I think the community in L.A. has always been really supportive," she says. "I think it was a really cool, fresh, new, exciting time in the music scene. There were a bunch of bands, and there were a bunch of house parties and shows going on. We were super passionate about it. And if we were being judged or if someone didn't like us, then I definitely didn't know about it."

Since the band began venturing out beyond the L.A. scene, though, Sanchez admits that she has had to make a point to remember the risks inherent with having a group of women traveling together in unfamiliar places—and that is especially true for rock musicians. "If you dress a certain way, you're going to really stick out—people are going to look at you. You're going to feel unsafe or uncomfortable," she says. "I'm sure that would happen if you were a guy, too, but I think [as a woman] you're probably a little bit more careful because if something goes down, you are less likely to be able to protect yourself than a man would, unfortunately."

Aggressive, overzealous fans are another problem that can prove particularly dangerous for female musicians. Sanchez says that, so far, she and her bandmates haven't had serious trouble with this, but they are always watchful for it. "There was one case where some drunk guy grabbed my boot during a show, and luckily there was a bouncer who kicked him out," she says, "but not all venues have someone keeping an eye out, and that's something I realized needs to change.

"I definitely think we need to make it a safer place for women—and in general," Sanchez continues. "The nature of the music scene can be really dark. You are surrounded by lots of drugs and alcohol. I think people need to keep an eye out for each other, and that especially includes promoters and venues."

She praises one venue, Metro in Chicago, that has already implemented an extra level of protection. "They asked us before we played, 'Do you have any fans or stalkers or anyone that we should keep an eye out for?' No other venue has ever done that before," Sanchez says. "It was a huge eye-opener for me because

I realized it's cool to have a venue looking out for you, because that *should* be part of their responsibilities."

Unfortunately, however, sometimes the problem comes from within the venue's own ranks. Sanchez recalls an infuriating incident in Las Vegas that happened five years ago: "I've been in a fight with a soundman before who was extremely rude. I was kicked out of the club," she says.

"I was asking him to make adjustments during a show, which is not abnormal. Sometimes you need a certain volume; it's nothing crazy." But instead of doing as she requested, the soundman responded by arguing with her over the sound system. "He was talking to me *while we were playing*. Even our audience was booing him. They were pissed because he was just being such a dick. And then after the show, he got a little bit physical and in my face. We got in an altercation, and then I got kicked out. It was pretty crazy." She sighs. "I hate talking about that because it was such a bummer, honestly."

She's certain her gender had something to do with the way she was treated in that case. "I think that this guy is a schmuck in general, but I think he gave me even extra sass because I am a small girl who, to him, knows nothing. So I think he felt really powerful speaking to me in that way."

Still, she's quick to add, "For the most part, people [working at venues] have been respectful. And on those occasions when someone does treat the band like they don't know what they're doing, we ignore it because we're like, 'You just wait and see. We're going to show you. We know how to play, and we know how to do a proper soundcheck, and we know what the fuck we're talking about.' You have to go in there with confidence, and they realize right away that they were wrong. But at the end of the day, their apology doesn't mean shit. Who cares? You're bigger than them."

That kind of occasional dispiriting episode aside, Sanchez has been pleased overall with how she's seen women in the music business increasingly being granted the same visibility and respect as their male peers. She believes that feminism has played a key role in making this progress possible—though she thinks that this means different things to different people.

"I think we all have our different ways of showing it," Sanchez says of being a feminist. "Some people are more vocal about it, and some of us are more leading by example." She counts herself, and L.A. Witch in general, as being more in that second camp. "Just by us being onstage, just by us accomplishing what we have accomplished, I think we have inspired people. I think that's my style of contributing to feminism. I do believe that I am a part of the movement, and I do think that we've had an impact. It's been really cool."

Afterword

Susan Rogers

"What's it like to be a woman in the music business?" is a question I've answered a lot over the past forty-five years. The questioner's curiosity is justified; the record-making industry was and is dominated by men. I began my career in 1978 and despite (and sometimes because of) my gender, I made a good living as an audio technician, recording engineer, and record producer, sometimes working with other women, but mostly with the men who hired me. Whether it was the novelty of working with a woman, social engineering, or my skills that got me the job didn't matter. I was living out my dream of making records. Over time I learned that life is the best teacher, and in the early days of my career, my failures were often due to simply not having had enough of it yet.

The women profiled in these pages have responded to this question, too, recalling their experiences and impressions from the 1970s through the decades to this century, as pioneering women in rock. We learn how the scene has changed over time, and we learn what has stubbornly stayed the same. Many of these stories have a familiar subtext that boils down to having to rapidly choose between what psychologist Daniel Kahneman calls our two systems of thinking: the fast one (gut instinct) and the slow one (reason). For young people, role models are useful in demonstrating how these two choices can pan out. Without role models, trailblazing women frequently had to reinvent the wheel and discover for themselves the right (or the least painful) way to counteract problems caused by not having a Y-chromosome. Stories in this book can help the youngest generation of women (and men) with problem-solving, while hinting at ways that the new music industry can avoid causing some of these problems in the first place.

Popular music's traditional function is to serve courtship behaviors, and humans are like most species in that the male leads the dance. The classic rock 'n' roll template is a twelve-bar song about sex with females and how to get more of it. As rock music lyrics embraced storytelling, politicizing, and self-expression in the 1960s and 1970s, it widened the gate for songwriters such as Joni Mitchell, Carole King, Suzi Quatro, Joan Jett, Ann Wilson, and Lydia Lunch. This advance allowed women songwriters to sell a lot of records. In the hermetically sealed world of the recording studio, however, and the alcohol-infused clubs and lounges, music stubbornly clung to its unofficial mandate that female singers come across as sexually attractive and available. This was a nontrivial problem for women, who needed to figure out how to integrate their artistic profile with their gender before stepping up to the mic.

To help answer the what-is-it-like question, women profiled in this book shared with readers a few catcalled invitations from the audience to flash their breasts or perform a sex act. Bonnie Bloomgarden described the club scene in a way that presumes readers know that the following is a step down in respect: "you are treated like a girl." My female engineering colleagues and I can tell stories of being intimidated, debased, or embarrassed in the recording studio. These stories are funny over the fullness of time (mainly because they feature some really asinine behavior), but the incidents don't feel funny in the moment.

A common theme is that the perpetrators didn't expect us to fight back. We had our reasons for that: fighting back risked being ejected from the game. To keep our jobs, we cloaked ourselves in tolerance and sangfroid. Our choices were: (a) tolerate it for the sake of our goals, (b) draw a line and come up with a punishment for crossing it, (c) work only with women, (d) work with romantic partners for protection, and (e) find a respectful cohort. (I was fortunate to have found the latter: producers such as Tony Berg, Michael Beinhorn, Matt Wallace, and T Bone Burnett worked with me, as did legendary artists, including Prince, David Byrne, and Barenaked Ladies.)

How many women earning a living as a novelist get accused of not writing their own books? If your answer is, "I can't think of any," then consider the strangeness of how often this used to happen to pioneering women rock stars and accredited journalists, as Katherine Yeske Taylor recounts in the introduction to this book. Readers from my generation (baby boomers) remember when "She writes her own songs!" was like hearing about a monkey heating up a can of soup. Donita Sparks recounts a journalist who praised L7 "regardless of gender," meaning, in other words, pay no attention to that monkey with the can opener. This isn't heard today but that's because a thing that *is* always seems obvious and natural. It's good to remember that "everything is the way it is because *it got that way*."[1] We arrived at an acceptance of women songwriters and music journalists thanks to the pioneers who publicly mutated the status quo until it became the new standard.

A different kind of catcall makes the demand that a woman onstage comes across as likeable. "Smile more!" Suzanne Vega was advised from the crowd. The implication was that the performer wasn't doing her appointed duty to be pleasing. Vega describes wanting to look natural for a photoshoot and to have her outside image be congruous with her inside image. For women artists of the past century, this was more of a challenge than it should have been, caused by the enormous vacancy in representation. Joan Osborne talked in these pages about the self-consciousness of appearance for women rock artists, and the value in being able to take the path up the mountain carved by women who started their trek earlier.

This reminded me of when I was a young audio tech in the late 1970s and early 1980s, in Hollywood. One of the biggest of many obstacles was figuring out what to wear. Dress as a typical audio tech—jeans and plaid shirts—and feel out of sync with myself. Or dress as a typical young woman—blouses and sandals—

and feel at odds with my profession. I opted to toe the party line and dress like my male cohort until the day that Prince leaned into the mic at rehearsal, capping off instructions to the band with, ". . . and Susan, *where did you get that stupid shirt?!*" Prince's success made a convincing argument for being oneself, and so I began to add items to my closet that let me show my world, for bigger and for smaller, what a female engineer looked like.

The personal histories in this book illustrate how far women in music have come and how long it has taken. Donita Sparks recounts a pitiful truth shared by a Warner Bros. record executive: some morning radio DJs had a "no chick" policy or quota and wouldn't give women rockers the airplay that was crucial to selling records. When you think about this in the context of the times (the 1990s) and recall that schoolgirls were learning that, thanks to the sacrifices of their foremothers, they could be anything they wanted to be, well, you can see the irony.

Stories like the ones Katherine Yeske Taylor has collected here are a cultural map of women rock musicians over the past fifty years. They describe high yet sharp peaks, sterile deserts, verdant fields, and lots of real or anticipated dangers. As the women pioneers settled this landscape, they transformed it into one that is more welcoming and productive for today's artists. How they accomplished this, and why, is a genuine love story between women and rock music.

*   *   *

Susan Rogers holds a doctoral degree in behavioral neuroscience from McGill University (2010). Prior to her science career, Susan was a multiplatinum-earning record producer, engineer, and mixer. She is best known for her work with Prince during his peak creative period (1983–1987). Her discography also includes records with David Byrne, Barenaked Ladies, Geggy Tah, Nil Lara, Robben Ford, Tricky, Michael Penn, Jeff Black, and many others. In 2021 she became the first female recipient of the Music Producers Guild Award for Outstanding Contributions to UK Music. She teaches psychoacoustics and record production for Berklee Online. Her book on music listening, This Is What It Sounds Like: What the Music You Love Says about You, *published by W. W. Norton & Co., is available everywhere.*

Acknowledgments

Enormous thanks to literary agent Lee Sobel for believing in me, and for coming up with the idea for this book and letting me run with it. Your help and unwavering enthusiasm were the driving force behind making this book happen.

The best editors in the world, Bernadette Malavarca and John Cerullo, helped me with this book. Both of them were extremely patient and supportive as I went through all the ups and downs of being a first-time author. You taught me things that I will carry with me for the rest of my career.

I am so grateful to the amazing women I interviewed for this—thank you all for being so generous with your time and so candid and thoughtful with your answers. It means the world to me that you agreed to do this book. All of you inspired me so much. (And thanks also to the many publicists and managers who helped me make these interviews happen!)

My writing career never would've happened if I hadn't had amazing parents, Ron and Maril Yeske, who encouraged my writing from the moment I put my first word on paper. Mom, special thanks for driving me to my earliest interviews, even though that was probably a weird thing for your kid to be doing! I wish Dad could still be here to see that I finally became a published author, but I know he'd be proud of me, too.

For being incredibly supportive of me throughout this process, much love goes out to Karen "Bebe" Stackpole, Celeste Orangers, Vince Gaudio, Colleen Baldino, Joseph Pisano, Nancy L. Weber, Jennifer Weitsen, Steve Pilon, Jenny Noren, Grace Chung Kim, Shani Blenden, Randi Tucker, Jesse Malin, Tom Clark, Diane Gentile, Tom Beaujour, Pearl and Kyle Wynne, Nathanael Hall, Kat Marie Mitchell, Hillary Meister, Lisa May, Laura Siegel, Mia D'Avanza, Jessica Palmer, Toby Maloney, and Katherine Turman. And an extra special shout-out to all of my Anderson, South Carolina, cheerleaders!

Finally, much gratitude goes out to all the unsung activists (of any gender) who've done so much to make life more equitable for women everywhere.

Notes

Introduction

1. J. Hopper, "The Invisible Woman: A Conversation with Björk," *Pitchfork* (January 21, 2015), retrieved February 21, 2022, https://pitch fork.com/features/interview/9582-the-invisible-woman-a-conversa tion-with-bjork/.

2. K. Yeske Taylor, "Interview: Donita Sparks of L7," *The Big Take-over* (May 6, 2020), retrieved February 21, 2022, https://bigtakeover .com/interviews/InterviewDonitaSparksofL7.

3. K. Yeske Taylor, "Suzi Quatro's Rock and Roll Rebirth," *The Aquarian Weekly* (May 20, 2021), retrieved February 21, 2022, https:// www.theaquarian.com/2021/05/20/suzi-quatro-interview-rock-and -roll/.

4. B. Tourtellotte, "A Minute with: Joan Jett on Life as a 'Runaway,'" *Reuters* (March 17, 2010), retrieved January 21, 2022, https://www .reuters.com/article/us-jett/a-minute-with-joan-jett-on-life-as-a-run away-idUSTRE62H0C520100318.

5. Billboard Staff, "Can Riot Grrrl TikTok Re-Imagine a Flawed Scene?" *Billboard* (August 13, 2021), retrieved January 21, 2022, https:// www.billboard.com/music/rock/riot-grrrl-tiktok-revival-9614584/.

6. J. Pelly, "Kathleen Hanna on What Bikini Kill Means Now," *Pitchfork* (November 22, 2019), retrieved February 21, 2022, https:// pitchfork.com/features/interview/kathleen-hanna-interview-what -bikini-kill-means-now/.

Chapter 9: Donita Sparks (L7)

1. E. True, "L7: V Is for Vixcore." *Melody Maker*, December 1, 1990.

Chapter 10. Amy Ray (Indigo Girls)

1. "Gender Dysphoria," Mayo Clinic, retrieved October 25, 2022, https://www.mayoclinic.org/diseases-conditions/gender-dysphoria/symptoms-causes/syc-20475255.

2. Facebook post, Michigan Womyn's Music Festival (April 21, 2015), retrieved December 29, 2022, https://www.facebook.com/michfest/posts/10153186431364831.

Chapter 13. Tobi Vail (Bikini Kill)

1. "Logging," United States Department of Labor, retrieved November 19, 2022, https://www.osha.gov/logging.

Chapter 15. Catherine Popper

1. J. Coscarelli and M. Ryzik, "Ryan Adams Dangled Success: Women Say They Paid a Price," *New York Times* (February 13, 2019), retrieved October 6, 2022, https://www.nytimes.com/2019/02/13/arts/music/ryan-adams-women-sex.html.

2. R. Adams, "EXCLUSIVE: 'I Will Never Be Off the Hook for My Harmful Behavior,'" *Daily Mail* (July 3, 2020), retrieved October 6, 2022, https://www.dailymail.co.uk/news/article-8480627/Musician-Ryan-Adams-reveals-hes-sober-pens-raw-apology.html.

Afterword

1. Biologist D'Arcy Wentworth Thompson (1860–1948) is credited with this quote but scholars believe he coined it in an unwritten speech.

Index

Page locators in italics indicate photographs